Urban-Rural Disparity in Literacy

About the Authors

Dr. (Mrs.) Sneh Sangwan, Associate Professor in the Department of Geography, BPSM Girls College, BPS Mahila Vishwavidyalaya, Khanpur Kalan (Sonepat), has two books and a dozen of research papers to her credit. She is a life member of several professional and academic bodies and has participated in more than 25 National and International conferences/seminars/workshops. She was unanimously elected as Member of Executive Committee for the two consecutive terms (2003-2005 and 2006-2008) of National Association of Geographers, India (NAGI), which is the premier academic body for geographers of India. She has been awarded Major Research Project by UGC as Principal Investigator.

Dr. (Mrs) Anju Dabas, is presently working as Assistant Professor in the Department of Geography, Kanya Mahavidyalaya, Kharkhoda (Sonepat). Dr. Anju's active involvement in research activities is just a beginning and, at present, she has only one book and two research papers to her credit. She has participated in various conferences/seminars/workshops of National and Regional level.

Dr. Randhir Singh Sangwan, at present, working in the Deptt. of Geography, M.D. University, Rohtak, has three books and more than a score of research papers, to his credit. He has participated in more than 50 National and two International Conferences of International Geographical Union (IGU) held at Glasgow, Scotland (Great Britain) and Tunis (Tunisia, Africa) in 2004 and 2008 respectively. He received "Prof. R.N. Dubey Memorial Award-2002"—for Academic Excellence in Teaching and Research in Geography. This Award was conferred on by Bhoovigyan Vikas Foundation, the august body of Earth Science Professionals and was presented by the then His Excellency, Vice President of India.

Urban-Rural Disparity in Literacy

Sneh Sangwan
Anju Dabas
Randhir Singh Sangwan

CONCEPT PUBLISHING COMPANY PVT., LTD.
NEW DELHI-110059

ISBN-13: 978-81-8069-856-9

First Published 2012

Published and Printed by

Concept Publishing Company Pvt. Ltd.
A/15-16, Commercial Block, Mohan Garden
New Delhi-110059 (India)
T: 25351460, 25351794, *F*: 091-11-25357109
E: publishing@conceptpub.com, W: www.conceptpub.com
Editorial Office: H-13, Bali Nagar, New Delhi-110 015, India.

Cataloging in Publication Data--*Courtesy:* D.K. Agencies (P) Ltd. <docinfo@dkagencies.com>

Sangwan, Sneh, 1966-
Urban-rural disparity in literacy / Sneh Sangwan, Anju Dabas, Randhir Singh Sangwan.
p. cm.
Includes bibliographical references (p.) and index.
ISBN 9788180698569

1. Literacy—India—Haryana—Regional disparities. 2. Literacy—India Haryana—Statistics. 3. Education, Urban—India—Haryana. 4. Education, Rural India Haryana. I. Dabas, Anju, joint author. II. Sangwan, Randhir Singh, 1956-joint author. III. Title.

DDC 302.22440954558 23

Foreword

Here is a book on *Urban-Rural Disparity in Literacy*, a theme of great importance in a country like India where nearly one-fourth of population is still illiterate. Education is one of the main determinants of the level of human development; it enables individuals and communities to earn their livelihood and secure their rights guaranteed under the Constitution and the laws framed by the Parliament and State legislatures. Literacy is the first step in educational achievements.

Census of India 2011 reveals that India's population has shot up to 1.21 billion. It exceeds the combined population of the US, Brazil, Indonesia, Pakistan and Bangladesh. The welcome features of the latest census returns are many. First the decadal rate of growth of population has fallen from 21.54 per cent in 2001 to 17.64 per cent in 2011. Second, 2001-2011 is the first decade since 1921 to add a smaller number to the population of the preceding decade. Third, the literacy rate climbed up from 64.83 per cent in 2001 to 74.04 per cent in 2011. Fourth, while literacy among males increased by 6.9 per cent (from 75.26 per cent to 82.14 per cent), it rose by 11.8 per cent (from 53.67 per cent to 65.46 per cent) among the females. The gap of 21.59 percentage points between men and women in 2001 now stands reduced to 16.68 points. In absolute terms, women (110,069,001) outnumber men (107,631,940) among the neo-literates. And fifth, the overall sex ratio (number of females for every 1,000 males) has improved from 932.91 in 2001 to 940.27 in 2011.

The only major disturbing data thrown open by Census 2011 is the steep fall in the child sex ratio, which measures the number of girls for every 1,000 boys in the 0-6 year age-group. It has been continually declining since 1961 but the fall during 2001-2011 (927.31 to 914.23) is the worst since Independence. The 2001 data revealed a regional split in child sex ratio. The decline is more pronounced in northern and western States. The southern and eastern States continue to have decent ratio. The split has continued in 2011 but less sharply. Bihar, Gujarat and J & K have recorded decline in child sex ratio; Haryana and Punjab have improved only marginally; and with 1,094 girls for 1,000 boys, Kerala leads other States in this respect.

The book centres on literacy in Haryana as revealed by the Census 2001. Figures for 2011 census have now started coming; they would help researchers find the strides the State has made in educating its people. The book gives details of the inter-district disparities in literacy; literacy among males and females; and literacy among different communities and religious groups in the State. The book goes deeper into spatial disparities and looks at rural-urban differentials; and intra-district disparities selecting certain talukas and villages. Although the conclusions of the book are based on 2001 census figures, the conclusions are relevant and useful for all those who would like to do further research on literacy in the State.

While the level of literacy in the country has secularly improved, the gains, as in the past are not uniformly distributed. Kerala with 93.91 per cent literacy in 2011 has consistently done far better than other States, while Bihar with only 63.82 per cent literacy in 2011 has consistently lagged behind. Haryana with 67.91 per cent literacy in 2001 and 76.64 per cent in 2011 falls in between. Sex-wise data reveal that the percentage of literate males in Haryana went up from 78.49 in 2001 to 85.38 in 2011 and that of females from 55.73 to 66.77 in the same period. Gurgaon district has recorded the highest literacy rate (84.44 per cent) followed by Panchkula (83.44 per cent), and Faridabad (83.04 percent). Lowest level of literacy has been reported from Mewat district which stood at 56.14 per cent. In female literacy too, Gurgaon district with 77.64 per cent female literacy tops the other districts; Mewat district with 37.58 per cent female literacy against 73 per cent for males in 2011 stands at the tail end.

It is often said that poor sex ratio and illiteracy go together. It does not hold good for Haryana where districts with poor literacy levels have the highest sex ratio and child sex ratio. The literacy rate of Mewat, one of the most backward districts of the State, has the worst literacy rate (56.1%) but the State's highest sex ratio of 906, the overall figure for the State being 877 females for 1,000 males. The situation is the same with respect to the 0-6 age group with 903 girls per 1,000 boys while the State has the worst child sex ratio of 830 in the country.

The other districts of Haryana with lowest literacy rates are Fatehabad, Palwal and Sirsa, but their sex ratios are among the highest in the State. While Fatehabad has the second lowest literacy rate of 69.1 per cent, the sex ratio is 903. Its child sex ratio is 845 girls for 1,000 boys, an increase of 17 points over the 2001 Census figures. Similarly, Palwal, with a literacy rate of 70.3 per cent, has the second highest child sex ratio of 862 in the State; and Sirsa's sex ratio of 896 goes with its literacy rate of 70.4 per cent, which is below the State's average literacy rate of 76.64 per cent.

Haryana's 2011 Census return points to strange anomalies in matters of literacy and sex ratios. The State has the worst sex ratio of 830 in the country in the 0-6 age group but high literacy rates. The literacy rates of Jhajjar, Rewari and Sonepat districts are above 80 per cent, but are marked with one the lowest child sex ratio. Jhajjar and Mahendragarh, have a very high literacy rate of 78.9 per cent but have the lowest child sex ratios at 774 and 778, respectively, in the entire country.

The 2011 Census returns show that high literacy, at least in India, is not necessarily a good indicator of healthy gender balance. Maharashtra, with a literacy rate of almost 83 per cent, has a CSR of 883, while Chhattisgarh, with just 71 per cent literacy (61 per cent for women) has a CSR of 964. It is well demonstrated in Gujarat, Rajasthan, Bihar, Haryana and West Bengal. Naturally then, education in the conventional sense is not enough to correct a deep societal and cultural bias that India seems to harbour against girls. The tribal societies and the schedules castes, have a better CSR than even Kerala, India's default model State.

The book authored by Dr. Sneh Sangwan, Dr. Anju Dabas and Dr. Randhir Singh Sangwan, offers an excellent background material to compare literacy levels in Haryana and its constituent district and ethnic areas through time. It would indeed be interesting and useful to incorporate the 2011 data as and when they become available in the next edition of the book. I congratulate the Sangwan due to live together lovingly as wife and husband but also to work together as researchers to enlighten the world around them.

Allahabad **Bhoogol Ratna Prof. R. P. Misra**
April 4, 2011

Preface

Population and region have mattered the most in national economic, social, cultural and planning studies. They shape the geography and environment of development comprehensibly. Region signifies the composite expression of territorial distinctiveness with reference to human and non-human attributes. Population contributes significantly towards defining the extent and intensity of regional distinctiveness.

Population is not a homogeneous comprehension and its quantitative and qualitative attributes vary spatially. Population attribute variations cause necessary disparities at sub-regional and regional scales. The quantitative and qualitative attributes of population produce differences in time and space perspective making the impact of technological innovations unequal in sectoral and areal development/planning. The process, the issues and the planning response to the cause of national/regional development vary widely and apparently. Population has unavoidably impacted to mould the geographical distribution and functioning of the components of spatial organization.

National development/regional planning has emerged as essential field of economic and socio-cultural amelioration. Along with this, there have come signs that more consistent, comprehensive and longer term population strategies have become imperative. It seems more imperative to, now, discuss and analyse the distinctive characteristics of population composition and related extent of spatial disparity.

The division of population into urban and rural components has appeared, perhaps, the most apparent and pervading. Any aspect of economy, society and developmental planning is essentially subjected to apparent dimensions of urban and rural.

Accordingly the literate-illiterate composition of regional population, like any other component of population, implies significant urban-rural distinctiveness. It is found that necessary differences in scale and rate of literacy as and when they are viewed in urban and rural perspectives. The urban segment always scores over the rural segment.

The book testifies the experiences in spheres of teaching and research of author/authors in the discipline which they are concerned with. The authors of the book have taught and pursued research activities in the field of population geography. Much of their attention focuses, in this book, on qualitative aspect of population, literacy in particular. Major focus relates to issues of urban-rural disparity in literacy with particular reference to the state of Haryana, India. Naturally readers are expected to derive the required contents or an account for as well as an account of the traditional subject matter of Population Geography with emphasis on geographic reality of analysis, viz., urban rural disparity in literacy. Besides introducing issues, methodology and organization of subject matters, the contents of the book imply the unifying theme that urban-rural disparity forms an integrated system of population or appropriately a set of interlocking subsystems of population components in spatial context. The literacy component defines the quality of population and releases flows of information, innovation and ideas the bases of national development and planning.

The authors do not claim the book an independent composition. The book is the outcome of help received from the need of student community and from those many geographers and scholars whose ideas have been drawn, insufficiently recognized in formal references. It is, however, authors' submission that the views and opinions expressed in the text do not necessarily represent those of the sources derived from. Although many facts and views of different sources have been incorporated, all errors, misinterpretations and other failings will remain authors' responsibility alone. Authors will derive some consolation from the interest in and acceptance of the book shown by readers.

January 21, 2011
Rohtak

Sneh Sangwan
Anju Dabas
Randhir Singh Sangwan

Acknowledgements

We are deeply indebted to Bhoogal Ratna Prof. R.P. Misra, Mahatma Gandhi National Fellow and former Vice Chancellor of the University of Allahabad, Allahabad; Prof. B. Thakur, Department of Geography, University of Delhi, Delhi; Prof. Nandeshwar Sharma, former Head, Department of Geography, L.N. Mithila University, Darbhanga; Prof. Suresh Misra, Indian Institute of Public Administration; Prof. S.P. Sinha, former Chairman, Department of Geography, Kurukshetra University, Kurukshetra; Dr. R.B. Singh, Associate Professor, Department of Geography, University of Delhi, Delhi; Dr. S.D. Singh, Associate Professor, Department of Geography, Government College, Bharatpur (Rajasthan); Sh. S.C. Gupta, Principal (Retd.), Department of Geography, Government P.G. College, Jhajjar; Dr. (Mrs.) Suresh Boora, Principal, Kanya Mahavidyalaya, Kharkhoda (Sonipat) for their valuable suggestions, encouragement and unstinted moral support in completing the work.

We would like to place on record our deep sense of gratitude to all those officers/officials of various departments belonging to Government of Haryana as well as Government of India for the help and co-operation they extended whenever we visited the offices. We are also grateful to the staff members of the libraries of Maharshi Dayanand University, Rohtak; Jawahar Lal Nehru University, New Delhi; University of Delhi (Ratan Tata Library), Delhi; and Panjab University, Chandigarh. We also owe our gratitude to various authors whose works have been consulted and quoted in the present study.

We are also greatly beholden to our parents and in-laws whose blessings helped us in completing this work. All our near and dear ones who helped us in any manner also deserve our thanks. Mr. Deep Dabas, Dr. Alka, Mahima and Himanshu Sangwan deserve our special thanks for the help rendered to us by solving all problems to be sorted out with the help of computer.

We also acknowledge the keen interest and dedication with which Sh. Rakesh Sangwan of Computer Zone, Shopping Complex, M.D. University, Rohtak typed the manuscript.

It would be highly gratifying for us if our humble effort proves to be thought provoking and opens up new vistas.

We take the opportunity to express our special thanks to Sh. Ashok Kumar Mittal, Concept Publishing Company Pvt. Ltd., New Delhi for readily agreeing to publish this book and bringing it out expeditiously and efficiently.

For a few errors that may have crept into the book, we crave the indulgence of readers and own sole responsibility.

January 21, 2011

Sneh Sangwan
Anju Dabas
Randhir Singh Sangwan

Contents

List of Tables

List of Maps

List of Figures

1 Introduction

1.1 Statement of the Problem

Literacy is that qualitative attribute of population which is considered as a fairly reliable index of the socio-cultural and economic advancement of the area (Chandna, 2008). Literacy and education are essential for social reconstruction, improvement in the quality of life and preparation of manpower for rapid development. However, literacy works for moulding the younger generation to assume future responsibilities and develop appropriate values of life. On the other hand, 'the lack of literacy can certainly be an impediment in tne development process. A certain level of literacy is, therefore, a basic requirement for the people to get out of ignorance and backwardness (Gosal, 1979). Thus, literacy is essential for economic development, and social advancement which measure overall development of a country.

The present study which examines the disparity in literacy in Haryana is, however, a departure from the usual spatial studies pertaining to literacy. It emphasizes upon the disparity in literacy of Haryana in terms of area, residence, sex, social group, etc. Such studies have special significance for heterogeneous societies like those of India in general and Haryana in particular. Although one would like to study the disparity in literacy in terms of religion as well, yet, the non-availability of data on literacy by religion restricts the scope of the present study to areas, residence, sex and major caste groups. Thus, while some attempts have been made to study the regional patterns of literacy in Haryana, no such attempt except Sangwan and Sangwan (1995) has been made so far to analyze the regional patterns of disparity in literacy. The purpose of the present study is to describe and interpret the spatial patterns of disparity in literacy in case of urban and rural areas, male and female population as well as non-scheduled castes and scheduled castes.

The rationale behind the selection of study area is the popular characteristics of the State in the terms of its high overall literacy as well as female literacy, high socio-economic level, high per capita income, high road density, more diversified nature of economy, more number of schools in rural areas as also for girls, out-migration of literate population and in-migration of illiterate population, all of which have a far reaching impact on the disparity in literacy. Further, there is considerable research work, already done on literacy as well as disparity in literacy in India in particular, but only a few studies to count, like that of Krishan and Chandna (1974) and Sangwan and Sangwan (1995), have appeared on the literacy disparity in Haryana so far. This fact has also motivated the authors to take up the present study.

1.2 Review of Literature

Literacy studies have been carried on at various levels in India. The pioneering works on literacy at national level were that of Parlulekar (1939) and Kingsley Davis (1951). In their studies, they enunciated the causes of illiteracy as rooted in the economic and social life of the country like India. Hilda H. Golden in 1955 gave his viewpoints regarding the impact of literacy on the social change in underdeveloped countries and the "level of economic development", in which "level of urbanization" is usually a component, has been thought able to "explain" much of national variation in literacy at the global scale. Joseph E. Schwartzberg (1961) has shown that the actual progress in literacy in India during 1951-61 has been considerably greater than is suggested by a comparison of the literacy rates for 1951 and 1961. Whereas, the "proportion" of literate persons increased by about 44 per cent during these 10 years, the increase in "actual number" of literates was 77 per cent. In fact, the increase during the decade is more than the total increase of the two earlier decades combined.

Several studies such as those of Gosal (1964, 1967, 1979) have been conducted on Indian literacy. Gosal in 1964 stated that despite remarkable progress in education in recent years, the Indian population is still one of the least literate in the world mainly because of prevalence of a rigid caste system and subsistence farm economy based on a very backward technology which has made it unnecessary for everyone to read and to write. In 1967, Gosal conducted a study on the regional aspects of rural literacy in India and told that the lack of literacy in rural areas is the result of influence of the caste with its hereditary occupations, subsistence farm economy and the appalling poverty among a large section of the rural population. Gosal (1979) also discussed the spatial patterns of literacy in India and explained that literacy rates are high in coastal areas because of long contact with overseas people and the concerted efforts of Christian missionaries in extending educational facilities to both men and women. Whereas, low literacy rates are found in those areas where urban development is low, the scheduled caste population forms a sizeable section of total population and non-Christian tribal population is predominant. In his studies on literacy in India, Gosal also commented that the gap between the levels of male and female literacy is the result of "a long, continued prejudice against the education of women and also against their employment outside the home".

But Krishan and Shyam told that this "prejudice" exists because an exclusively domestic role is seen as the ideal for women. Man fear that education may unsuit women for that role, because "an educated female may become of doubtful character or may not be capable of adjusting herself in the joint family system, or may not participate in obligatory agricultural operations, or may not remain under the control of her husband". While discussing pattern of city literacy, they said that the low literacy rate is the characteristic of area of Muslim dominance and the literacy is negatively correlated with Hindi speaking areas (Krishan and Shyam, 1974a). This was followed by a detailed description about the literacy patterns of Indian cities (Krishan and Shyam, 1974b). Krishan and Shyam (1977) also have referred that India is market not only by a low literacy rate but also by wide disparity in literacy by sex, residence and area and these disparities reflect the necessity, propensity and opportunity of various degrees for getting literate among different population groups. Apart from this, both have done a detailed study on regional aspect of urban-rural disparities of literacy rates in India in a separate article (Krishan and Shyam, 1985). The discussion in this chapter is based on the differential index value, calculated at district level for India. Tirtha's (1966) study tells about the extent of literacy among the population of any country which reflects its educational and cultural level and indirectly the stage of its development. Vyas in 1967, explained various factors which influence the levels of literacy. George (1978), a social scientist, presented an article on the status of women in India and explained that the status of women in India has never been at par with that of in the developed countries. Low levels of living, illiteracy and inter-spouse communication combined with economic dependence, ignorance and tradition stand in the way of improving it. Of these factors, literacy and education play a predominant role. This article attempts to examine the progress of Indian women in respect of education and educational opportunity. It further states that the contribution of Christian missionaries have been the most outstanding in the spread of education in India. Similarly, Raju (1988) made a socio-geographic analysis of female literacy both for the non-scheduled and scheduled caste segments of the population in Class-I cities of India and found that the distinction is more strongly marked between non-scheduled and scheduled castes than between the male and female components of either groups. That is, caste disparity is greater than sex disparity in literacy.

Jolly (1991), while describing strategies to attain universal literacy in India by 2001, identified the rural-urban differentials in literacy.

Premi (1991) studied the literacy scenario in India and found that as a result of National Policy on Education and other new policy thrusts, the literacy rates have improved gradually despite tremendous increase in population, but the rural-urban literacy differentials continue to be high even in 1991.

Mehta (1995) focused on patterns and correlates of tribal literacy in India. Physical and economic distance to schools as well as lack of opportunity for schooling in mother tongue were found to be the main deterrents in the way of tribal literacy in the country.

Hazra (1997) has compared performance of major regions in female literacy of the world, and highlighted low position of the South Asian countries realm in this regard. Discussing the pattern of female literacy in India, the author pointed out that the vicious circle of female illiteracy, poverty and low status in society needs to be broken down.

In his district-wise Census data based detailed study on "Spatial dimensions of literacy in India", Gosal (2002) points out that there has been not much change in the regional patterns of literacy in the country during 1961-2001. However, rural-urban and male-female differential in literacy rates have narrowed down considerably over these years. Male-female differential in literacy rate showed significant inverse correlation with general literacy rate.

Nath (2001) draws attention to lowest literacy rates in Uttar Pradesh and Bihar, which together have about one-fourth of the population of the country. Also, despite having a large number of illiterates, the progress in increasing literacy has been noteworthy, resulting in phenomenal growth of the print media—weekly and daily newspapers, magazines and books, films and television serials, all in regional languages.

Krishan (2002) emphasizes a major rise in female-male ratio in higher education from 14 : 100 in 1951 to 6 : 100 in 2001. Women's participation in medical, engineering and technical education has also gone up noticeably in the past few decades. The State level data reveals that 'the presence of women in higher education finds a stronger correlation with female literacy rate, than with level of urbanization or per capita income.

Some meso and micro level studies on literacy regarding certain States of India have also been made by various scholars. Sharma (1971) made a valuable study on the literacy in Rajasthan, whereas Siddique (1977) made an effort to study the phenomenon of literacy in Uttar Pradesh and found that there are considerable variations in rural-urban, male-female literacy and that among the different regions mainly caused by social, economic and historical factors. Employing 1981 Census data, Gill (1992) studied spatial patterns of literacy in Punjab.

Bhardwaj (1999) has found the rapid expansion in educational facilities, free education in schools and emergence of middle class section of society following rapid growth in service sector as major factors responsible for speedy rise in literacy level in Himachal Pradesh during 1971-2001.

Joshi (2002) attempted to analyze the patterns of gender related educational development (GEDI) in Rajasthan. The GEDI goes down when the literacy achievement of males and females declines. The GEDI value of 1 indicates full equality, and the maximum disparity is devoted by a value of 0. Similarly, the index of deprivation was found as I = 1 – GEDI. In 2000, the GEDI for Rajasthan stood at 0.693 and the Index of Deprivation (IOD) comes to 0.307.

Kaur (2003) focused on gender disparity in literacy in Indian Punjab. It was found that gender disparity bears strong inverse correlation with level of general literacy. Similarly, gender disparity in literacy was low among the urbanities than that among the ruralities. Khan (2004) explained the regional imbalances and changing pattern of literacy in Jammu and Kashmir State (1961-2001).

In case of Haryana, the valuable study on literacy was made by Krishan and Chandna (1974) to examine the literacy patterns with special reference to its growth in the past and existing inequalities by sex, residence and area. They found that the spatial pattern of literacy in Haryana is bi-modal, with literacy peaks characteristic of the zone peripheral to the Union Territory of Delhi and of Ambala district. Literacy rates go on declining as one moves away from these two areas and the lowest literacy rates are found in the southeastern part of the State where Meo-Muslim population dominate.

At a still lower spatial scale, Banerjee (1975), in her study on literacy in the district of Singhbhum, Bihar, made an effort to correlate literacy with modernization and said that the high male-female and rural-urban differential in the district indicates the fact that modernization is only superficial or skin deep in this district.

Dutta (1982) analyzed literacy rates in southern district of West Bengal to conclude that high literacy rate is associated with more urbanized districts such as Hugli, 24 Parganas, Howrah. On the other hand, low literacy is found in Purulia, Bankura due to high proportion of scheduled caste and scheduled tribe population. Chib (1994) discussed literacy pattern in the trans-Himalaya district of Kinnaur in Himachal Pradesh.

Misra (1997) analyzed level of literacy among *dalit* population in Atarra tehsil of Uttar Pradesh. As expected, the *dalits* were behind in this regard from their non-*dalit* counterparts which was mainly due to (i) literacy does not have much functional value for their family chores; (ii) a child is considered more useful for the family's day-to-day activities than sending her/him to school; and (iii) physical distance to school play its own part in this regard.

Das and Betal (2005) analyzed the role of educational institutions on literacy in Hugli district of West Bengal and found strong correlation between literacy and number of different category of educational institutions.

Region has found attention in a few studies. Yavatmal and Shastri (1985) analyzed spatial pattern of tribal literacy in Vidarbha region of Maharashtra using 1981 Census data and also examined disparity in literacy by caste, sex and residence.

Tripathi (1993) analyzed the impact of urbanization on literacy in rural areas of Bundelkhand region in Uttar Pradesh and found close association between literacy and degree of urbanization.

Sharma (2004) deals with the present status and variations in literacy and educational levels in north-eastern India. He examines in the study the factors behind the low level of literacy and education and their social consequences in the region.

Thus, most of the studies, pertaining of literacy, have been confined to the spatial analysis of this attribute either at national or at regional level.

1.3 Geography and Urban-Rural Differential Studies

The available literature on rural-urban differentials reveals that the issue has received slight attention from geographers.

As far as disparities in the sphere as well as education are concerned, a systematic attempt to measure the nature and patterns of regional disparities in education was made in a series of studies sponsored by the International Institute of Educational Planning (Carron and Ngoc, 1980a). The relationship between intra- as well as inter-regional disparities in education and the process of socio-economic development was illustrated with the help of specific case studies that made use of a number of innovative tools in the diagnosis of the existing malaise. Smith and Zopf (1970) have examined the inequalities in education in U.S.A. in terms of sex, residence, colour or race and State.

A comparative study of male and female illiteracy in the world has shown that the magnitude of disparities between the sexes with regard to literacy is very high in some cases and that this attribute would continue to persist. Reference may be made to the fact that in a number of countries—Chad, Mali, Upper Volta, Ethiopia, Somalia and Niger in Africa as well as Yemen,

Afghanistan and Saudi Arabia in Asia—literacy rate was close to the zero mark as late as in 1971 (Carron and Ngoc, 1980b). Ryba in 1979 examined the territorial aspects of educational achievements. He showed that territorial inequalities may be noticed at every scale of analysis and that these have tended to persist over time. Williamson's study on the patterns of educational inequality in West Germany validated the hypothesis that educational inequalities are deeply rooted in the social milieu and continue to constrain development even in the otherwise developed countries of Europe (Williamson, 1977). Baker (1986), in his study of northern Ethiopia, explained that distinction between rural and urban areas is firmly established in census reports and social and economic statistics.

A number of studies on the nature and the patterns of disparities in the context of Indian literacy have been undertaken by scholars during post-independence period. Davis in 1951 described that with the solitary exception of Kerala, the male-female disparity in literacy is very great everywhere in India. This unusual disparity is the result of a long, continued prejudice against the education of women and also against their employment outside the home. Ghosal (1964) studied the rural-urban disparity in literacy in India and said that the rural and urban areas stand in marked contrast to each other in the field of literacy. Krishan and Chandna (1974) explained that rural-urban disparity in literacy had an adverse correlation with general literacy. Tilak (1978) described the regional inequality in literacy in India. Krishan and Shyam (1978) described and interpreted the regional aspects of the urban-rural differential in literacy in India on the basis of 1971 Census data. They had also incorporated new techniques to measure the literacy differences between rural and urban areas. Ghosal (1979) made a study of literacy in spatial perspective and found that as in several other characteristics of population, so in literacy and education, the villages and towns in India stand in marked contrast to each other. Mishra (1980) in his book *An Introduction to the Study of Population* covered almost all demographic aspects of population. He considered rural-urban differences in sex-ratio, population composition, age at marriage and marital composition, rural-urban distribution of non-workers and differences in literacy rates among scheduled castes and scheduled tribes residing in rural and urban areas. Sopher (1980) made another notable contribution in this regard. By using his own formula (1974), he made a detailed study of sex disparity in Indian literacy in terms of residence, religion, caste and age groups of population on the basis of 1971 Census data at district level. These apart, he had also studied the spatio-temporal trends in both male and female literacy. Mamoria (1981) also studied the State-wise rural-urban differentials in literacy.

A comparative study on the nature and patterns of inequities in literacy rates between 1961 and 1971 has been undertaken by Kundu and Rao (1982). The study is based on the State as the unit of analysis. Inter-State differences in the rural and urban literacy rates have been examined for the year 1981 by D'Souza (1982). Raza and Aggarwal (1986) made an attempt to examine the different aspects of inequalities that have acted as impediments in the path of the educational development of the third world countries in general and that of India in particular. With a view to unraveling these complexities, the issues relating to the identification, measurement and explanation of inequalities in the territorial spread of literacy in India have been examined with the help of district-wise data and proposed an alternative formulation of Sopher's disparity index.

Nain (1988) examined inter-State change of rural-urban differentials in literacy, vital rates, sex ratio and size of household in India during 1971-81.

Sangwan and Sangwan (2003) undertook a study on rural-urban divide in terms of changing spatial pattern of social variables like literacy, sex ratio, size of the household, and vital rates in India.

At the national scale, although Premi (1980), Rice and Rice (1984), Raza and Aggarwal (1986) had identified the vertical disparities in literacy by area, sex, residence, caste, tribe, age and religion, yet the spatial analysis of these disparities had suffered a neglect.

At micro levels, Ram (1981), Mathur (1981), Usha Rao (1982), Kaur (1983) and Sharma (1985) have also studied the literacy differential in Punjab, Uttar Pradesh, Karnataka, Patiala and Assam respectively.

Shah (1981) made a probing study into variations in the literacy rates of Gujarat and some of the economic correlates of the same has shown that the proportion of agricultural workers in the rural workforce exerts a significantly strong influence on literacy rates in the selected villages. Usha Rao (1982) has studied the intra-State disparities in literacy rates for the scheduled castes population in Karnataka. Ahmad (1982) has examined inter-district inequities in literacy rates of the tribal population of Bihar for the year 1971. Aggarwal and Murlidhar (1986) made a spatio-temporal analysis of literacy between scheduled castes and non-scheduled castes population in Maharashtra and computed intra-group disparity indices among scheduled castes for a variety of binomial elements by using modified Sopher's disparity index. Ahmed and Nuna (1986) carried a detailed study based on the literacy data of the 1971 census for the scheduled castes and tribes of Maharashtra, on the one hand, and the non-scheduled population on the other.

Sangwan (1990) made a spatial analysis of sex disparity in the levels of literacy in Haryana. Sangwan and Sangwan (1995, 2010 and 2011) have studied the literacy differentials by sex and residence in Haryana.

Finally, some scholars have devised new techniques and methodology for studying various aspects of literacy. These have been explained under the subtitle of methodology.

The studies having their focus on the differentials in literacy in Haryana are only a few to count. Thus, the present work will be a contribution in this regard in which the literacy differential between one area and the other, males and females, urban and rural population in Haryana shall be subjected to a geographic analysis.

1.4 Objectives of the Study

The main objectives of the present study are as follows :

1. To interpret the regional imbalances in literacy in the State.
2. To describe the urban-rural disparity in literacy.
3. To analyse the male-female disparity in literacy.
4. To examine the literacy rates and literacy disparity between Scheduled Castes and Non-Scheduled Castes.

1.5 Hypotheses

The following hypotheses are formulated to be tested in order to give specificity and direction to the problem under study:

1. Literacy disparity would be lower in urban areas because the urban society will be less prone to prejudices against females' mobility.
2. Male-female disparity in literacy is high where sex ratio is high and the proportion of scheduled caste as well as Muslim population is high.
3. Male-female disparity in literacy is low in urban areas as compared to rural areas.
4. Urban-Rural disparity in literacy is of a higher dimension in the case of scheduled castes as compared to the rest of the population.
5. Literacy disparity between scheduled castes and non-scheduled castes would be very high in poor region and where less mechanization of farms has taken place, because in such areas most of the scheduled castes people work as agricultural labour which needs little education.

1.6 Sources of Data

The study refers to the spatial analysis of disparity in literacy in Haryana for the year 2001. The study banks heavily upon the census data which are fairly reliable. The data have been mainly obtained from the office of the Registrar General, New Delhi Various occasional papers published by Census of India, Office of the Registrar General, New Delhi, were also consulted. The various census publications from which the data have been collected are notably, "District Census Handbooks for each District", "Statistical Abstract of Haryana", "Social and Cultural Tables", "Special Tables on Scheduled Castes", "Primary Census Abstract", and "General Population Tables", pertaining to Census of India 2001. The Tehsil has been considered to be the most suitable unit of study, for which data are available in the published records of the Census of India. The data were then processed to find the relevant ratios.

1.7 Methodology

Methodology that has been adopted in the present study is in consonance with the basic objectives of the study, and hypotheses that have been framed for testing. In every geographic inquiry, spatial concept occupies the central position in its methodology where the preparation of a map is the most important tool. The disparity in literacy and the literacy rates have been represented cartographically as to see them in the regional perspective. The Census Map of Haryana (2001) showing the district/tehsil boundaries has been adopted as the base map (Map 1.1).

Wherever necessary, correlations have been calculated to determine the relationship between the dependent as well as the independent demographic and socio-economic variables.

For measuring the disparity or inequality in the literary rates of two relevant population groups, different scholars have employed different techniques.

Gosal (1964) had used the simple technique of scanning the two sets of data (male literates and female literates), visually comparing the two mapped patterns and getting the ratio between the two groups.

Sopher (1974) made a notable contribution in computing disparity by using his own formula, i.e.

$$D_s = \log (X_2/X_1) + \log (100 - X_1)/(100 - X_2)$$

Where,

X_2 ³ X_1 and X_1 and X_2 are demographic indicators of *alphas* and *non-alphas* respectively.

Krishan and Shyam (1978) described the regional aspects of the rural-urban differential in literacy in India on the basis of 1971 census data by using the formula, i.e.

$$ID = Urban\text{-}Rural/Total$$

Krishan and Rana (1980) studied rural-urban differentials in size of the household in India by using crude method of rural-urban differential, i.e.

$$ID = Rural - Urban$$

Naik (1971), Chitnis (1972, 1974), Sen (1973), Banerjee (1975), Shastri (1985), Gosal (1988) and Nain (1988) calculated rural-urban differentials in literacy with the help of this method. Nain (1988) used this method also for calculating rural-urban differential in sex ratio, vital rates and size of the household in India. Goel (1994) also calculated rural-urban differentials in size of the household in Uttar Pradesh by this method.

Victor S. D'Souza (1980) evolved a new formula for the

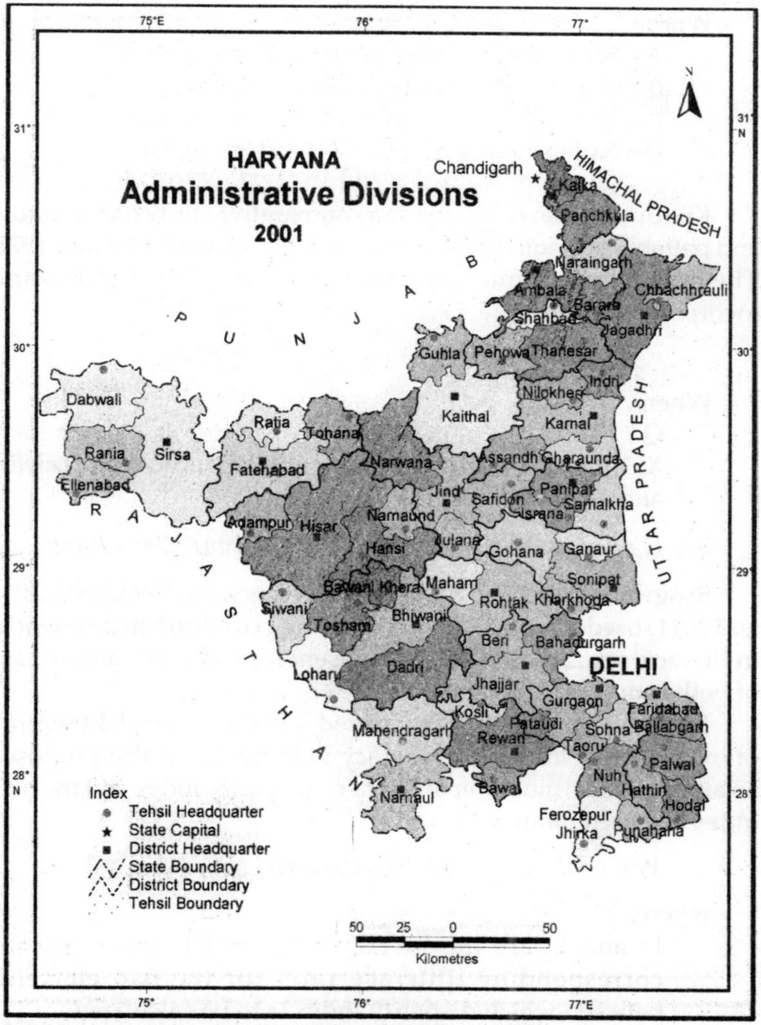

Map 1.1: Haryana: Administrative Divisions, 2001

measurement of educational inequalities among scheduled castes of Punjab, i.e.

$$\text{Coefficient of Equality} = \frac{A/B}{C/D} \times 100$$

Where,

A = Scheduled Castes Literate Population
B = Scheduled Castes Total Population
C = Non-Scheduled Castes Literate Population
D = Non-Scheduled Castes Total Population

Kundu and Rao (1982) made a comparative study on the nature and patterns of inequalities in literacy rates between 1961 and 1971. They modified Sopher's formula of differential index and incorporated a new one, i.e.

$$Ds = log\ (X_2/X_1) + log\ (Q - X_1)/(Q - X_2)$$

Where,

$Q\ ^{3}\ 200$,
$X_2\ ^{3}\ X_1$ and X_1 and X_2 are demographic indicators of *alphas* and *non-alphas* respectively.

So, $D_s = log\ (Rural/Urban) + log\ (200 - Urban)/(200 - Rural)$

Sangwan (1990), and Sangwan and Sangwan (1995, 2003, 2010 and 2011) used this formula for calculating rural-urban differential in literacy, sex ratio, size of the household, and vital rates in case of both India and Haryana.

Raza and Aggarwal (1986) looked into the regional dimension of inequality in the level of literacy in India. They also proposed an alternative formulation of Sopher's disparity index and the new index has been defined as:

$$W = log(L_2/L_1) + log\ [(100+I_1)/(100+I_2)]\ L_2\ 3/8\ L_1 > 0$$

where,

L_1 and L_2 are the literacy rates and I_1 and I_2 are the corresponding illiteracy rates for the two elements between which disparity index is to be calculated.

Sagar (1990), in his study of rural-urban differentials in literacy, has modified D'Souza's formula and gave his own to calculate differentials, i.e.,

$$DI = 100[1 - (Y_i/X_i)]$$

where,

DI stands for the differential index.
X_i stands for the ratio of the property of one item in the i = th areal units.

Y_i stands for the ratio of the property of the other item in the i = th areal unit.

In order to measure the differentials or inequality of various demographic aspects among two relevant population groups, these statistical techniques have been adopted by different scholars. As we can see from the above methodological studies, most of these have been conducted to calculate literacy differentials mainly.

Disparity or differentials can be absolute or relative. In an absolute sense, it may be calculated by simply subtracting the lesser values from the higher values. For instance, if literacy rate for urban population in a region is 60 per cent, for rural population it is 40 per cent, then absolute disparity will be equal to 20 per cent (i.e., 60 – 40 = 20). The relative disparity may be derived by working out the ratio between the literacy rates of both the regions, i.e., Urban : Rural = 60 : 40 = 3 : 2. Though these are two different views of disparity from different angles, but both suffer from a common vagary of grouping dissimilar areas into the same type. An area with urban literacy rate of 80 per cent and rural literacy rate of 60 per cent would have the same absolute disparity as an area with 50 per cent of urban literacy and 30 per cent of rural literacy rates.

Likewise, the relative disparity in an area with 80 per cent male and 40 per cent female literacy rates would be the same as in an area having 60 per cent urban literacy and 30 per cent rural literacy rates.

Thus, both absolute and relative measures have been used to measure disparities between various binomial elements. However, the major difficulty with both of these measures is that the disparity between alphas and non-alphas is not the same as between non-alphas and alphas. Hence, a more sophisticated technique for the measurement of disparity is required to overcome this difficulty. David E. Sopher (1974) has proposed an alternative measure known as *Sopher's Disparity Index*, that gives the same value in the two cases mentioned above. Sopher's disparity index was originally stated as follows:

$$Ds = \log (X_2/X_1) + \log (100 - X_1)/(100 - X_2)$$

Where,

$X_2 \geq X_1$ and X_1 and X_2 are literacy rates of *alphas* and *non-alphas* respectively.

But this disparity index has also some limitations such as (i) for a given set of data, the disparity between alphas and non-alphas would be numerically the same but directionally opposite to that between non-alphas and alphas. This seriously restricts the analytic application of the index; (ii) It fails to distinguish between situations, each defined by two observations, when one of the two observations is zero or 100.

Therefore, in measuring the urban-rural disparity in literacy rates, an index that satisfies all the four axioms of additive and multiplicative monotonicity, redistribution and repetitive transfers (Kundu, 1986) has been employed. This is the Sopher's index which was further modified by Kundu and Rao (1982), i.e.,

$$Ds = \log (X_2/X_1) + \log (200 - X_1)/(200 - X_2)$$

where,

$X_2 \geq X_1$ and X_1 and X_2 are various demographic aspects of *alphas* and *non-alphas* respectively.

It was found that most of the other techniques suffer from a limitation that the areas of high as well as low literacy may display similar differential index value if the two segments being differentiated are at the same level of literacy although they are simple and easy to comprehend.

Keeping in view the above mentioned disparity index, the first and foremost step in the analysis was the selection of binomial elements, in terms of which disparity was to be measured. The differential index for literacy rates for the different tehsils of Haryana was computed on the basis of disparity index given by Kundu and Rao (1982).

1.8 Organisation of the Study

The present study has been organised into six main chapters followed by summary and conclusions.

The first chapter is introductory in nature and deals with the problem under study, review of literature, methodology and data sources.

The second chapter depicts the physico-cultural profile of the study area.

In the third chapter, the spatial patterns of literacy by urban-rural residence and sex have been discussed at tehsil level.

The fourth chapter is devoted to disparity in literacy by sex, wherein the male-female disparity in literacy has been examined especially.

The fifth chapter is also devoted to disparity in literacy by residence, wherein the urban-rural disparity in literacy has been examined especially.

The sixth chapter brings out the spatial variations in the patterns of disparity in literacy between scheduled castes and non-scheduled castes population.

The last chapter presents a summary and conclusions. It is followed by References and Bibliography.

The organizational scheme of the thesis is as follows :

CHAPTER SCHEME

1. Introduction
2. The Study Area—A Physico-Cultural Profile
3. Spatial Patterns of Literacy
4. Male-Female Disparity in Literacy
5. Urban-Rural Disparity in Literacy
6. Literacy Disparity between Scheduled Castes and Non-Scheduled Castes
7. Summary and Conclusions

   References and Bibliography

2 A Physico-Cultural Profile of Haryana

2.1 Location and Extension

Haryana State came into existence as an independent State on 1st November 1966, after the reorganization of composite State of Punjab on linguistic basis. It is located in north-western part of India (Map 2.1). It stretches from 27°38′ N to 30°55′5″ N latitudes and from 74°27′ 8″ E to 77°36′5″ E longitudes. It is bounded by the orchard State of Himachal Pradesh in the north and north-east; by Uttar Pradesh, the most populous State and Union Territory of Delhi in the east; and by the Union Territory of Chandigarh and Punjab, the State of adventurist farmers and toiling workers, in its north-west. Rajasthan with its rich cultural heritage and history replete with most heroic deeds bounds the State of Haryana on south and south-west.

The administrative boundaries of Haryana State have been changed from time to time due to the political conditions but the geographical and natural boundaries of the State have remained the same. Geographically, the boundaries of Haryana State are found in river Ghaggar in the north-west, Siwalik hills in the north-east, River Yamuna in the east, Aravali hills in the south and the Thar desert in the south-west.

Haryana is one of the smaller States of India. According to Census of India (2001), the area of the State is 44,212 km^2 and is inhabited by 211.45 lakh persons. The area and population of the State constitute 1.35 and 1.93 per cent of the total area and population of India respectively. Thus, Haryana ranks 17th in terms of area and 16th in population size among the 28 States and 7 union territories in 2001 Census. The administrative divisions of Haryana comprises 19 districts and 67 tehsils as per 2001 Census (Map 2.2).

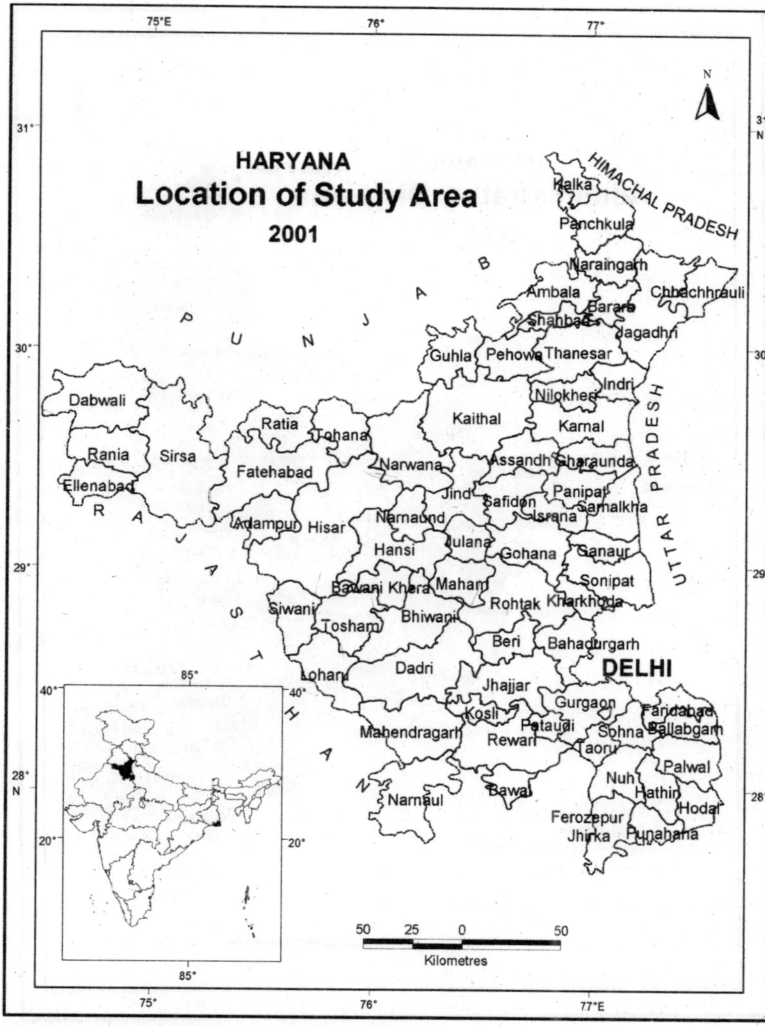

Map 2.1: Haryana: Location Map, 2001

2.2 Physical Environs

2.2.1 *Physiography*

Physiography deals with the study of the surface features and landforms of the earth. A large portion of Haryana forms the part

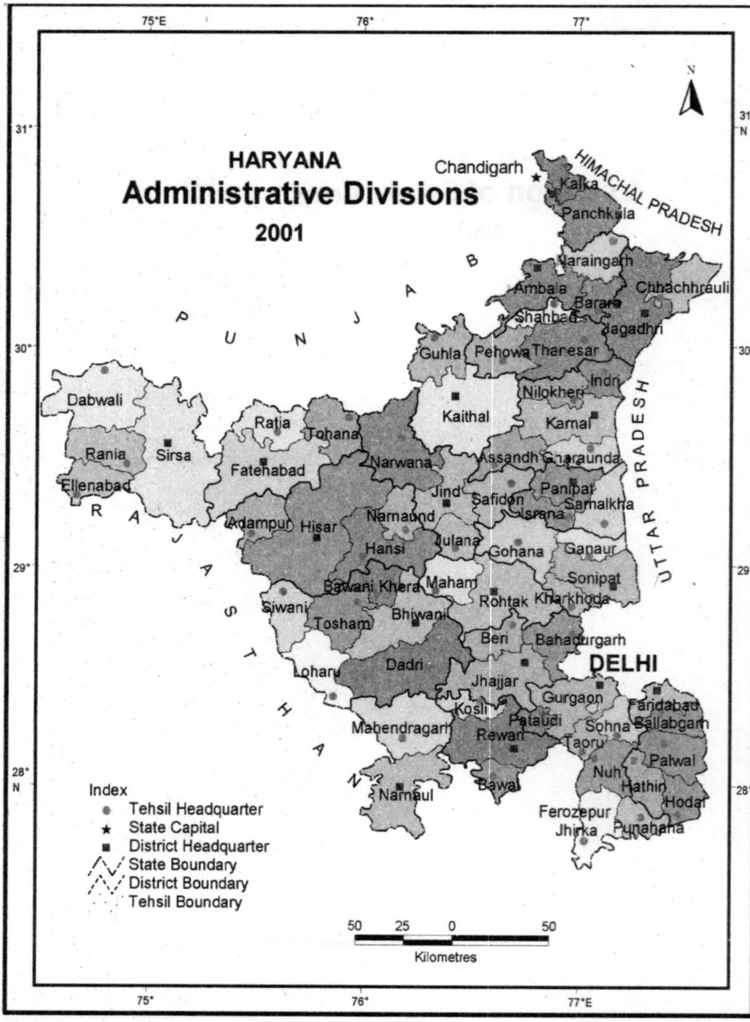

Map 2.2: Haryana: Administrative Divisions, 2001

of Indo-Gangetic plain which was formed by the deposition of alluvium brought down by the Himalayan rivers. Geographers now demarcate Haryana as 'Haryana Tract' as a sub-division of Punjab Plain. Haryana is generally a broad level plain with the exception of Outer Shiwalik ranges in the north-east in Panchkula, Ambala and Yamunanagar and Aravali ranges in the south in Mahendergarh and Gurgaon districts.

Physiographically, Haryana may be divided into five sub-regions which provide a suitable framework upon which a systematic outline of the landform environment may be founded (Singh, 1976 and Haryana State Gazetteers, 2004). These regions are:

1. The Shiwaliks Hills (over 600 metres in height);
2. The Piedmont Plain or The Foothill Rolling Plain (300-400 metres in height);
3. The Alluvial Plain or the Ghaggar-Yamuna Plain (below 300 metres in height);
4. The Bagar—An Undulating Sandy Plain (230-350 metres in height); and
5. The Aravalli Outliers (300-600 metres in height).

1. The Shiwalik Hills (Over 600 metres in Height)

The Shiwalik Hills, which form a sub-mountainous narrow belt in the extreme north/north-east of Haryana, are the sharply-rising and straight high hills and flank the northern boundary of Panchkula district. The Siwaliks are made, for the most part, of 'barely coherent' sandrock, with occasional clays, gravels and conglomerates, an ideal formation for gullying (Spate and Learmonth, 1967).

The Shiwalik hills constitute three main pockets of hilly tracts, viz., the Chandigarh Shiwalik Hill Tract, Morni Hill Tract and Kalesar Hill Tract. The Morni Hill tract is the largest pocket hilly area within the Panchkula district and comprises two north-west and south-east running parallel ridges separated by the deep and narrow valley of the river Ghaggar. Of the two ridges, the southern one is more massive and extensive, but the highest peak, viz., Dharot Kahlong, 1,499 metres above mean sea level, lies on the northern ridges (Haryana State Gazetteer, 2004). The highest peak on the southern ridge is only 1,246 metres high. The crest of the southern ridge supports a number of small settlements including that of Morni from which the tract derives its name. However, some scholars consider Karoh peak as the highest point of Morni hills as well as of Haryana whose absolute relief is 1,514 m (Singh, 1976; Verma and Singh, 2001).

The slopes in the Siwaliks are generally steep and characterized by frequent vertical drops. Many streams after indenting these hills come to the piedmont. The Ghaggar, the Markanda, the Tangri, the Chautang, and the Rakshi are the important ones. These monsoon torrents are dry except during the rainy season, when they in sudden spate come down armed with masses of sand and pebbles and are agents of rapid erosion on the Piedmont Plain below.

The low lying areas of varying widths between these mountain ranges, running from north-west to south-east, are known as Pinjore and Nalagarh *duns* (Geological Survey of India, 1989). *Pinjore Dun* is a structural velley, about 5-8 kilometres wide, sandwiched between the outer Himalayas in the north and the Shiwalik range in the south. It extends from the river Ghaggar in the south-east to the river Satluj outside the limits of the Panchkula district, in the north-west. However, within the area, its extent is limited between the river Ghaggar and *Balad nadi*, a distance of about 25 kilometres.

2. *The Piedmont Plain or The Foothill Rolling Plain (300-400 metres in Height)*

The Piedmont Plain, locally known as *Ghar*, is sandy undulating plain with a perceptible slope near the hills (Singh, 1976). This is a long belt of undulating, fairly sloping plain with elevation between 300-400 metres, adjoining the Shiwalik range stretching from the river Ghaggar in the north-west to the river Yamuna in the south-east. Its width, varying from 10 to 25 kilometres, is maximum in Naraingarh tahsil. Collateral coalescence of alluvial fans at the foot of the Shiwalik range has created a continuous belt of steeply sloping undulating land all along the hills. These alluvial fans have been formed by the deposit of material brought down by the seasonal streams from the Shiwalik range near the hills. The deposited material is very coarse like sand and gravel but as one move away from the hills, the material gets finer and finer. Gully formation on the alluvial fans and its extension into the adjoining clay uplands has extended and accentuated the undulations in the area. Gully formation on the two major clay uplands, one between *Dangri nadi* (*Tangri stream*) and *Begna nadi* and the other between the *Markanda River* and *Somb nadi* is most intense. Here, the flat land has been devoured extensively by the gullies. Generally, these gullies are entrenched 2-5 metres deep but at places these are as deep as 10 metres. Drainage density in the tract is very high and the streams are fairly closely spaced (Haryana State Gazetteers, 2004).

3. *The Alluvial Plain or the Ghaggar-Yamuna Plain (Below 300 metres in Height)*

The alluvial plain of Haryana as usual has the alluvial richness. It is one of the socio-economic hinterlands of India, contributing a major and significant share to the foodgrain reserve of the nation. Besides, it occupies an important position in the sub-continent as it forms the water divide between the two mighty River systems of the Ganga and the Indus flowing into the Bay of Bengal and the Arabian Sea respectively. It comprises vast riverine plains of the older and the newer alluvium and, therefore, the lithological diversity in alluvial monotony has a strong bearing upon the distributional pattern of land-use, cropping pattern and agricultural productivity.

The Ghaggar and Markanda streams and Yamuna River have left their imprint on the local relief of the alluvial plain. The region is considerably vast, more fertile and populous.

Indeed, the 300 metres significant contour represents a more meaningful boundary between the plain and the upland (Singh, 1976). The plain imperceptibly slopes from north-east to south and south-west, the gradients to which follow the lines of natural drainage. The plain is remarkably flat in the districts of Ambala, Yamuna Nagar, Kurukshetra, Karnal, Kaithal, Jind, Sonipat and the north-eastern part of Hisar.

Within the alluvial plain are the narrow low lying flood plains, known as *Khadar* of Yamuna, *Naili* of Ghaggar, and *Bet* of Markanda. Besides, the flat of the saucer in Sonipat and northern parts of Rohtak districts forms a part of the said plain. At places, there are occasional local undulations forming old rolling alluvial plains which include the *Rohi* of Dabwali and Sirsa tahsils (Sirsa district). The *Rohi* has many abandoned beds of old streams, in particular that of the Ghaggar, which provide fertile land suited to agriculture. The *Rohi* is not completely flat because of the presence of *tals* and *tibbas*. The local relief of the *tibbas* is very insignificant and these have either been under the process of levelling or completely graded on account of the extension of irrigation facilities with *Bhakra Canal.*

The older alluvial plain is covered by the Pleistocene deposits. The old alluvial Plain (*Bangar*) at varying depths contains carbonate of lime, usually occurring in nodules called *Kankar,* which are from less than one centimetre to more than 5 centimetres in diameter. In *Bangar*, these *Kankar* formations occur much below the root-zone of the soil and such parts of the land are known as *Nardak*. In the upper reaches of the Saraswati stream in Thanesar tahsil of Kurukshetra district, the *Kankar* seems to occur in the form of a pan close to the root-zone and this tract is termed as *Chhachhra*. The older alluvium of the *Nardak* and the *Chhachhra* has lower level of fertility as compared to the *Bangar* alluvium on account of the *Kankar* formations in the former. On the whole, the *Bangar* region is characterized by patches of saline efflorescence which is the result of the mechanical composition of alluvium, gentle slope of the land and the capillary action during the hot dry season. The damage caused by salinity has, however, been considerably minimized by the tube well and canal irrigation facilities.

On the east of the alluvial plain is the flood plain of the Yamuna extending from its existing course to its old high bank. It is narrow in the tahsil of Jagadhri in Yamuna Nagar district, it broadens towards Sonipat after passing through the districts of Karnal and Panipat and again narrows down in the district of Faridabad. In the north-west of the alluvial plain lie the flood plains of the Ghaggar and the Markanda called *Naili* and *Bet* respectively. Gulha *Naili,* Shabad *Bet,* and Sirsa *Naili* are wide and a larger area is liable to inundation during the floods. The wide flood plains gradually merge into adjacent old plains. On the other hand, the flood plain in Fatehabad tahsil is narrow with a recognizable change into the old plains. Ghaggar *Naili* is gently sloping, and largely cleared of natural vegetation for cultivation. This area has experienced agricultural revolution of significant magnitude during the fifties resulting from agricultural colonization of the cultivable waste land, where the irrigation facilities provide through the minor irrigation schemes and the Bhakra Canal brought dynamic changes in agrarian economy.

Sisra *Naili* is wide and shallow. The result is that a far larger area is flooded in the south-east of Sirsa tahsil, known as the *Ankai Swamp*. In this part, sand dunes are common as it lies close to the

Marusthali of Rajasthan. These dunes are of shifting nature and crescentric in shape. Their march has been checked with the extension of irrigation facilities.

The water-table in the *Khadar, Naili,* and *Bet* regions is fairly high, facilitating irrigation from tubewells. The regions have fertile soils of recent deposits which are replenished every year.

4. The Bagar—An Undulating Sandy Plain (230-350 metres in Height)

Sand dunes of various shapes and sizes form a thirsty land, covered by steppe vegetation in the south-western parts of Haryana. The *Bagar* lies in parts of Sirsa, Fatehabad, Hisar and Bhiwani districts. Of great significance is the large amount of wind-blown sand, piled-up several metres high above the local flats or *Tals,* and stretched for several kilometres in length. This forms a continuous strip of significant concentration of *sandy billows* adjacent to the *Thar Desert* on about 11.23 per cent of the total area of the State. Sand dunes, found on a massive scale in this belt, extend from the south-east of Sirsa district along the Rajasthan border with Hisar district and this sand dune belt widens gradually through the Bhiwani district. The region resembles practically treeless undulating arid desert, and is locally known as *Bagar* (Singh, 1976).

Sand dunes, locally known as *Tibbas,* of varying magnitude are the main features of the south-west. At places, the local relief is as high as 15 metres but generally the dunes are 3 to 6 metres above the ground level. Some of the dunes are mobile, while most are stationary. Their axes may be parallel to the wind direction. Generally, longitudinal dunes are common. The mobile sand dunes, at places, present a serious problem of erosion by wind and threaten to impair the prosperity of fertile alluvial plains lying to their north and north-east.

The region is not altogether, as the name implies, a desolate treeless waste, but it does support a thin scrubby vegetation in *Tals*. The places of the region, which are useful for cultivation and where sand does not accumulate due to some reason or the other, are locally known as *Tals*. Further, the monotony of sand heaps is broken by the rocky projections in Bhiwani district particularly. The region gradually rises in elevation towards the south-eastern part terminating in *Sohana Plateau* of Aravalli ranges.

As a result of meagre rainfall and its highly unreliable

character, the climatic conditions of the *Bagar* and the undulating sandy plains are arid. Most of the arid region possesses a very scanty vegetation partly due to cultivation and grazing practices, and primarily due to the prevailing desert conditions. The soil moisture deficit is very acute and it persists throughout the year.

5. The Aravalli Outliers (300-650 metres in Height)

The Aravallis, consisting of Alwar and Ajabgarh series, extend for 90 km in the Gurgaon rolling plain and Mahendragarh *Tals* and *Tibbas*. The hills traverse a northeast-southwest direction and at places extend upto Delhi and reach the Yamuna River like isolated ridges. Besides Gurgaon, the Aravalli outliers are scattered as rocky outcrops in Mahendragarh, Rewari, and Bhiwani districts, and stand out distinctly against the level horizon above the sand dunes. Tosham hills, attaining an absolute relief of 398 metres, in the district of Bhiwani have steep drops. Similarly, the Aravalli extensions in Gurgaon have also moderately steep falls. In Haryana, the absolute relief of the Aravalli outliers is at no point higher than 640 metres. *Dhosi hill* is considered as the highest peak of southern Haryana, which stands at 640 m and is about three km west of Narnaul city, whereas the general ground level is at about 220 metres (Geological Survey of India, 1989).

These hills with bold and rounded forms present wind-worn and water-eroded topography. Equally apparent is the abundance of debris produced by mechanical disintegration of the bare surfaces. The main southwest-northeast alignment of the hills is remarkably regular in the district of Gurgaon.

On the whole, the Aravalli outliers form series of flat-topped ridges with gentle slopes on both the flanks, and thin bony fingers half-buried either in the alluvium or the aeolian deposits giving a low local relief.

The Aravallis are fairly dissected by generally dry but, at times, violently flowing *nullahs* (small seasonal streams of dissipating nature). The drainage in the area is mostly ephemeral and northerly. The important rivers are Dohan, Krishnawati and Sahibi. Dry channels, guillies and ravines, the relict hills, the boulders scattered over gullied surfaces, and the undulating dales and vales have made the Aravallis (Haryana State Gazetteers, 2004).

The water-table may be as much as over 150 metres down

making traditional irrigation impracticable. It is observed that about 50 per cent of the hills, comprise sharply rising areas where soil erosion is active and soil cover is either thin or absent.

Due to inadequacy of rainfall and rocky nature of the terrain, the Aravalli hills generally lack vegetation cover. At best, these support some stunted trees of Kikar and Karir or thorny shrubs or bushes of *ber* and other hardy varieties. Pastures are not widespread but, on gentler slopes, there are patches of grass and shrubs which support a certain amount of pastoral activity.

2.2.2 *Drainage*

Haryana is devoid of any perennial river except the Yamuna, which flows not exactly through Haryana, but along the extreme eastern side of the State and provide irrigation facility to the region. A large number of rainfall torrents flow down the outer slopes of the Shiwalik and spread much gravels and pebbles in their beds. The Ghaggar, the Markanda, the Saraswati, the Chautang and the Rakshi are the important ones. All these streams flow in the south-west direction as the general slope of Haryana is from north-east to south-west. But in southern Haryana, the slope is towards north. That is why, a number of small rainy season rivulets carry the water from Rajasthan. Among these, the Dohan, the Krishnawati (Kasaunti), the Indori and the Sahibi are worth mentioning. All the streams of Haryana are seasonal and look like streaks of water only during summer and very often become formidable bodies of water during the rainy season. Since many of the streams have broad sand course and go below surface, the entire tract is region of inland drainage.

2.2.3 *Climate*

The climate of Haryana can be classed as a Sub-Tropical Continental Monsoon Climate possessing the following characteristics; (a) seasonal rhythm, (b) hot summer, (c) cool winter, (d) mostly dry except for two to three months (July to September), (e) meagre and aberrant rainfall, (f) unreliable rainfall, and (g) great annual range of temperature. According to Koppen's climatic classification, most of Haryana falls under climatic type '*Cwg*' (Sub-Tropical Monsoon Climate with Ganges type of temperature regime, i.e., dry winter and hot summer) except some parts of south-western Haryana, particularly Sirsa district, where '*BShw*' (Subtropical steppe climate or low latitude hot and dry climate) climatic type dominate the scene. Some of the characteristic climatic elements of the State are as follows:

(a) Temperature

Day temperatures are more or less uniform over the plains except winter and monsoon when the temperatures increase southwards and north-westwards respectively. Temperature is far less inconsistent from year to year than rainfall, but in Haryana great annual range of temperature is highly significant. The large temperature ranges are because of the magnitude of continentality and differences in the characteristics of prevailing air masses. The average annual temperature in Haryana ranges from 23°C in north-east to more than 25°C in north-west and south-west. This gradual increase from north to east and south to west is mainly because of dominance of hilly tracts and sand-dunes topography respectively.

The climate of Haryana in summer season is also characterized by hot winds known as *loo* in local language and frequent dust storms. May is the hottest month with the mean maximum temperature of 41°C in the plains, the plateau regions and elevated places recording 2 °C to 5 °C lower. The highest temperature recorded at an individual satiation in the plains is 48.4 °C at Hisar observatory, on the 19th June, 1981, which was about 6.8 °C higher than normal of the warmest month. The highest temperature recorded at an individual satiation in the plains is 48.4 °C at Hisar observatory, on the 19th June, 1981, which was about 6.8 °C higher than normal of the warmest month (Haryana State Gazetteers, 2004).

January is the coldest month when the minimum temperature for the State as a whole is 6.6 °C varying from 5 °C in the west to 7 °C in the east and also from 7.5 °C in the south 6 °C in the north. During winter, much lower temperatures may be experienced in the wake of western disturbances. On such occasions minimum temperatures may drop below the freezing point at few stations of western parts of the State. The lowest temperature on record at an individual plain station was 3.9 °C at Hissar observatory on 31st January, 1929 and this was about 9.4 °C lower than the normal of the coldest month (Haryana State Gazetteers, 2004).

(b) Rainfall

The feeble currents of south-west monsoon extend over the entire State by the last week of June. The months of July and August are the rainiest months, each accounting individually to about 30 per cent of annual rainfall. In each of these months, there are 5 to 11 rainy days (with daily rainfall of at least 2.5 mm.) for the State (Haryana State Gazetteers, 2004).

During winter (November to March), Haryana receives 6.0 cm of rainfall which although small in amount is of great significance for agriculture. The winter rainfall occurs in association with western disturbances which move from west to east across the State.

The State as a whole receives a total annual rainfall of 59.3 cm, which varies from 30 cm over the extreme western parts adjacent to Rajasthan, 56 cm on the extreme south to 108 cm over the extreme north along the eastern border of the State.

The monsoon rainfall decreases from east to west and northwest to southwest. But the cyclonic rainfall fades from north to south and there is a significant variability in rainfall from month to month.

The southern and south-western half of Haryana is bounded on its north by a 500 mm isohyet. In the northern half, rainfall gradually increases towards Shiwalik where it approaches to about 1000 mm. So, annual precipitation varies between over 1000 mm on the Shiwaliks, the Sub-Shiwaliks and the Piedmont Plain in the northeast to less than 300 mm along the southwestern borders of the State.

The northern-most district of Panchkula constitutes the area of maximum rainfall in the State and western-most district of Sirsa receives minimum amount of rainfall. Rainfall over Sirsa district and Punchkula district are 32.5 cm and 98.8 cm respectively. In the central portion of the State, annual rainfall varies from 40 cm to 48 cm. The districts adjacent to Rajasthan are much more dry than those adjacent to Uttar Pradesh.

In nutshell, rainfall over most of Haryana is unreliable, variable, aberrant, meagre and often truant.

(c) Relative Humidity

The relative humidity is generally high during the period from July to September. The mean monthly relative humidity fluctuates between 42 per cent in June and 72 per cent in August. It is lowest in the summer months of March to June, when it becomes about 25 per cent to 33 per cent, because this is the period when the temperatures are rising and the wind speed is at its maximum. On the other hand, it has been observed highest in the month of August (72 per cent). The diurnal variation of relative humidity is least during monsoon season. By contrast, the diurnal variation of relative humidity is highest during the winter period. Among the winter months (December to February), the month of January is the most humid (63 per cent). In regional perspective, the western parts of the state are less humid than the eastern parts.

2.2.4 Soils

The soils of Haryana can be classified into six major categories (Singh, 1976) as given below :

1. *Very Light Soils (i.e., Sandy and Loamy Sand Soils)*

In the southwest, where the Great Indian Desert makes an entry on to the plains of Haryana, severe aridity prevails. The most predominant component in these stretches is desert sand of quartz origin having well-rounded grains with a fair proportion of calcium. The soil cover is mostly sandy and loamy sand, lying on the undulations of Bhiwani Bagar (sandy), Western Mahendragarh district (sandy) and Hisar Bagar (loamy sand). A high content of salt is present and the sub-soil water is mostly unsuitable for irrigation purposes because of its brackish nature. The chief characteristics of these soils are that they are vey deep, light, well-drained and highly permeable.

2. *The Light Soils (i.e., the relatively Sandy Loam and Sandy Soft Loam Soils*

The light soils have two sub-categories, viz., (a) The relatively Sandy Loam, and (b) The Sandy Soft Loam.

The relatively sandy loam belt stretches between the sandy soils and the loams. It covers the dominantly *barani* areas of Fetehabad, Hisar, Bawani Khera and Bhiwani tehsils. Sandy loam locally known as *rausli* needs little ploughing and readily retains moisture. *Rausli* being capable of retaining moisture is the best soil for dry farming, i.e., barani cultivation.

The sandy soft loam is found in Sirsa tehsil north of the Ghaggar silty clayey and clayey silt belt and in the whole of Dabwali tehsil. The soil is generally a light loam interspersed here and there with sandy insulations which become more common in the western part of Dabwali tehsil. It is soft, with almost ideal proportions of sand and silt and clay.

The light soils (sandy loam, soft loam and light loam) have advantage over the medium soils because in the former less moisture is required for germination, growth and assured harvest. They provide the better agricultural soils and are generally easily ploughed. These soils are capable of producing variety of crops, such as wheat, gram, barley, cotton and oilseeds.

3. *The Medium Soils (Light Loam, Coarse Loam and Loam Soils)*

Medium soils constitute the major part of Haryana and comprise soils of widely different nature resulting from varying physical compositions in terms of silt, sand and clay proportions. These embrace three sub-categories, viz., (a) Light Loam (*Seoti*), (b) Coarse Loam (*Dahar* and *Chaekonte*), and (c) Loam (*Bangar* and *Nardak*).

Light Loam is encountered in western and central Ambala and south Naraingarh tehsils where sand is the dominant constituent. Outside this major belt, there are patches or blocks of light loam in the north of Gurgaon and the northwest of Nuh and a big block in the centre of Rewari.

Coarse loam is found in the south-eastern part of Jhajjar, central Nuh and western Firozepur Jhirka tehsils, where in low lying areas the proportion of coarse silt deposits is significant.

Loam covers a major part of Haryana which forms the old and prosperous agricultural area of the State. The soil is deep, well-drained and fertile, capable of producing a variety of crops such as wheat, cotton sugarcane and rice.

4. *The Moderately Heavy Soils (Silty Loam Soils)*

The silty loam soils, locally known as *Khaddar,* are found along the major river course of the *Yamuna* in Yamuna Nagar, Karnal, Panipat, Sonipat and Faridabad districts.

Khaddar soil is very inferior, poor, grey-coloured sandy loam in Yamuna Nagar and north Karnal districts. Towards south through southern Karnal, Panipat, Sonipat, and Faridabad (Ballabgarh and northeastern tip of Palwal tehsils) districts, it is fertile loam. The proportion of silt and clay components in silty loam is higher than in loam, hence it has a blocky structure which reduces its water-holding capacity.

5. The Heavy Soils and Very Heavy Soils (Clayey Silt and Silty Clay Soils)

These soils are found along the Ghaggar-Markanda seasonal drainage system. The *heavy soil* is clayey silt which forms a good area of alluvium known as *bet*. The *very heavy soil* consists of silty clay or stiff loam or stiff clay which is confined to drainage lines and hollows. Hard clay (*sotar*) or loam prevails in Ghaggar valley in Hisar and a stiffer clay or loam in *Naili, Anderwar* and *Chhachhra* assessment circles of Gulha and Thanesar tehsils.

A yet more stiff loam is found in the low lying areas where the action of the water has washed out the sandy particles. It is locally known as *Dakar* and characterized by its clods not crumbling in hands. *Dakar* (clay), a stiff or hard iron clay area, to the west of Jagadhari tehsil and extreme east of Ambala around Mulana, is formed by the Shiwalik seasonal streams. Stiff clay is also common in *Chhachhra* of Thanesar, the area intersected by several hill streams.

In nutshell, *the heavy soils* are rich in organic matter and poor in salt content. Generally, their quality appears to be good. In years of good rainfall and regular supply of agricultural water, yields are high. These soils are suitable for grain crops like gram and barley from *barani* (rain fed) fields, and wheat and rice from irrigated fields.

6. The Soils on Shiwaliks, Piedmont Plain and the Rocky Surfaces (Aravallis)

The soils on Shiwaliks in Kalka, Naraingarh, and Jagadhari tehsils are composed of very friable and only partially consolidated sandstone containing beds of clay, sand and conglomerate with frequent boulder and pebble beds. Soil is confined to small strips and terraces along the intervening valleys. Sandy hills sprinkled with boulders are a usual phenomenon.

The Piedmont Plain is mostly covered by sandy shingly soil much overgrown with thorn bushes and cut by ravines. The area is known as *Ghar* in Kalka and Naraingarh and *Kandi* in Jagadhari tehsils. The soils are poor and sandy, lying on uneven surface, and pebbles, shingles and boulders often lie close to the surface.

The soil of the rocky outcrops in Gurgaon, Rewari, and Mahendragarh districts is coarse, not sufficiently thick and favourable for crop production. It is too shallow, too stony, too infertile to be used for the raising of field crops.

2.2.5 *Sub-Soil Water Table*

In the Siwaliks of Haryana, the ground water-table is quite deep. Over the rest of the region, the ground water-table rises as one moves from south and south-west to north and east. In the districts of Mahendragarh, Bhiwani, Hisar, Jind and Sirsa, the sub-soil water is deep seated and is generally found at a depth of more than ten metres except in the Hansi depression and Ghaggar bed. The greatest depths range from 40 to 50 metres. In the districts of Ambala, Karnal, Kurukshetra, Sonipat and Rohtak the water-table is often found at an average depth of 3 metres, though it never exceeds a depth of nine metres (Chib, 1977).

2.2.6 *Forest Cover*

Haryana is an intensively cultivated State and deficient in natural forests. With only 3.61 per cent forest cover of the total geographical area of the State (Government of Haryana, 2010), the Haryana is one of the least forested States of the country. In terms of minimum forest cover, Haryana ranks second (3.61 per cent) after Punjab (3.30 per cent) amongst 35 States and union territories of India (Forest Survey of India, 2009). Prevailing arid conditions and long human occupance have been responsible for its poor vegetation cover.

The forests found in the State are grouped into three types (Census of India, 1991), viz. :

(i) Tropical Dry Deciduous Forests

(ii) Tropical Thorn Forests, and
(iii) Sub-Tropical Pine Forests

(i) Tropical Dry Deciduous Forests

These forests are distributed in the foothills of Shiwalik in the north-eastern parts of Panchkula, Yamunanagar and Ambala districts. Some patches of these forests are also found in Jind district and eastern to north-western parts of Faridabad district. Among Tropical Dry Deciduous Forests, *Kikar* (*Acacia nilotica*) dominates in northern parts and *Shisham* (*Dalbergia sissoo*) in the southern parts. The shrub jungle mainly consists of coral flowered leafless *Karir (Capparis decidua), Jal (Salvadora oleoides)* and *Jand (Prosopis cineraria).*

(ii) Tropical Thorn Forests

These forests are found in the districts of Rewari, Mahendragarh, Gurgaon, Bhiwani, Kaithal, Kurukshetra and Ambala. A few land patches are also covered with these forests in the districts of Hisar, Karnal, and Sonipat. This sort of flora is found in areas getting annual rainfall from 20 cm to 40 cm. These forests are dominated with short stunted thorny bushes and the trees of *Neem (Azadirachta indica), Pipal (Pious religiosa), Babul (Acacia jacquemontii)* and *Kikar (Acacia nilotica).*

(iii) Sub-Tropical Pine Forests

These forests are available in the higher parts of Shiwalik in Panchkula, Yamunanagar, and Ambala districts. In these forests, *pine* (Pinus), especially the *'lower Shiwalik pine'*, is found mixed with shrubs and thorny species of trees.

At the district level, wide regional variations are found in the forest cover of the State. Panchkula district has the highest proportion of forest cover of the total geographical area of the district (31.55 per cent) and is followed by Yamuna Nagar district (10.92 per cent). By contrast, the lowest forest cover is the characteristic of Fatehabad district (0.71 per cent) followed by Sonipat district (0.94 per cent) (Forest Survey of India, 2009).

2.2.7 *Fauna*

Haryana is rich in animal wealth. Animals like cows, buffaloes, bulls, horses and ponies, mules, donkeys, camels, goats, sheep, pigs and dogs are found in larger numbers in the State. Haryana is known throughout the country for its milch and draught cattle and claims the honour to be the home of two of the best Indian breeds of cows and buffaloes. This is because its soil and the climate are suitable for breeding good stock.

Due to poor vegetal cover, very few wild animals are found in the forests of Haryana. Nonetheless, the areas of Karnal, Panipat, Kaithal and Kurukshetra still hold a good position as regards the stock of wild life. In the Kaithal district and the area bordering Jind territory, *black buck* and *chinkara* are still available, though not in plenty. *Hog deer* which was once quite abundant in swampy parts and along the banks of the Yamuna, is now available in traces only. Some of the noted wild animals still available in Haryana, of course in lesser numbers than before, are *Sambhar, barking deer, spotted deer, wild boar, black buck, ravine deer, blue bull, panther,* and *hyena.* The *tiger* and *leopard* are rarely seen in the State. *Tiger* is a casual visitor to the Kalesar forests and Avavalli hills. Sometimes, the *leopard* may also be seen near Kalka or hilly areas. The fauna regions of Kalka, Pinjore, Morni hills, Kalesar and Kalsia forests possess good potential for wild life development in future.

Under the highest category of mammals, the common *langur* and *bandar* are the main species. Some other carnivorous animals which may be available in the State are the *jungle cat, the small Indian civet, the common mongoose, jackales (giddar)* and *the Indian fox.*

Various kinds of birds are also available in different fauna regions of Haryana. Amongst them, the game birds like the *black partridge, snipe, duck, geese, teals* and *cranes* are common in suitable localities near lakes and ponds. *Blue rock pigeon* is commonly found throughout the State. There is no shortage of *peafowl. Common sand-grouses* are found is open, barren plains, stubble fields and land away from water. *Black partridge* is a State bird.

Apart from the game birds described above, there are numerous other common birds such as sparrow, crow, kite, vulture, babbler, kingfisher, hornbill, egret, heron, stork, tit, bulbul, cuckoo and the dove. *Baya,* tailor-bird, is also common in Haryana State. It mostly makes its nests in the trees of *kikar* which are in abundance.

2.2.8 Mineral Resources

Haryana is not very rich in mineral resources. Mineral-bearing tracts are confined to Mahendragarh, Rewari, and Gurgaon districts in the south; and to a narrow belt along the north-western border of Panchkula and Ambala districts. Some of the important minerals found in the State are slate, iron ore, limestone, lime kankar, china clay, silica sand and sulphur.

Though, Mahendragarh and Rewari are backward both economically and industrially but these are the richest districts as far as mineral deposits are concerned. Only small deposits of high phosphorus *iron ore* are located in Mahendragarh district and another small occurrence is located in Bhiwani district. Total iron ore deposit in Mahendragarh district is of the order of 8.084 metric tonnes, out of which 3.398 metric tonnes is indicated and the rest is inferred (Haryana State Gazetteers, 2004).

The chief deposits of *slate* occur in Mahendragarh and Rewari districts and are situated near Kund, Bahali, Rampura and Bas. In Kund area alone, *slate* reserves have been estimated at 8.78 metric tonnes, out of which nearly 60 per cent is of multicoloured variety (Haryana State Gazetteers, 2004). Because of its desirable flat drainage nature, the slate mined here is used for various purposes.

The geological survey has revealed that deposits of calcite, copper ore, dolomite, granite, mica, feldspar, quartz and other deposits are found in the Mahendragarh district. But, by and large, these deposits are small in quantity and are of low quality.

China clay is found in Faridabad and Gurgaon districts. The important occurrences are located near Alipur, Aurangpur, Ghamrang, Ghosgarh and Sikandarpur. Other occurrences in the area are located near Kasan, Ghata, Mangar and Nathupura. The clay contains mostly poorly-crystallised Kaolinite with little quartz. Chemical analysis of clay from different localities indicate that silica is normally over 60 per cent, while alumina is around 20 per cent and that these are of refractory type. An estimate of pegmatite material, which yields roughly about 50 per cent clay on washing at Aurangpur, Ghogarh, and Sikandarpur is 890, 800 and 5,250 tonnes per metre depth respectively. Total Kaolin deposits of the two districts are of the order of 0.22 metric tonnes, out of which 0.07 metric tonnes is indicated and the rest is inferred (Haryana State Gazetteers, 2004). *Silica sand* is found in Gurgaon and

Faridabad districts. There are many *sand quarries* in the Aurangpur area in Faridabad district. *Sulphur* is found in Panipat district.

Limestone is mostly confined to Mahendragarh and Panchkula districts of Haryana. Total deposits of cement limestone in the State are of the order of 50.25 metric tonnes. Of which, 24.01 or 25 metric tonnes is measured and the rest in inferred (Haryana State Gazetteers, 2004). In Panchkula district, good quality *limestone* is mined which is used in Bhupindra Cement Works at Surajpur. The *lime Kankar* is being worked out in Loharu (Bhiwani) and Kaliawas (Rohtak) for cement manufacturing at Charkhi Dadri in Bhiwani district.

2.3 Cultural Setting

The cultural profile of Haryana comprises a brief account of the economy of the State as well as the demographic characteristics of the population.

2.3.1 *Economic Characteristics*

(a) Agriculture

Agriculture is a primary activity and the mainstay of more than 70 per cent of the population living in the villages of Haryana. Agriculture still continues to occupy a significant position in State economy, despite the fact that its share in the Gross State Domestic Product is continuously declining. The State was deficit in food-grains at the time of its formation in 1966. From a largely food deficit area, Haryana has today become one of the most uniquely developed agricultural regions of the nation and has a pivotal position in the economy of the State. It has emerged as the "*grain bowl of the country*". Resultantly, foodgrains production touched an impressive figure of 161.66 lakh tonnes during 2008-09 as compared to 25.92 lakh tonnes during 1966-67 registering a more than six-fold increase (Government of Haryana, 2010).

In Haryana, the gross area sown was 45.99 lakh hectares during 1966-67 and it has increased to 65.10 hectares during 2008-09.

It means agriculture in Haryana is progressing at a faster rate due to the latest agricultural techniques, scientific appliances, chemical fertilizers, use of high yielding varieties of seeds and provision of increased water supply. Most of the agricultural land of the State is under foodgrains where wheat, rice, maize, jawar, bajra are important ones. However, surgarcane, cotton, and oilseeds are also the important crops of Haryana.

(b) Industries

Although Haryana is primarily an agricultural State, the progress made on the industrial front is also tremendous. This tremendous progress is the result of concerted efforts and large scale incentives such as exemption from electricity duty, property tax and grant of interest free loan in lieu of inter-State sales tax, etc., announced by the Government from time to time for setting up of new industrial units throughout the state. Proximity of Delhi, a large consumer market, offers special locational advantages to industries in Haryana.

In Haryana, the total number of registered working factories increased from 1,168 in 1966 to 9,282 in 2005. It is about eight times increase in the number of registered working factories of the total existing at the time of formation of Haryana as a separate State. There was also a phenomenal increase in the estimated number of workers employed in these factories from 7,10,116 in 1966 to 5,74,591 in 2005 (Government of Haryana, 2007).

At the district level, the total number of registered working factories in 2005 is the highest in Faridabad district (2,563) followed by Yamuna Nagar (1,251) and Gurgaon (1,165). By contrast, the lowest figure has been observed in Mahendragarh district (60) followed by Bhiwani (114) and Fatehabad (117) districts.

On the basis of strength of labour force, the registered working factories can be grouped into three types of industries, viz., (i) large scale industries, (ii) medium scale industries, and (iii) small scale industries. From a mere 162 large and medium scale industries in 1966 when Haryana came into existence as a separate State, the number has touched a figure of 1,203 by December, 2002, an increase by eight times. In regional perspective at district level, the highest number of large and medium scale units are in Gurgaon district (375) followed by Faridabad (254) and Sonipat (132) districts. On the other hand, Mahendragarh district (02) is having the lowest number of large and medium scale units and is followed by Fatehabad (04) and Kaithal (05) districts (Government of Haryana, 2002).

The State accounts for about 80 per cent of the total number of cars, 60 per cent of tractors, 70 per cent of motor-cycles and 20 per cent of bicycles manufactured in the country. About 25 per cent of India's total production of sanitary wares is also from Haryana. (Government of Haryana, 2002).

Besides this, about 80,000 SSI units are functioning in the State. Twenty per cent of the country's total export of scientific instruments, 60 per cent of the demand for ammunition boxes of the country's defence forces and 60 per cent of the total needs of woollen blankets of Indian Army are met by SSI units of Haryana. The SSI units of Haryana are also manufacturer of the largest number of electrical mixes, food processors and gas stoves in the country (Government of Haryana, 2002).

Faridabad-Ballabgarh industrial corridor has assumed a place of pride on the industrial map of the country. There are more than 100 large and medium and over 1,200 small scale units. Faridabad is the biggest industrial centre in the State. About half of the State's industries are located here. The wide range of goods produced covers such items as agricultural tractors, automobile parts, motor-cycles, hand tools, machine tools, scientific instruments, radio and electric equipments, sanitary wares, textiles, shoes and other numerous articles. Industrial units like Goodyear, Bata, Escorts, Eicher, Metal-box, Hyderabad Asbestos, Kelvinators have an all-India status.

Yamuna Nagar, Sonipat, Bahadurgarh and Gurgaon are also important industrial centres of the State. Bahadurgarh and Hisar have become important centres for rolling mills, steel tubes and other steel processing industries. Dharuhera in Rewari district is new and fast developing industrial centre of southern Haryana. Kundli in Sonipat district and Roz Ka Meo in Gurgaon are also being developed for the location of certain small scale industries. The world famous Atlas cycles are manufactured at Sonipat city. Marked industrial development has also been recorded in Rohtak, Panipat, Jagadhari, Ambala, etc. The Refinery in Panipat is the first of its kind in the State.

(c) Transport Network

It has been rightly observed that '*if agriculture and industry are the body and bones of the national organism, transport and communications are its nerves'*. Kipling goes further and says *'Transport is Civilization'*. The importance of road transport in the growth of economy can hardly be over emphasized. It has played significant role in shaping the economic, social and political life of the communities. Cheap and efficient transport system helps in the specialization of production, cheap consumer goods of large varieties, close inter-dependence between the individual, groups, and nations. It is, indeed, inconceivable to think of modern economic life without transport facilities.

Haryana State was carved out of the territories of composite State of Punjab on 1st November, 1966. At the time of its creation, it was underdeveloped State with poor road network and inadequate transport facilities. The total road length (metalled and unmetalled) maintained by Public Works Department (B&R) as well as Local Bodies was 8,187 km during 1966-67, which increased to 24,383 km during 2009-10, about threefold increase within a span of 34 years.

Haryana Roadways is one of the better run State Road Transport Undertaking of the country. It had a fleet of 475 buses in 1966, that increased to a fleet of 3,257 buses (as on 31.12.2009), which are being operated by 20 Depots and 17 Sub-Depots. The Roadways covers about 10.63 lakh km daily and carries more than 11.07 lakh passengers everyday with a staff of 17,679 persons (Government of Haryana, 2010). So, the State has the enough transport facilities where each and every village is connected through road network.

The rail network of Haryana is well established. Under the 'National Capital Region' (NCR) scheme, the Central Government cooperates with the State government in promoting the rail transport of the State that shall facilitate the people around this region. The government has proposed to develop a rail corridor connecting towns around Delhi and linking the major satellite towns like Faridabad, Gurgaon, Bahadurgarh, Kundli, etc., to other cities and towns in Haryana. Similarly, there is a proposal to provide rapid mass transportation system between Delhi and these Satellite towns. Some of the major railway routes that are laid across the State are :

- Ambala - Delhi
- Ambala - Ferozepur

- Amritsar - Howrah
- Amritsar - Delhi
- Bhiwani - Rohtak-Delhi
- Bhiwani - Rohtak-Kalka
- Delhi - Ferozepur
- Delhi - Shimla
- Kalka - Howrah
- Kalka - Jodhpur
- Rewari - Ahmedabad
- Rohtak - Rewari

Ambala, Kurukshetra, Panipat, Rohtak, Hisar and Rewari are the main railway junctions in the State. Rewari has the distinction of being the biggest Metre Gauge Railway Junction of North India. There is also one railways workshop in Yamuna Nagar. The Government of Haryana is implementing plans to promote the growth of the rail transport in the State.

2.3.2 *Demographic Characteristics*

(a) Distribution of Population

The population of Haryana accounts for 2.1 per cent of the country's population and ranks 16th amongst the States and Union Territories. As per 2001 Census, the total population of the State is 2,11,44,564 persons consisting of 1,13,63,953 males and 97,80,611 females. It is unevenly distributed. The most thickly populated district is Faridabad having a population of 21,94,586 persons (10.4 per cent population of the State). The second position is occupied by Gurgaon with 7.9 per cent (16,60, 289). By contrast, Panchkula is the smallest district in population size with only 2.2 per cent (4,68,411) population of the State (Table 2.1 and Map 2.3).

Haryana has an urban population of 61,15,304 persons living in 106 towns, while the number of villages is 6,955 (6,764 inhabited and 191 uninhabited villages), having a population of 1,50,29,260 persons. It means only 28.9 per cent population live in urban areas and 71.1 per cent population live in rural areas of Haryana. It shows the predominantly rural characteristics of the population of the State. Amongst the districts, Faridabad is the most urbanized district with 55.65 per cent of its population living in urban areas.

At the other end of the scale, Mahendragarh with 13.49 per cent of its total urban population is the least urbanized district of the State (Table 2.2 and Map 2.4).

Table 2.1: Haryana: Distribution of Population by Districts, 2001

District/State	*Population*	*Per Cent to Total Population of State*
Haryana	**21144564**	**100.00**
Faridabad	2194586	10.37
Gurgaon	1660289	7.85
Hisar	1537117	7.27
Bhiwani	1425022	6.74
Sonipat	1279175	6.05
Karnal	1274183	6.03
Jind	1189827	5.63
Sirsa	1116649	5.28
Ambala	1014411	4.93
Yamunanagar	1041630	4.80
Panipat	967449	4.58
Kaithal	946131	4.47
Rohtak	940128	4.45
Jhajjar	880072	4.16
Kurukshetra	825454	3.90
Mahendragarh	812521	3.84
Fatehabad	806158	3.81
Rewari	765351	3.62
Panchkula	468411	2.22

Source: *Census of India (2001), Primary Census Abstract*, Haryana, Series-7, Directorate of Census Operations, Haryana.

Note: Districts have been arranged in descending order of population percentage

(b) Density of Population

Density of population conveys land-man ratio and is normally calculated as number of persons per square kilometre/mile. It is a significant measure of degree of population concentration. The density of population in Haryana has increased from 372 persons per km^2 in 1991 to 478 persons per km^2 in 2001Census registering an increase of 106 persons per km^2. With the passage of time, an increase in density of population is a natural phenomenon in a developing State like Haryana.

As per 2001 Census, the density of population in Haryana (478 persons per km^2) is significantly above the national average of 324

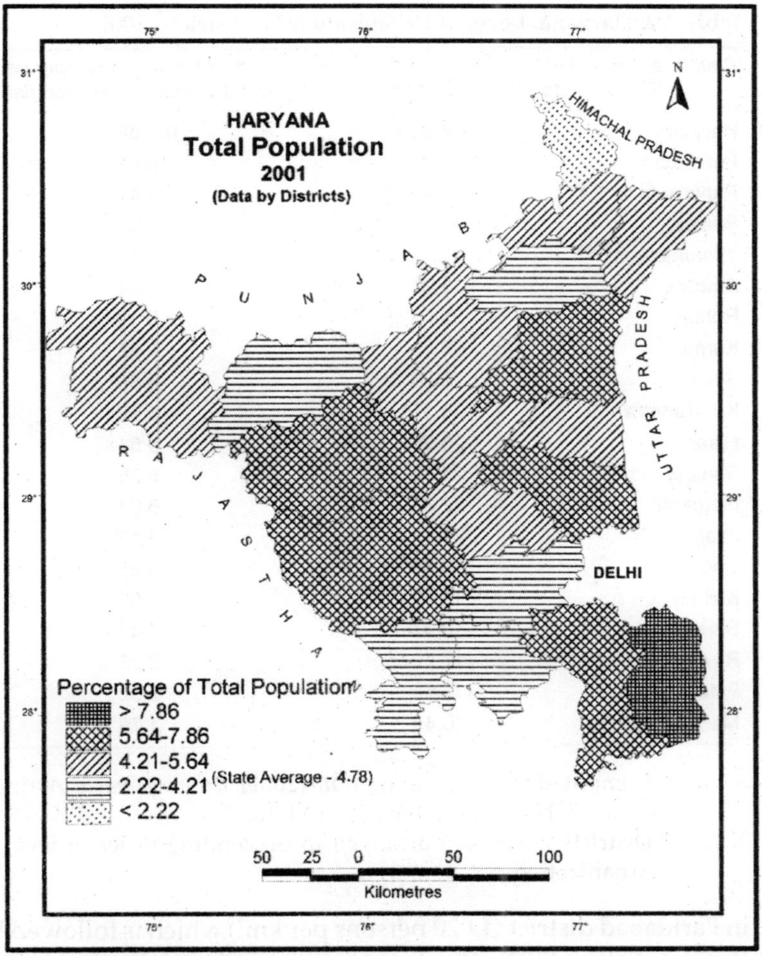

Map 2.3: Haryana: Total Population, 2001

persons per km², and is also higher than adjoining State of Himachal Pradesh (109 persons per km²) but lower than Punjab (482 persons per km²). As the density of population is influenced by various factors such as productivity of soils, climate, topography, minerals, industrial development, urbanization, irrigational facilities, and other factors of the economic development of the area, so density of population is strikingly uneven in the State. The highest density of population is recorded

Table 2.2: Haryana: Level of Urbanisation by Districts, 2001

State/Districts	*Urban Population as per cent to Total District Population*	*Urban Population as per cent to Total State Urban Population*
Haryana	**28.92**	**100.00**
Faridabad	55.65	19.97
Panchkula	44.49	3.41
Panipat	40.53	6.41
Yamunanagar	37.73	6.43
Ambala	35.20	5.84
Rohtak	35.06	5.39
Karnal	26.51	5.52
Sirsa	26.28	4.80
Kurukshetra	26.11	3.52
Hisar	25.90	6.51
Sonipat	25.12	5.26
Gurgaon	22.23	6.03
Jhajjar	22.17	3.19
Jind	20.30	3.95
Kaithal	19.39	3.00
Bhiwani	18.97	4.42
Rewari	17.79	2.23
Fatehabad	17.63	2.32
Mahendragarh	13.49	1.79

Source: Computed from Census of India (2001), *Primary Census Abstract*, Series-7, Haryana, Table A5, pp. 1-10.

Note: Districts have been arranged in descending order of level of urbanization.

in Faridabad district (1,020 persons per km^2) which is followed by Panipat district (763). These districts are industrially developed, so attracting in-migration resulting into higher density. On the other hand, Sirsa district has the lowest density of population (261 persons per km^2) and is followed by Bhiwani district (298) (Table 2.3 and Map 2.5). The topography of these districts is mostly dotted with sand dunes which hamper the agriculture and agricultural based household industries. Dry tropical climate, paucity of water and truancy of rainfall are other causes of low density of population. There are only three districts in Haryana, viz., Fatehabad (318), Bhiwani (298) and Sirsa (261) where density is below the National average (324 persons per km^2). In the

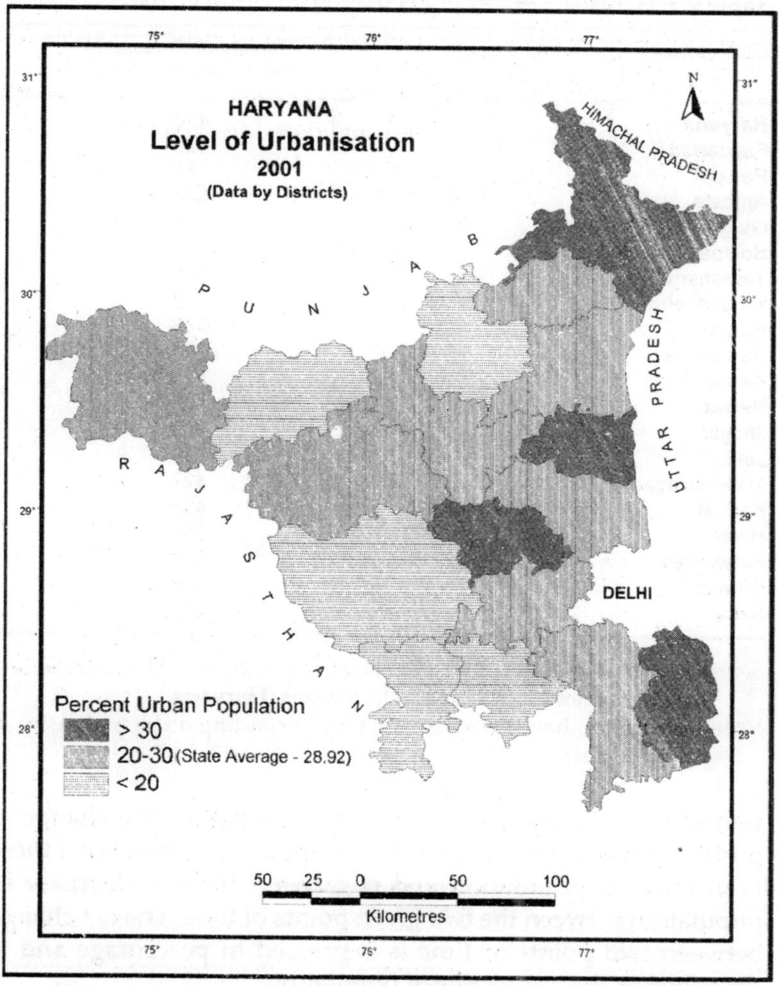

Map 2.4: Haryana: Level of Urbanisation, 2001

concluding remarks, density of population in the eastern half of Haryana is relatively more than its western half (Map 2.5).

(c) Growth of Population

The growth of population is often used to connote the change in the number of people living in a particular area during a specific

Table 2.3: Haryana: Density of Population by Districts, 2001

District/State	*Density of Population (Persons per km²)*
Haryana	**478**
Faridabad	1020
Panipat	762
Ambala	644
Gurgaon	611
Sonipat	602
Yamunanagar	589
Kurukshetra	539
Rohtak	539
Panchkula	521
Karnal	505
Rewari	480
Jhajjar	479
Jind	440
Mahendragarh	427
Kaithal	408
Hisar	385
Fatehabad	318
Bhiwani	298
Sirsa	261

Source : Census of India (2001), *Primary Census Abstract,* Haryana, Series-7, Directorate of Census Operations, Haryana.

Note : Districts have been arranged in descending order of density of population.

period of time, irrespective of the fact whether the change is positive or negative. The growth of population is positive if there is increase in population and negative if there is decrease in population between the two given points of time. The net change between two points of time is expressed in percentage and is described as the *growth rate* of population.

Haryana has had a very chequered demographic history, more so during the twentieth century (Table 2.4 and Fig, 2.1). The decadal growth of population in Haryana is 28.43 per cent which is higher than the National average of 21.5 per cent and kept on changing during the twentieth century (Table 2.5). The comparatively low growth rate of population during 1941-51 was attributed to the partition of the country by which Muslim population out-migrated to Pakistan. The relatively low growth rate during 1971-81 and thereafter may be attributed to the impact of family welfare

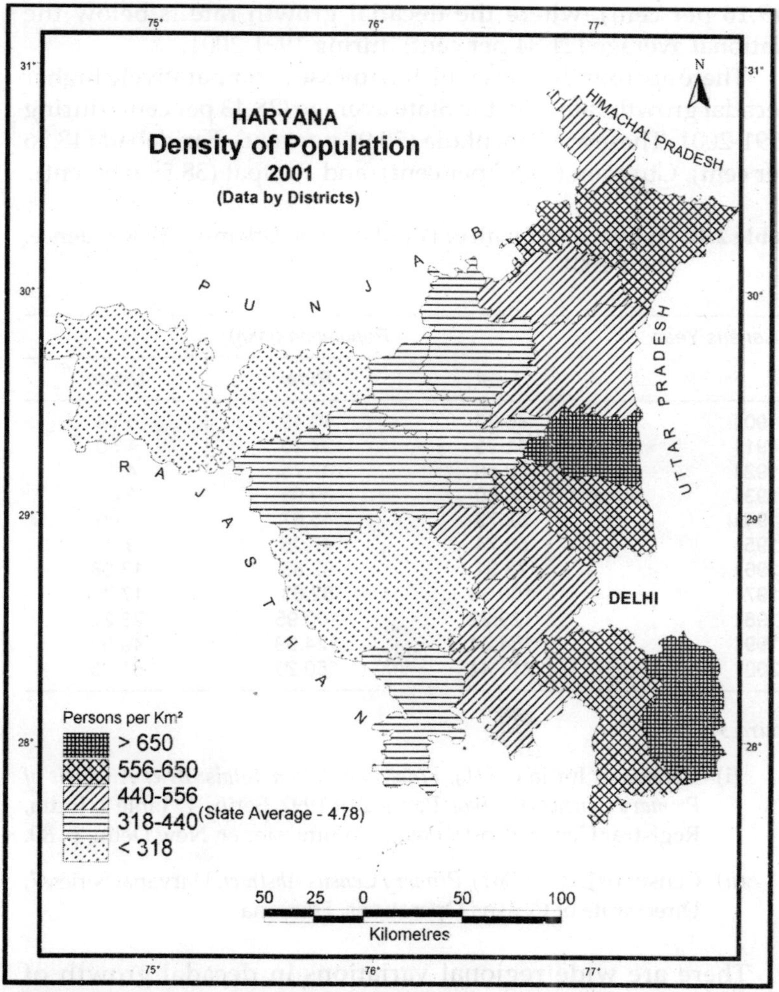

Map 2.5: Haryana: Density of Population, 2001

schemes in the State and awareness of the people in limiting their families with the spread of education. However, it is a matter of concern that at National level, the *population growth rate* has declined, whereas the percentage decadal growth rate of Haryana has risen slightly from +27.41 per cent (1981-91) to +28.43 per cent during 1991-2001.

Surprisingly, there are only three districts in Haryana, namely Kaithal (21.02 per cent), Rohtak (21.00 per cent), and Mahendragarh

(19.16 per cent), where the decadal growth rate is below the National average (21.34 per cent) during 1991-2001.

There are four districts which witnessed comparatively higher decadal growth rate than the State average (28.43 per cent) during 1991-2001. These are Panchkula (50.91 per cent), Faridabad (48.56 per cent), Gurgaon (44.87 per cent), and Panipat (38.58 per cent).

Table 2.4: Haryana : Growth of Population by Urban-Rural Residence, 1901-2001

Census Year	*Population (lakh)*		
	Total	*Rural*	*Urban*
1901	46.23	40.49	5.74
1911	41.75	37.25	4.50
1921	42.56	37.75	4.81
1931	45.60	39.95	5.65
1941	52.73	45.67	7.06
1951	56.74	47.05	9.69
1961	75.91	62.83	13.08
1971	100.36	82.63	17.73
1981	129.22	100.95	28.27
1991	164.64	124.09	40.55
2001	211.44	150.29	61.15

Sources :

(i) Census of India (1991), *Final Population Totals: Brief Analysis of Primary Census Abstract,* Paper 2 of 1992, Series-1, Table 2, India, Registrar General and Census Commissioner, New Delhi, p. 89.

(ii) Census of India (2001), *Primary Census Abstract,* Haryana, Series-7, Directorate of Census Operations, Haryana.

There are wide regional variations in decadal growth of population in Haryana. Among the districts, the highest growth rate of 50.91 per cent has been recorded in Panchkula district followed by Faridabad (48.56 per cent) and Gurgaon (44.87 per cent) during 1991-2001. Its main reason is that these districts are characterized with high level of urbanization and industrialization, so attract the large number of in-migrants in search of job. On the other end of scale, the lowest decadal growth rate of 19.16 per cent has been recorded in Mahendragarh district (Table 2.6 and Map 2.6).

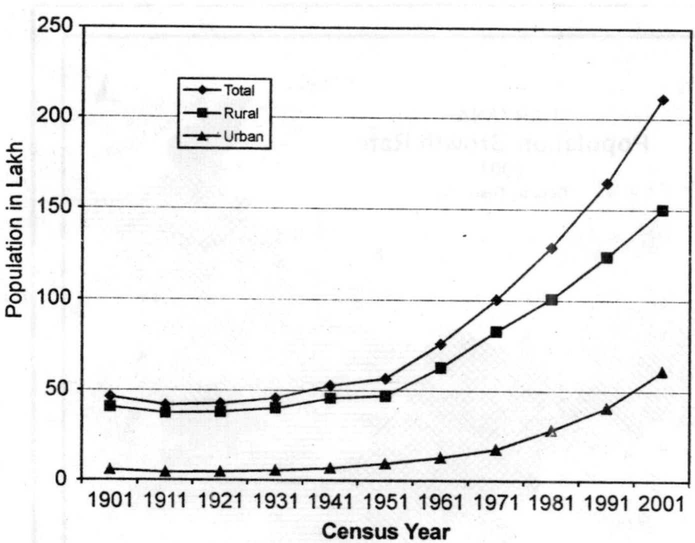

Figure 2.1: Haryana: Growth of Population, 1901-2001

Table 2.5: Haryana: Per Cent Decadal Variation of Population by Urban-Rural Residence, 1901-2001

Census Year	*Decadal Variation of Population (%)*		
	Total	*Rural*	*Urban*
1901-11	-9.70	–8.00	–21.66
1911-21	+1.95	+1.33	+7.00
1921-31	+7.14	+5.84	+17.36
1931-41	+15.63	+14.31	+25.00
1941-51	+7.60	+3.03	+37.19
1951-61	+33.79	+33.53	+35.02
1961-71	+32.22	+31.53	+35.58
1971-81	+28.75	+22.16	+59.47
1981-91	+27.41	+22.92	+43.41
1991-2001	+28.43	+21.12	+50.82

Sources :

(i) Census of India (1991), *Final Population Totals: Brief Analysis of Primary Census Abstract*, Paper 2 of 1992, Series-1, Table 2.1, India, Registrar General and Census Commissioner, New Delhi, p. 98.

(ii) Census of India (2001), *Primary Census Abstract*, Haryana, Series-7, Directorate of Census Operations, Haryana.

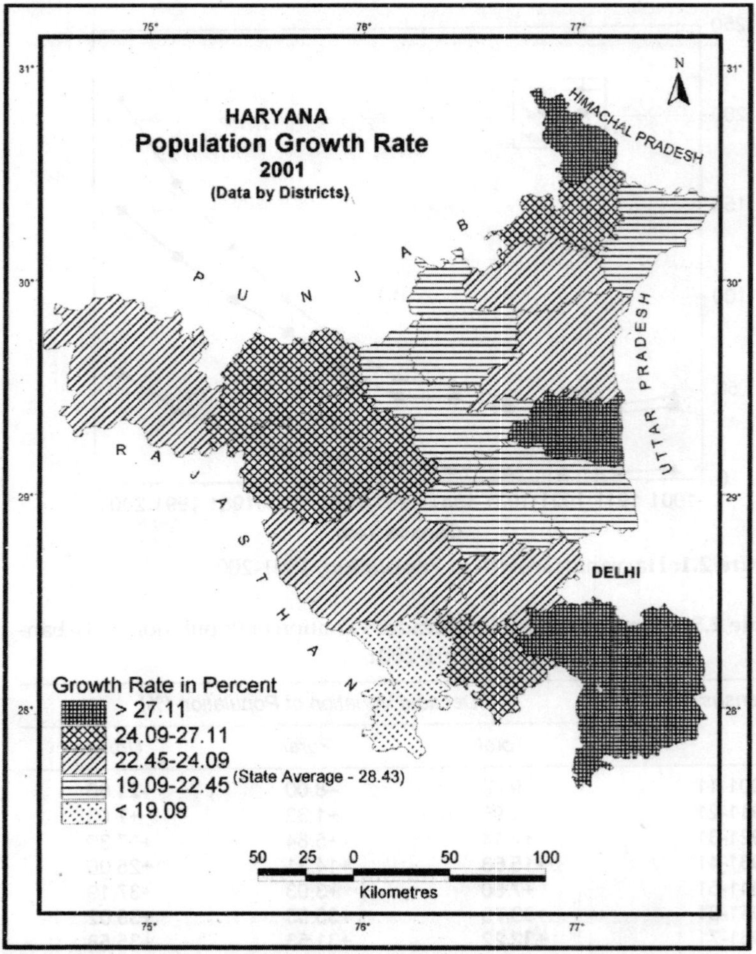

Map 2.6: Haryana: Population Growth, 2001

(d) Sex Ratio

Haryana is a State with deficiency of females. Right from the beginning of twentieth century, sex ratio in Haryana had always remained unfavourable to females (Table 2.7 and Figure 2.2). It is notable that with certain ups and downs from 1901 onwards, the sex ratio of Haryana has declined continuously since 1981 and is at its lowest in 2001 (861 females per 1,000 males).

Table 2.6: Haryana: Growth of Population by Districts, 2001

Districts/State	*Population Growth Rate (%)*
Haryana	**28.43**
Panchkula	50.91
Faridabad	48.56
Gurgaon	44.87
Panipat	38.58
Hisar	27.11
Ambala	25.78
Rewari	25.34
Fatehabad	24.76
Jhajjar	24.06
Kurukshetra	23.32
Karnal	23.06
Sirsa	22.69
Bhiwani	22.49
Sonipat	22.39
Yamunanagar	29.19
Jind	21.36
Rohtak	21.00
Kaithal	21.02
Mahendragarh	19.16

Source : Census of India (2001), *Primary Census Abstract,* Haryana, Series-7, Directorate of Census Operations, Haryana.

Note : Districts have been arranged in descending order of population growth rate.

Table 2.7: Haryana: Sex Ratio by Rural-Urban Residence, 1901-2001

Census Year	*Females Per 1000 Males*		
	Total	*Rural*	*Urban*
1901	867	861	908
1911	835	834	842
1921	844	848	811
1931	844	851	792
1941	869	879	806
1951	871	877	845
1961	868	874	842
1971	867	870	853
1981	870	876	849
1991	865	864	868
2001	861	866	847

Source : Census of India (2001), *General Population Tables, Haryana,* (Tables A-1 to A-4), Series-7, Statement-3, Directorate of Census Operations, Haryana, pp. 84-85.

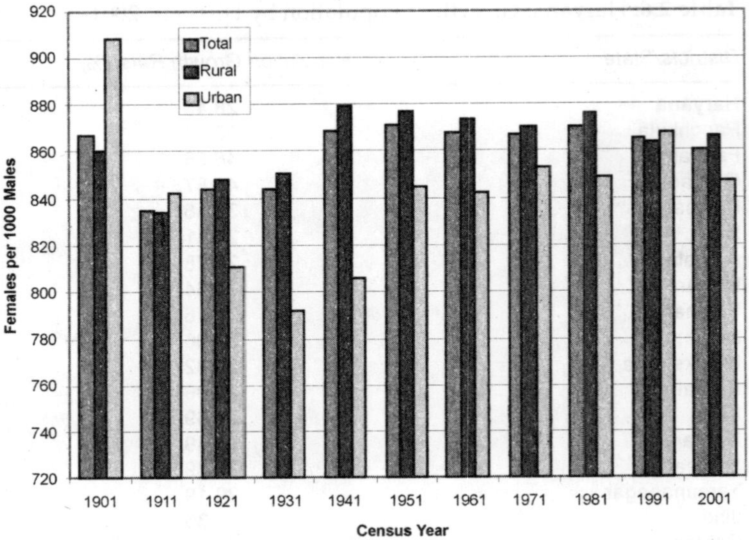

Figure 2.2: Haryana: Sex Ratio, 1901-2001

As per 2001 Census of India, the sex ratio of Haryana is 861 females per thousand males which is very much below the national average of 933 females per thousand males. The sex ratio of total population of the State has declined from 865 in 1991 to 861 in 2001 census. The tendency to conceal the birth of females, sex ratio at birth favourable to males, and higher mortality rate among females may be some of the reasons which explain this phenomenon of low sex ratio in Haryana.

The sex ratio is generally high in rural areas than that of their urban counterparts. For the State as a whole, the sex ratio is 866 females per thousand males in rural areas as compared to 847 in urban areas. In rural areas, the agriculture is the mainstay of the people which absorbs most of the family members in its activities and keeps them at home. Whereas, people go to urban areas in search of employment and take their families with them if they feel that their job are secure and they can get a satisfactory residential accommodation. Sometimes, they keep their families at their native village, as a result of which the rural areas are attributed with the improvement in sex ratio and urban areas are adversely affected.

Spatially, in all the districts, except Mahendragarh, sex ratio of total population is below 900. So, the highest sex ratio is found in Mahendragarh district (918 females per thousand males). By contrast, the lowest sex ratio has been recorded in Panchkula district (823 females per thousand males) (Table 2.8 and Map 2.7).

At the time of 2001 Census, there are 10 districts where sex ratio is higher as compared to State's average (861 females per 1000 males). These are Ambala (868), Yamunanagar (862), Kurukshetra (866), Karnal (865), Fatehabad (884), Sirsa (882), Bhiwani (879), Mahendragarh (918), Rewari (899), and Gurgaon (873) districts.

A decline in sex ratio between 1991 and 2001has been recorded in the districts of Panchkula (–16 points), Ambala (–35 points), Yamunanagar (–21 points), Kurukshetra (–13 points), Panipat (–23 points), Sonipat (–1 point), Sirsa (–3 points), Hisar (–2 points), Rohtak (–2 points), Jhajjar (–14 points), and Rewari (–28 points). Sex ratio remained constant in Kaithal district (853) in both the censuses. The remaining districts of Karnal (+1 point), Jind (+14 points), Fatehabad (+7 points), Bhiwani (+1 point), Mahendragarh (+8 points), Gurgaon (+2 points) and Faridabad (+11 points) have shown improvement in their respective sex ratio. Karnal was the only district where sex ratio in 1991 was below the State's average, but it has improved its sex ratio to the extent to come up above the State's average in 2001.

Contrary to the expectation that the sex ratio is generally high in rural areas as compared to their urban counterparts, the districts of Panchkula, Kaithal, Sonipat, Jind, Fatehabad and Rohtak have experienced lower sex ratio in rural areas as compared to urban areas. The reasons for this disparity in the sex ratio between rural and urban areas need further examination. Rural character of Haryana towns coupled with cheaper residential accommodation might have attracted family migration to urban centres where better educational facilities are available. Moreover, with certain social change leading to somewhat greater attention towards the girl child in recent years and availability of better medical facilities in urban areas may be responsible in the reduction of female mortality rate, resulting in high sex ratio in urban areas. Besides, people are relatively more inclined to family planning in urban areas in limiting their family size where birth of a female child is not usually considered bad may also be responsible for high sex ratio in urban areas.

In rural areas, the highest sex ratio is found in Mahendragarh district (924 females per thousand males) and the lowest in Panchkula district (798 females per thousand males). By comparison, in urban areas, the highest sex ratio is the characteristic of Mahendragarh district again (883 females per thousand males) and the lowest sex ratio is found in Panipat district (819 females per thousand males).

Table 2.8: Haryana: Sex Ratio by Districts, 2001

District/State	*Sex Ratio (Females/1000 males)*
Haryana	**861**
Mahendragarh	918
Ambala	899
Fatehabad	884
Sirsa	882
Bhiwani	879
Gurgaon	873
Rewari	868
Kurukshetra	866
Karnal	865
Yamunanagar	862
Kaithal	853
Jind	852
Hisar	851
Jhajjar	847
Rohtak	847
Faridabad	839
Sonipat	839
Panipat	829
Panchkula	823

Source: Census of India (2001), *General Population Tables, Haryana,* (Tables A-1 to A-4), Series-7, Statement-3, Directorate of Census Operations, Haryana, pp. 84-85.

Note: Districts have been arranged in descending order of sex ratio.

(e) Literacy

Literacy has been treated as an important indicator of social development. For the purpose of the Census, a person who can read and write with understanding in any language is treated as literate. During the post-independence period from the census of 1961 onwards and especially since its formation as a separate State in 1966, Haryana has experienced a continuous increase in literacy

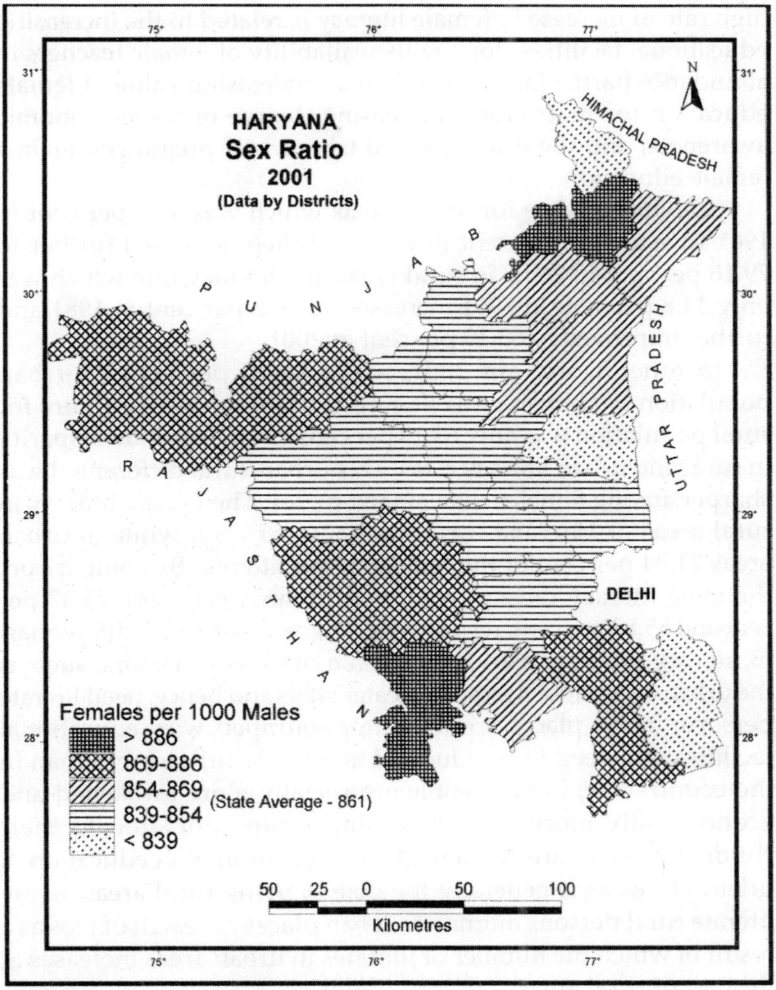

Map 2.7: Haryana: Sex Ratio, 2001

rate during the span of 50 years which increased from 19.9 per cent in 1961 to 67.91 per cent in 2001—an increase of more than three times.

The same trend has been observed in case of both male and female literacy rates. However, in case of female literacy rate, a remarkable increase of more than six times (from 9.2 per cent in 1961 to 55.73 per cent in 2001) has been observed. The relatively high rate of increase in female literacy is related to the increasing educational facilities along with availability of female teachers in abundance particularly in rural areas, increasing value of female education for matrimony, increasing degree of socio-economic awareness, and the waning social taboos and prejudices against female education.

The literacy rate for urban areas which was 44.7 per cent in 1961 rose to 56.9 per cent in 1981 and then increased further to 79.16 per cent in 2001. In rural areas, the literacy rate which was only 14.8 per cent in 1961 increased to 30.3 per cent in 1981 and further improved to 63.19 per cent in 2001.

In other words, in 2001, while 79.16 per cent of urban population in Haryana was literate, the corresponding figure for rural population was only 63.19 per cent, implying wide disparity in rural and urban literacy rates. This urban-rural differential was sharper among females than among males. The female literacy in rural areas of Haryana was only 49.26 per cent, while in urban areas 71.34 per cent of the females were literate. By comparison, the male literacy rates in rural and urban areas were 75.37 per cent and 85.83 per cent, respectively. These urban-rural differentials in literacy rates are associated with a number of factors, such as the urban occupations require greater skills and hence, need literate persons; urban places are far better equipped with educational facilities; the need to be educated is more in urban areas than in the countryside; urban people are socially more awakened and economically more capable of imparting education to their children; females are not denied the opportunities of education in urban places as is generally the case in many rural areas; many literate rural persons migrate to urban places in search of jobs as a result of which the number of literates in urban areas increases at the cost of rural areas.

As per Census of India (2001), Haryana has literacy rate of 67.91 per cent, which is comparatively higher than the National average (64.84 per cent). The literacy rates for males (78.49 per cent) and females (55.73 per cent) as well as for urban (79.16 per cent) and rural (63.19 per cent) areas are also higher than the National average. There are five districts, namely Gurgaon (62.91 per cent), Jind (62.12 per cent), Kaithal (59.02 per cent), Hisar (64.83 per cent) and Sirsa (60.55 per cent) where literacy rate is lower than the National average. So far as female literacy rate is concerned, it is below the National average (53.67 per cent) in six districts, viz., Fatehabad (46.53 per cent), Hisar (51.08 per cent), Kaithal (47.31 per cent), Jind (48.51 per cent), Bhiwani (53.00 per cent) and Gurgaon (47.78 per cent) during 1991-2001.

In regional perspective, the highest literacy rate has been recorded in Ambala district (75.31 per cent) and the lowest in Kaithal district (59.02 per cent) (Table 2.9 and Map 2.8). There are 12 districts where literacy rates are higher as compared to State's average (67.91 per cent). These are Panchkula (74.00 per cent), Ambala (75.31 per cent), Yamunanagar (71.63 per cent), Kurukshetra (69.88 per cent), Panipat (69.17 per cent), Sonipat (72.79 per cent), Fatehabad (67.98 per cent), Rohtak (73.72 per cent), Jhajjar (72.37 per cent), Mahendragarh (69.89 per cent), Rewari (75.25 per cent), and Faridabad (70.03 per cent) districts. It can be concluded that the literacy rate is comparatively low in the north-western parts of Haryana, while it is relatively high in the peripheral zone of Delhi and Chandigarh.

Male literacy rate is relatively higher than female literacy rate in all the districts. Rewari district, with male literacy rate of 88.45 per cent, ranks first in the State, while lowest male literacy has been recorded in Fatehabad district (68.22 per cent) (Table 2.9 and Map 2.9). Female literacy rate is the highest in Ambala district (67.39 per cent) and is followed by Panchkula district (65.65 per cent). By contrast, it is the lowest in Fatehabad district (46.53 per cent) which is followed by Kaithal district (47.31 per cent) (Table 2.9 and Map 2.10).

Similar inequalities exist between the literacy rates of rural and urban population of Haryana. While 79.16 per cent of State's urban population is literate according to 2001 Census, in the countryside only 63.19 per cent of population can read and write (Table 2.10). This supports the fact that literacy rate is relatively higher in urban areas than rural areas because better facilities are available for schooling in urban areas and urban people are even more vigilant to impart education to their children. On the other hand, the relatively low percentage of literacy in rural Haryana was associated with adverse feelings of the elders in sending female children to schools, need more hands to work, poor agricultural conditions and backwardness of the area in the past.

Spatially, urban literacy rate is relatively higher than rural literacy rate in all the districts. The highest literacy rate in urban

Table 2.9: Haryana: Total Literacy Rates by Sex, 2001

State/District	*Literates as Per Cent of Total Population*		
	Total	*Male*	*Female*
HARYANA	**67.91**	**78.49**	**55.73**
Panchkula	74.00	80.86	65.65
Ambala	75.31	82.30	67.39
Yamunanagar	71.63	78.81	63.39
Kurukshetra	69.88	78.06	60.61
Kaithal	59.02	69.15	47.31
Karnal	67.74	76.29	57.97
Panipat	69.17	78.50	57.97
Sonipat	72.79	83.06	60.68
Jind	62.12	73.82	48.51
Fatehabad	67.98	68.22	46.53
Sirsa	60.55	70.05	59.93
Hisar	64.83	76.57	51.08
Bhiwani	67.45	80.26	53.00
Rohtak	73.72	83.23	62.59
Jhajjar	72.37	83.27	59.65
Mahendragarh	69.89	84.72	54.08
Rewari	75.25	88.45	60.83
Gurgaon	62.91	76.17	47.78
Faridabad	70.03	81.52	56.31

Source: Computed from Census of India (2001), *Primary Census Abstract*, CDs 1-12, Office of the Registrar General and Census Commissioner, India, New Delhi.

areas has been recorded in Ambala district (85.47 per cent) and the lowest in Kaithal district (72.33 per cent). There are nine districts where urban literacy rates are higher as compared to State's average (79.16 per cent). These are Panchkula (82.91 per cent), Ambala (85.47 per cent), Yamunanagar (81.67 per cent), Kurukshetra (80.86 per cent), Karnal (80.02 per cent), Sonipat (80.64 per cent), Rohtak (81.26 per cent), Rewari (82.25 per cent), and Gurgaon (81.71 per cent) districts (Table 2.10 and Map 2.11).

By contrast, Rewari district, with rural literacy rate of 73.70 per cent, ranks first in the State and is followed by Jhajjar district (70.36 per cent). On the other end of the scale, the lowest literacy rate in rural areas has been recorded in Fatehabad district (54.56 per cent) which is followed by Kaithal district (55.78 per cent). There are eleven districts where rural literacy rates are higher as compared to State's average (63.19 per cent). These are Panchkula (66.62 per cent), Ambala (69.63 per cent), Yamunanagar (65.35 per cent),

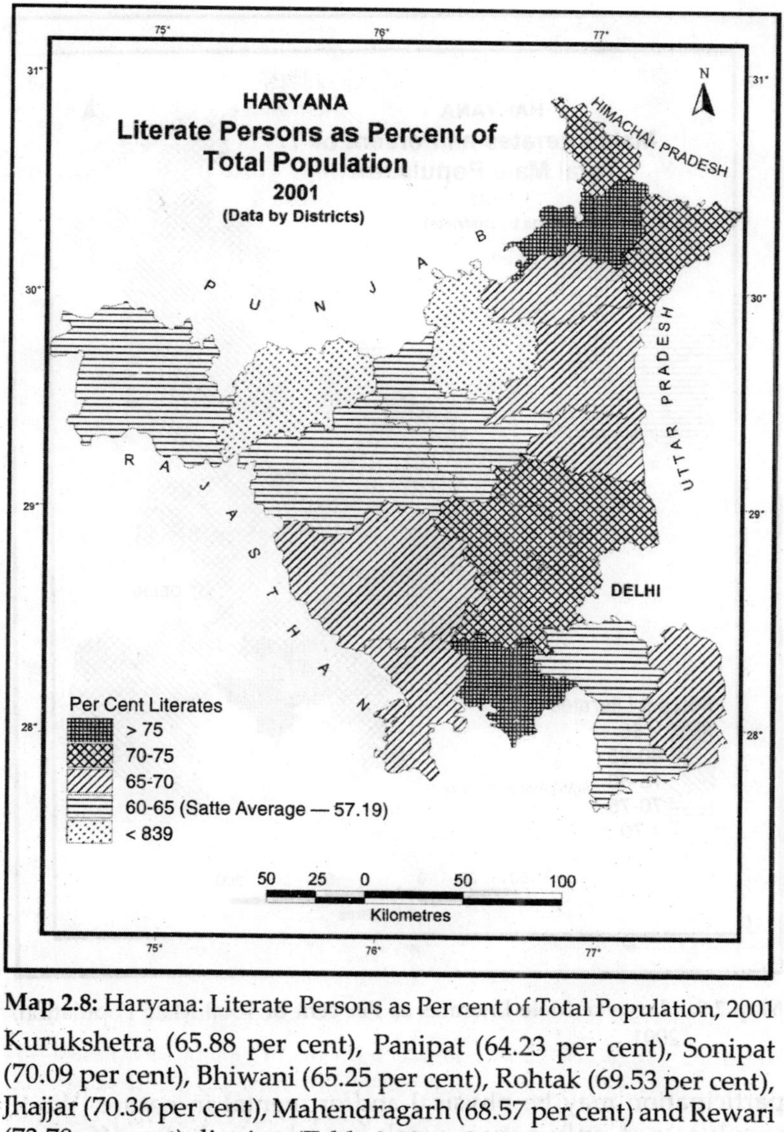

Map 2.8: Haryana: Literate Persons as Per cent of Total Population, 2001

Kurukshetra (65.88 per cent), Panipat (64.23 per cent), Sonipat (70.09 per cent), Bhiwani (65.25 per cent), Rohtak (69.53 per cent), Jhajjar (70.36 per cent), Mahendragarh (68.57 per cent) and Rewari (73.70 per cent) districts (Table 2.10 and Map 2.12).

(f) Working Force

Work is defined as participation in any *economically productive activity* with or without compensation, wages or profit. Such

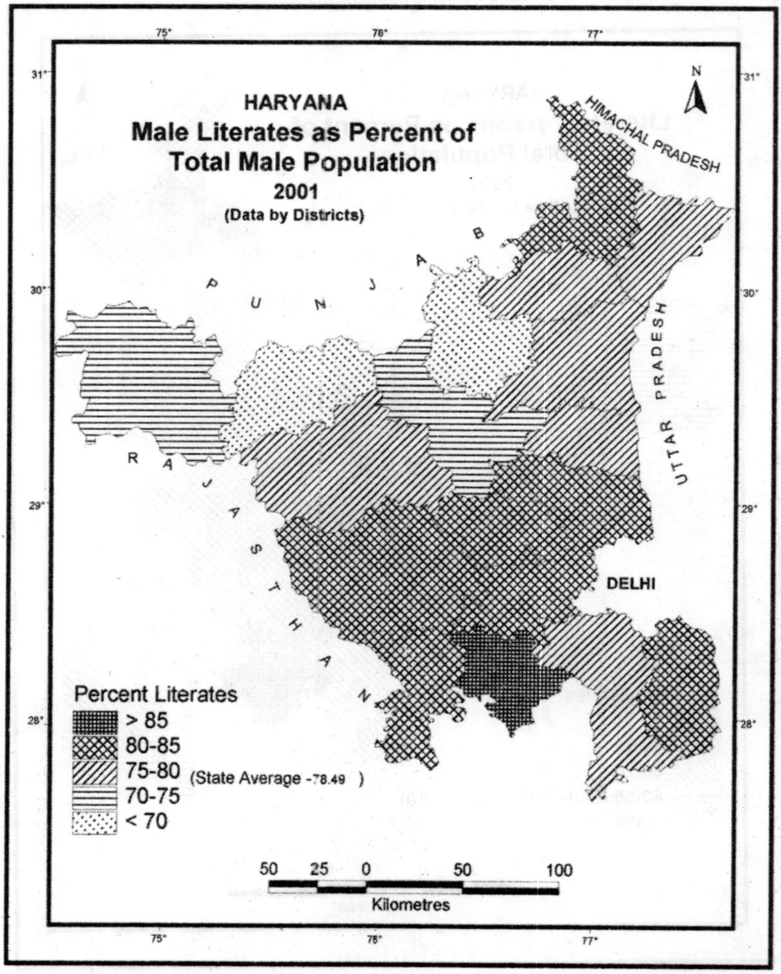

Map 2.9: Haryana: Male Literates as Per cent of Total Male Population, 2001

participation may be physical and/or mental in nature. Work involves not only actual work but also includes effective supervision and direction of work. It even includes part-time help or unpaid work on farm, family enterprise or in any other economic activity.

The *economically active population* of a country, which is engaged in gainful economic activities like production of goods and services, is known as its *working force*. The working force of a

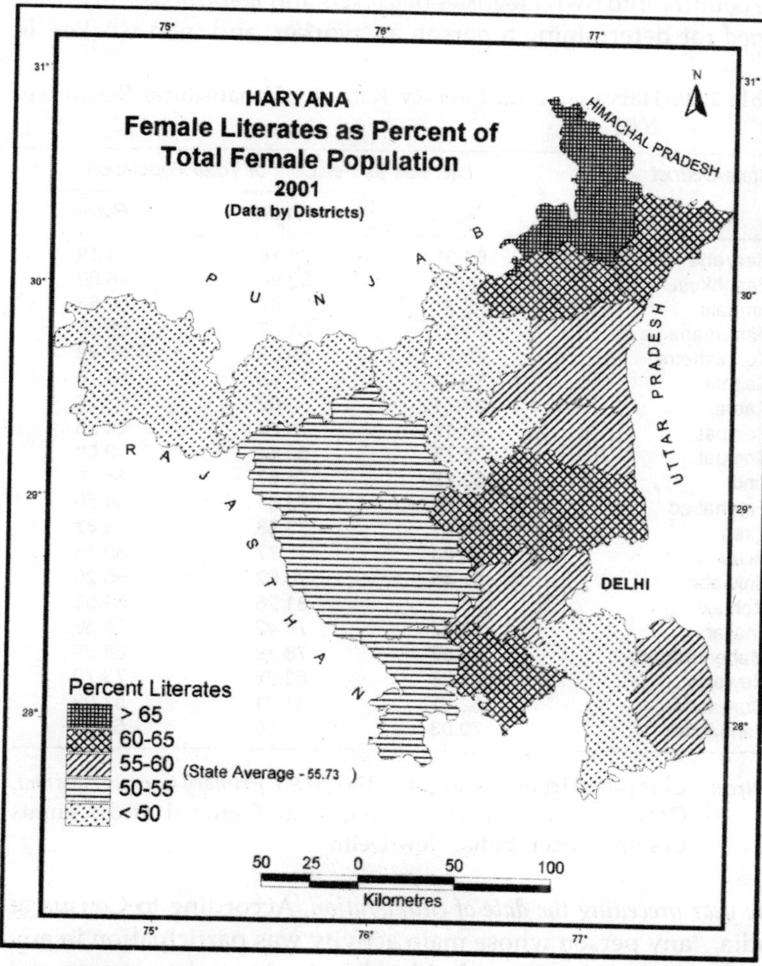

Map 2.10: Haryana: Female Literates as Per Cent of Total Female Population, 2001

country is understood to be made up of people between 15 to 59 years of age. But many people in this working age group are not actually workers due to various reasons. Many people continue to work beyond 60 years of age. Many are willing to work but only a few get the opportunity to work.

Census of India, therefore, divides the entire population of the country into two categories of *workers* and *non-workers*. *Reference period* for determining a person as 'worker' and 'non-worker' is

Table 2.10: Haryana: Total Literacy Rates by Urban-Rural Residence, 2001

State/District	*Literates as Per Cent of Total Population*		
	Total	*Urban*	*Rural*
Haryana	**67.91**	**79.16**	**63.19**
Panchkula	74.00	82.91	66.62
Ambala	75.31	85.47	69.63
Yamunanagar	71.63	81.67	65.35
Kurukshetra	69.88	80.86	65.88
Kaithal	59.02	72.33	55.78
Karnal	67.74	80.02	63.16
Panipat	69.17	76.24	64.23
Sonipat	72.79	80.64	70.09
Jind	62.12	75.87	58.55
Fatehabad	67.98	73.61	54.56
Sirsa	60.55	73.58	55.82
Hisar	64.83	77.77	60.16
Bhiwani	67.45	76.62	65.25
Rohtak	73.72	81.26	69.53
Jhajjar	72.37	79.42	70.36
Mahendragarh	69.89	78.19	68.57
Rewari	75.25	82.25	73.70
Gurgaon	62.91	81.71	57.09
Faridabad	70.03	78.80	58.36

Source: Computed from Census of India (2001), *Primary Census Abstract*, CDs 1-12, Office of the Registrar General and Census Commissioner, India, New Delhi.

one year preceding the date of enumeration. According to Census of India, "any person whose main activity was participation in any *economically productive work* either by his physical and/or mental activity was classified as *worker* ". As per Census of India (2001), all persons engaged in '*work*' as defined above are '*workers*'. Persons who are engaged in cultivation or milk production even solely for domestic consumption are also treated as 'workers'.

In historic perspective, the concept of '*worker*' was introduced in 1961, for the first time, in India. In 1961, any person who had worked for at least one hour a day on an average during the reference period was classified as 'worker'.

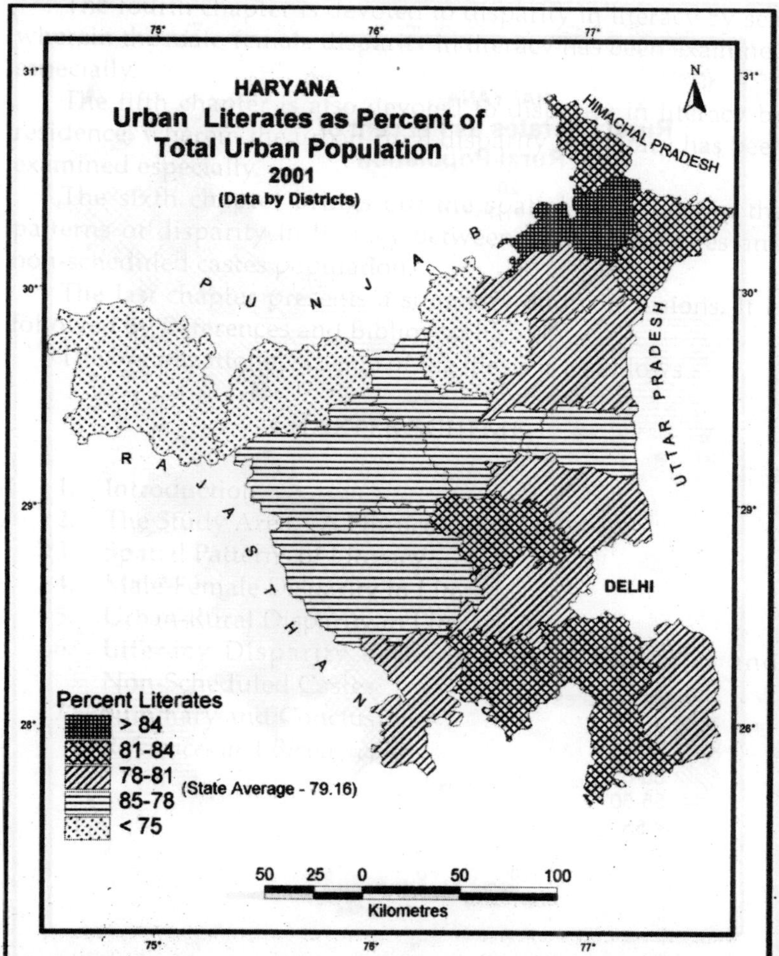

Map 2.11: Haryana: Urban Literates as Per cent of Total Urban Population, 2001

In 1971, "if a person worked on any one of the days during the reference period of one week prior to the date of enumeration was considered as a '*worker*' provided his/her main activity was economically productive work". Thus, persons engaged primarily in household duties (housewives), those getting education (students), those receiving income without participating in any productive activity (pensioners, rent receivers, thieves, pick-pocketers, prisoners, beggars, etc.) were classified as '*non-workers*'.

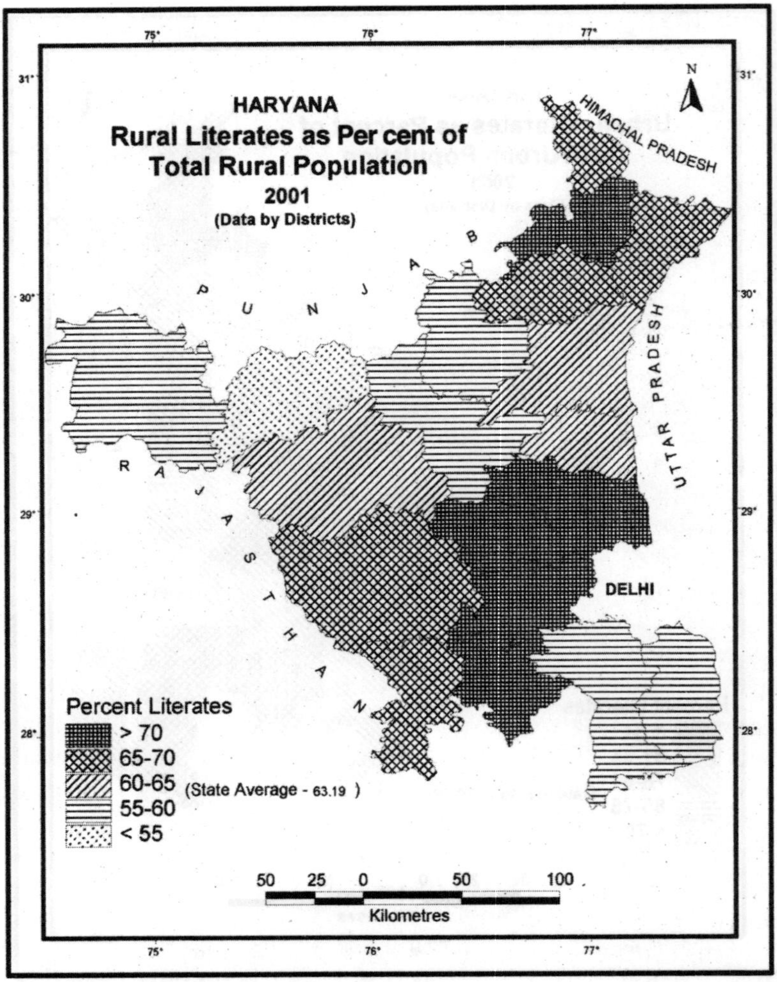

Map 2.12: Haryana: Rural Literates as Per cent of Total Rural Population, 2001

However, in 1981, the *workers* were divided into two groups of *'main workers'* [those persons who had worked for the major part of the reference period, i.e., 6 months (183 days) or more] and *'marginal workers'* [those persons who had worked for less than 6 months (183 days) during the reference period].

The 1991 and 2001 Censuses of India also adopted the aforesaid definitions. The *working force* in India, thus, comprises both the *main workers* as well as *marginal workers* and is computed as percentage of workers to total population.

The size of working force is determined by population growth and work participation rate (WPR), i.e., the percentage of total workers (main and marginal) to total population. Population growth depends upon fertility, mortality and migration, whereas work participation rate depends upon a variety of demographic, social and economic factors like fertility, mortality, migration, age composition, age of retirement, life expectancy, wage levels, household income, educational attainments, the availability of work and attitude towards work. Since these factors differ from one country to another and within each country from State to State and city to city, WPR is subject to variation over regions and time (Suri, *et al.*, 1988).

As per Census of India (2001), the total work participation rate (WPR) of 39.62 per cent is a significant improvement over that of 31.00 per cent recorded in 1991 in Haryana. This is quite close to National average of 39.1 per cent in 2001. The work participation rate among scheduled castes population of the State is 38.7 per cent. Among the districts, the highest proportion of 45.03 per cent of total workers has been recorded in Fatehabad followed by Jhajjar (44.17 per cent). At the other extreme, the lowest work participation rate of 31.99 per cent is recordred in Ambala district. The work participation rate of the scheduled castes population varies between 31.4 per cent in Ambala district and 44.0 per cent in Fatehabad district.

Male work participation rate (MWPR) for the State as a whole increased from 48.51 per cent in 1991 to 50.30 per cent in 2001 Census. On the other hand, female work participation rate (FWPR) has shown remarkable improvement in the State. It improved to 27.22 per cent in 2001 from a paltry 10.76 per cent in 1991. Among the districts, the highest male work participation rate has been observed in Panchkula district (54.54 per cent) and is followed by Fatehabad district (54.42 per cent). By contrast, the lowest male work participation rate has been recorded in Gurgaon district (46.84 per cent) and is followed by Mahendragarh district (48.00 per cent). By comparison, the highest female work participation rate has been observed in Mahendragarh district (38.20 per cent) and is followed by Rewari district (36.77 per cent). At the other end of the scale, the lowest female work participation rate has been recorded in Ambala district (10.16 per cent) and is followed by Yamunanagar district (11.66 per cent) (Table 2.11).

2.11: Haryana: Proportion of Workers to Total Population by Sex, 2001

State/District	*Workers as Per cent of Total Population*		
	Total	*Male*	*Female*
Haryana	**39.62**	**50.30**	**27.22**
Panchkula	38.14	54.54	18.22
Ambala	31.99	50.95	10.16
Yamunanagar	32.31	50.10	11.66
Kurukshetra	37.36	51.19	21.40
Kaithal	39.32	50.87	25.79
Karnal	35.74	50.18	19.05
Panipat	39.57	51.03	25.75
Sonipat	40.89	49.65	30.44
Jind	43.87	51.56	34.85
Fatehabad	45.03	54.42	34.40
Sirsa	42.59	53.05	30.73
Hisar	43.30	51.87	33.22
Bhiwani	42.76	49.24	35.38
Rohtak	39.47	49.33	27.83
Jhajjar	44.17	51.38	35.66
Mahendragarh	43.31	48.00	38.20
Rewari	43.59	49.72	36.77
Gurgaon	37.92	46.84	27.72
Faridabad	35.80	48.32	20.90

Source: Computed from Census of India (2001), *Primary Census Abstract*, CDs 1-12, Office of the Registrar General and Census Commissioner, India, New Delhi

In rural-urban perspective, the work participation rate is relatively high in rural areas as compared to their urban counterparts. Out of 19 districts, Ambala is the only district in the State where urban work participation rate (UWPR) (32.64 per cent) is higher than the rural work participation rate (RWPR), i.e., 31.64 per cent. Urban work participation rate (UWPR) for the State as a whole increased from 28.32 per cent in 1991 to 31.49 per cent in 2001 census. On the other hand, rural work participation rate (RWPR) has shown remarkable improvement in the State. It improved to 42.93 per cent in 2001 from 31.87 per cent in 1991. Among the districts, the highest urban work participation rate has been observed in Panipat district (36.13 per cent) and is followed by Panchkula district (33.59 per cent). By contrast, the lowest urban work participation rate has been recorded in Yamunanagar district (29.51 per cent) and is followed by Sonipat district (29.84 per cent). By comparison, the highest rural work participation rate has been observed in Fatehabad district (48.01 per cent) and is followed by Jhajjar district (47.32 per cent). At the other extreme, the lowest rural work participation rate has been recorded in Ambala district (31.64 per cent) and is followed by Yamunanagar district (34.00 per cent) (Table 2.12).

Table 2.12: Haryana: Proportion of Workers to Total Population by Rural-Urban Residence, 2001

State/District	*Workers as Per cent of Total Population*		
	Total	*Rural*	*Urban*
Haryana	**39.62**	**42.93**	**31.49**
Panchkula	38.14	41.79	33.59
Ambala	31.99	31.64	32.64
Yamunanagar	32.31	34.00	29.51
Kurukshetra	37.36	39.96	30.00
Kaithal	39.32	41.56	30.01
Karnal	35.74	37.29	31.46
Panipat	39.57	41.91	36.13
Sonipat	40.89	44.59	29.84
Jind	43.87	47.28	30.46
Fatehabad	45.03	48.01	31.09
Sirsa	42.59	46.34	32.06
Hisar	43.30	47.02	32.06
Bhiwani	42.76	45.65	30.39
Rohtak	39.47	44.63	29.91
Jhajjar	44.77	47.32	33.10
Mahendragarh	43.31	45.19	31.21
Rewari	43.59	46.50	30.14
Gurgaon	37.92	39.58	32.14
Faridabad	35.80	41.83	31.01

Source: Computed from, Census of India (2001), *Primary Census Abstract*, CDs 1-12, Office of the Registrar General and Census Commissioner, India, New Delhi.

According to 2001 Census, the proportion of main workers to total workers in Haryana is 74.5 per cent as against the all-India average of 77.8 per cent. There is a significant decline in the percentage of main workers from 92.5 per cent recorded in 1991. This decline in main workers is mainly due to high increase in female marginal workers in all categories of population in 2001. Maximum percentage of main workers are reported in Ambala district (84.9 per cent) followed by Panchkula (84.2 per cent). By contrast, the lowest proportion of main workers of 58.2 per cent is recorded in Mahendragarh district.

The relatively low proportion of main workers, on the one hand, reveals the higher capacity of a worker to support the large family and on the other hand, it reflects the growing magnitude of unemployment and economic health of the region.

Out of the total working population, 51.3 per cent workers are engaged in primary activities since overwhelming majority of the population resides in rural areas in the State. Among the two important primary activities, the proportion of cultivators (36.03 per cent) is much higher than that of agricultural labourers (15.27 per cent). The proportion of cultivators is also higher than that recorded at the National level (31.7 per cent). Among the districts, the highest percentage of cultivators is in Mahendragarh district (54.7 per cent) and the lowest in Ambala district (16.3 per cent) which is the industrially developed district of the State. In case of scheduled castes, the proportion of cultivators is also the highest in Mahendragarh district (62.6 per cent) and the lowest in Panchkula district (18.4 per cent).

So far as agricultural labourers are concerned, their proportion in total workers has declined from 19.7 per cent in 1991 to 15.3 per cent in 2001 in the State. Among the districts, the highest percentage of agricultural labourers is in Sirsa district (23.89 per cent). By contrast, the lowest percentage of agricultural labourers has been recorded in Panchkula district (6.1 per cent). The proportion of agricultural labourers among the scheduled castes is high at 42.2 per cent in 2001 Census.

The household industries (HHI) as one of the secondary activities are less developed in Haryana as only 2.6 per cent of the total workers are engaged in these industries. However, the household industry workers have increased from 1.5 per cent in 1991 to 2.6 per cent in the 2001 Census. Among the districts, the highest proportion of workers in household industries is found in Panipat (4.6 per cent) and the lowest in Jind (1.7 per cent). In case of scheduled castes also, the highest and the lowest proportion of HHI workers has been recorded in both the same districts of Panipat (4.6 per cent) and Jind (1.6 per cent) respectively.

In 2001 Census, the percentage of 'other workers' (OW) to total workers is 46.1 per cent which increased from 37.8 per cent in 1991. The proportion of other workers is highest in Panchkula, i.e., 73.9 per cent and lowest in Fatehabad, i.e., 30.3 per cent. Among the scheduled castes, 47.5 per cent are 'other workers' in the 2001 Census. In case of scheduled castes also, the highest and the lowest proportion of 'other workers' has been recorded in both the same districts of Panchkula (74.7 per cent) and Fatehabad (31.2 per cent) respectively.

In 2001 Census, the percentage of marginal workers in Haryana is 25.5 which is a significant increase from 7.5 per cent recorded in 1991. The proportion of marginal workers in the State is higher than that recorded at the National level (22.2 per cent). Among the districts, the highest proportion of marginal workers is recorded in Mahendragarh (41.82 per cent) followed by Rewari (38.60 per cent) and Bhiwani districts (30.22 per cent) (Table 2.13).

Table 2.13: Haryana: Proportion of Marginal Workers to Total Workers by Sex, 2001

State/District	*Marginal Workers as Per cent of Total Workers*		
	Total	*Male*	*Female*
HARYANA	25.50	13.69	50.85
Panchkula	15.84	09.36	39.41
Ambala	15.06	11.23	37.17
Yamunanagar	16.58	11.78	40.50
Kurukshetra	18.74	09.11	45.33
Kaithal	27.92	12.86	62.74
Karnal	21.95	12.69	50.18
Panipat	24.50	11.55	55.45
Sonipat	26.69	15.75	47.96
Jind	28.72	15.12	52.32
Fatehabad	27.92	14.19	52.50
Sirsa	23.47	11.51	46.88
Hisar	22.35	11.20	42.82
Bhiwani	30.22	16.90	51.30
Rohtak	22.33	13.58	40.63
Jhajjar	28.94	17.83	47.85
Mahendragarh	41.82	22.63	68.09
Rewari	38.60	20.40	65.96
Gurgaon	26.21	13.30	51.20
Faridabad	22.41	12.44	49.89

Source: Computed from, Census of India (2001), *Primary Census Abstract*, CDs 1-12, Office of the Registrar General and Census Commissioner, India, New Delhi.

By contrast, the lowest proportion of marginal workers is in Ambala district (15.06 per cent) followed by the districts of Panchkula (15.84 per cent) and Yamunanagar (16.58 per cent). In case of scheduled castes, the proportion of marginal workers is also the highest in Mahendragarh district (50.5 per cent) and the lowest in Panchkula district (22.9 per cent).

The highest proportion of male marginal workers has been observed in Mahendragarh district (22.63 per cent) and is followed by Rewari district (20.40 per cent). By contrast, the lowest male marginal workers have been recorded in Kurukshetra district (9.11per cent) and is followed by Panchkula district (9.36 per cent). By comparison, the highest female marginal workers have also been recorded in Mahendragarh district (68.09 per cent) followed by Rewari district (65.96 per cent). At the other end of the scale, the lowest female marginal workers have been observed in Ambala district (37.17 per cent) and is followed by Yamunanagar district (39.41per cent) (Table 2.13).

3 Spatial Patterns of Literacy

3.1 Introduction

Prior to the advent of the skills of reading and writing, society could be classified as being in the pre-literate cultural stage. The change from pre-literate to literate society is said to have begun somewhere during the fourth millennium B.C. through a gradual transition from pictography to the use of an alphabet (Golden, 1968). After the advent of the dual skills of reading and writing, the relevance of literacy to the cultural advancement enhanced significantly. It is in this context that in Population Geography, literacy is considered as a fairly reliable index of socio-cultural and economic advancement.

Literacy is essential for eradicating poverty and mental isolation, for cultivating peaceful and friendly international relations and for permitting the free play of demographic processes (Chandna, 1980). Illiteracy, on the other hand, takes away from man his dignity, perpetuates ignorance. Poverty and mental isolation, deters peaceful and friendly international relations and free demographic processes and hampers social advancement, economic growth and political maturity. Above all, literacy influences other such attributes of population as fertility, morality, occupation, etc. No wonder, the trends in literacy are considered as an index of the pace at which the socio-economic transformation of a society is taking place. Thus, the analysis of literacy patterns and trends therein is of immense significance for a population geographer.

3.2 Literacy: The Conceptual Analysis

The concept of literacy, that varies from country to country, generally refers to the minimum level of literacy skills. This minimum level of skills varies from ability to communicate orally, to make a check of a variety of difficult arithmetical computations. However, the length of schooling has often been considered as a basis of distinguishing between a literate and illiterate. Trewartha, (1969) considers the basis of length of schooling not a valid measurement of educational accomplishments. He also disapproves of the ability to read and write one's name in the language of his country as the criterion for defining a literate. In 1930, Finland applied perhaps the most strict definition where only those persons were classified as literate who passed a rather difficult test. Those who failed were divided into two categories: the semi-literates, persons who could read and write but made orthographic errors; and the illiterates, who could neither read nor write (UNESCO, 1957). By contrast, the Hong Kong Census of 1961, any person who claimed that he could read a language was assumed by inference also to be able to write and was classified a literate. Although the acceptance of what the enumerator is told may result in inflating the literacy percentages (Davis, 1951), yet there is no justification in confronting the respondents with a difficult test either. Therefore, the census enumerator has no option with him but to accept what he is told by the respondents. But the questions can be so framed as to get the most accurate information.

The Population Commission of United Nations considers the ability to both read and write a simple message with understanding in any language a sufficient basis for classifying a person as literate. The Indian census has adopted this definition. Gradually, many countries are shifting to this definition. If literacy is defined in terms of a person's ability to both read and write a simple message with understanding, the collection of accurate information by the census enumerators may not pose any serious problem. However, a distinction can be made between the literates and the educated, as has been done in case of India. All those persons who are classified as literates on the basis of their ability to both read and write are further subdivided into number of categories on the basis of their length of schooling.

In International usage, literacy is defined as the ability to read and write at least a simple message in any language; illiteracy, in contrast, refers to the lack or absence of this ability. The proportion of literate persons in a population is known as literacy level. Conversely, illiterates comprise of two sub-groups, pre-literate and unliterate. The former includes societies that have never encountered any language even after the invention of written language. The latter refers to people in societies that otherwise have written language, but due to one or the other reason, do not possess the ability to read and write. Further, a distinction is generally made between a person who is simply literate and a person who is functionally literate. Functional literacy is attained when a person is able to read newspaper, magazines and books of non-specialized nature with fair amount of understanding and is also in a position to write legible letters or comparable statements.

In India, during the earlier censuses up to 1981, it was customary to work out the literacy rate taking into account the total population. Since literacy rate is more meaningful if population in the age group 0-6 is excluded from the total population, it was decided in 1991 to use the term literacy rate for the population aged seven years and above. At the 1991 Census, it was also decided that all children in the age-group 0-6 years will be treated as illiterate by definition and the population aged seven years and above only is to be classified as literate or illiterate.

The same criterion has been retained at the Census of India (2001) which defines a literate as that person, aged seven years and above, who can both read and write with understanding in any language. A person who can only read but cannot write, is not literate. The literacy rate taking into account the total population in the denominator has now been termed as *crude literacy rate.* However, the per cent of literates among population aged seven years and above has been referred to as *effective literacy rate* or simply as *literacy rate.*

3.3 Literacy in Haryana: A Temporal Analysis, 1961-2001

During the post-independence period from the Census of 1961 onwards and especially since its formation as a separate State in 1966, Haryana has experienced an increasing trend in literacy rates (Table 3.1 and Fig. 3.1).

Table 3.1: Haryana: Literacy Rates by Sex, 1961-2001

Census Year	*Per cent Literates to Total Population*			*Male-Female Differential*
	Persons	*Males*	*Females*	
1961*	19.9	29.2	9.2	20.0
1971*	26.89	37.3	14.9	22.4
1981*	36.14	48.20	22.27	25.93
1981**	43.88	58.51	26.93	31.58
1991**	55.85	69.10	40.47	28.63
2001**	67.91	78.49	55.73	22.76

Sources: (i) Sharma, O.P. and Retherford, R.D. (1987), *Recent Literacy Trends in India,* Occasional Paper No. 1 of 1987, Office of the Registrar General and Census Commissioner, India, Government of India, New Delhi, Statements 8, 10 and 12, pp. 17-23.

(ii) Census of India (1991), *Final Population Totals: Brief Analysis of Primary Census Abstract,* Paper 2 of 1992, Office of the Registrar General and Census Commissioner, India, Ministry of Home Affairs, Government of India, New Delhi, Statements 17 and 18, pp. 57-59.

(iii) Census of India (2001), *Primary Census Abstract,* Haryana, CD2, Office of the Registrar General and Census Commissioner, India, New Delhi, Table 7.

* Literacy rates for 1961, 1971 and 1981 censuses relate to the population aged five years and above

** Literacy rates for 1981, 1991 and 2001 relate to the population aged seven years and above.

Table 3.1 shows a continuous increase in literacy rate during the span of 50 years which increased from 19.9 per cent in 1961 to 67.91 per cent in 2001—an increase of more than three times. The same trend has been observed in case of both male and female literacy rates. However, in case of female literacy rate, a remarkable increase of more than six times (from 9.2 per cent in 1961 to 55.73 per cent in 2001) has been observed. The relatively high rate of increase in female literacy is related to the increasing educational facilities along with availability of female teachers in abundance particularly in rural areas, increasing value of female education for matrimony, increasing degree of socio-economic awareness, and the waning social taboos and prejudices against female education.

It is also revealed from the Table 3.1 that the literacy rate (67.91 per cent) in Haryana is more than that of the country as a

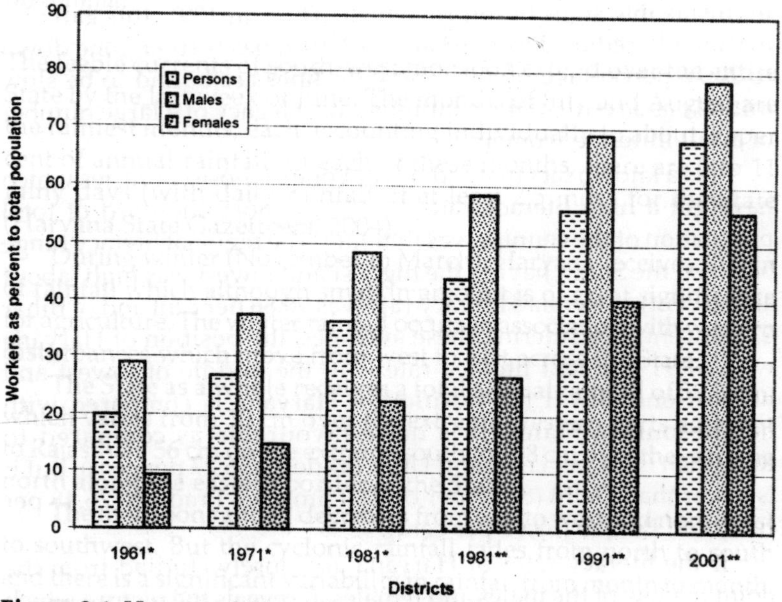

Figure 3.1: Haryana: Literacy Rates by Sex, 1961-2001

whole (64.8 per cent) in 2001. It is also true in case of male literacy rate (State average—78.49 per cent and National average—75.2 per cent) and female literacy rate (State average—55.73 per cent and National average—53.6 per cent).

Thus, more than three-fourth of the male and more than half of the female population aged seven years and above are literate in the State today. The State has continued its inexorable march in improving its literacy rate by recording a jump of 12.06 percentage points from 55.85 in 1991 to 67.91 in 2001. The increase in literacy rates in males and females is of the order of 9.39 and 15.26 percentage points respectively. Thus, the increase in literacy rates observed during 1991-2001 in respect of persons and females has been the highest recorded in comparison to earlier decades since 1961, whereas in case of males it is lowest recorded. This improvement in literacy rate augurs well for the country and needs not only to be sustained but requires a fillip particularly in the case of fairer sex.

The gap in male-female literacy rates of 20.0 percentage points in 1961 increased to 31.58 in 1981, but since then there are unmistakable signs of improvement. Thus, in 1991, this gap was marginally reduced to 28.63 and in 2001 it has further gone down to 22.76 percentage points. These declines are bound to be slow initially as a result of the continuing past legacy of a large number of adult illiterate women.

It is a known fact that India is not one of those countries which have got a high literacy rate. In 2001, almost one-third of total population of the country was illiterate. The regional literacy range between the States having the highest and lowest was high (about 40 per cent) as Kerala's literacy rate was 90.86 per cent and of Bihar 47 per cent. Considering these averages, the position of Haryana with 67.91 per cent literacy rate is in the middle of lowest and highest one. But if the position of Haryana is compared with neighbsouring States, it is quite favourable as compared to Rajasthan (60.4 per cent) and Uttar Pradesh (56.27 per cent). But it is lower than Delhi (81.67 per cent), Himachal Pradesh (76.48 per cent) and Punjab (69.65 per cent).

If the literacy rates of Haryana are closely studied from the point of view of the males and females, it reveals the picture which is generally true for the whole India. The male literacy is higher than female literacy rates.

It is very much similar to male-female ratio of literacy in the neighouring States where male literacy is higher than female literacy as indicated in Table 3.2.

Table 3.2: Literacy Rates of Haryana and the Neighbouring States (2001)

States/Union Territory	*Per cent Literates to Total Population*		
	Person	*Male*	*Female*
Delhi	81.67	87.33	74.71
Himachal Pradesh	76.48	81.35	67.42
Punjab	69.65	75.23	63.36
Haryana	67.91	78.49	55.73
Rajasthan	60.41	75.70	43.85
Uttar Pradesh	56.27	68.82	42.22

Source: Computed from Census of India (2001), *Primary Census Abstract*, CDs 1-12, Office of the Registrar General and Census Commissioner, India, New Delhi.

3.4 Spatial Patterns of Literacy

Economic development and literacy of a region are closely linked. A strong positive correlation has often been observed between the diffusion of literacy and economic progress. A large number of factors influence the literacy of region, but the important among these are (Chandna, 2008):

1. Type of economy.
2. Degree of urbanization.
3. Standard of living.
4. Cost of education.
5. Availability of educational institutions.
6. Degree of development of means of transportation and communication.
7. Stage of technological advancement.
8. Religious background.
9. Status of women in the society.
10. Prejudices against the females' mobility and education.

Among various determinants of literacy rates, the type of economy seems to be the most powerful parameter. Agricultural economies present a contrast to the industrial societies in the levels of literacy. In a predominantly agricultural economy, the literacy is generally low, in contrast to those areas where the industries constitute the main activity and the workers are employed in service sector.

Similarly, the degree of urbanization also affects the rate of literacy. Those areas which are more urbanized are also characterized by higher rates of literacy in comparison to those which still are at low level of urbanization. There also exists a positive correlation between literacy rates and standard of living. Higher the standard of living, higher the literacy rates and *vice versa.*

Literacy to a large extent is dependent upon the number of educational institutions. The larger the number of schools and other sources of getting education, the higher are the literacy rates.

The development of means of transportation and communication has opened new vistas in the field of literacy. Because, it has increased the degree of spatial interaction and the educational institutions in the urban areas now have become accessible to the countryside.

After considering the impact of various aforesaid socio-economic factors on the literacy rates in any area, it has been observed that there are striking spatial disparities in literacy rates within Haryana ranging from only 37.41 per cent in Punhana tehsil to 80.81 per cent in Gurgaon tehsil (Table 3.3).

On the basis of literacy rates as shown in Table 3.3, the tehsils of Haryana can be classified into five categories (Map 3.1):

1. Regions having Very High Literacy Rate (Above 80 per cent)
2. Regions having High Literacy Rate (70 to 80 per cent)
3. Regions having Moderate Literacy Rate (60 to 70 per cent)
4. Regions having Low Literacy Rate (50 to 60 per cent)
5. Regions having Very Low Literacy Rate (Below 50 per cent)

1. Regions having Very High Literacy Rate (Above 80 per cent)

In Haryana, there is only one tehsil, which has been characterized by literacy rate above 80 per cent. Gurgaon tehsil has the highest level of literacy (80.81 per cent), because this is industrially developed, economically sound and also has the favourable impact of big town like New Delhi as National Capital of India. Gurgaon has many industries, which are engaged in manufacturing cotton yarn, sanitary ware, glass bottles, steel pipes and tubes, ghee and milk powder, cattle feed, agricultural implements, Maruti Udyog Ltd., etc.

Thus, being an industrial based region, several other factors have also helped in the growth of its literacy rate, e.g., high job opportunities, high standard of living and well developed means of transportation and communications. The development of transportation and communication network has increased the degree of spatial interaction resulting into the breaking up of rural isolation (Chandna, 2008).

2. Regions having High Literacy Rate (70 to 80 per cent)

This category covers 28.44 per cent area of the State and comprise a total of 20 tehsils. High level of literacy has been observed in the

Table 3.3: Haryana: Literacy Rates by Tehsils, 2001

Sr. No.	*State/Tehsil*	*Literacy Rate (Per cent)*	*Sr. No.*	*Tehsil*	*Literacy Rate (Per cent)*
	Haryana	*67.91*	34.	Julana	66.32
1.	Gurgaon	80.81	35.	Hisar	66.31
2.	Ambala	78.33	36.	Palwal	65.43
3.	Faridabad	77.98	37.	Ballabgarh	65.35
4.	Rewari	76.56	38.	Israna	65.23
5.	Sonipat	76.43	39.	Samalkha	65.01
6.	Rohtak	75.15	40.	Hansi	64.34
7.	Bahadurgarh	75.13	41.	Safidon	64.10
8.	Pataudi	74.49	42.	Gharaunda	64.07
9.	Panchkula	74.44	43.	Loharu	63.90
10.	Kosli	74.26	44.	Pehowa	63.78
11.	Jagadhri	73.57	45.	Bawani Khera	63.44
12.	Kalka	72.92	46.	Tosham	62.54
13.	Shahbad	72.63	47.	Sirsa	62.23
14.	Barara	72.38	48.	Assandh	61.77
15.	Beri	72.10	49.	Siwani	61.71
16.	Panipat	71.67	50.	Adampur	60.87
17.	Thanesar	71.35	51.	Chhachhrauli	59.83
18.	Karnal	71.01	52.	Hodal	59.60
19.	Sohna	70.73	53.	Kaithal	59.49
20.	Mahendragarh	70.57	54.	Narnaund	59.48
21.	Bhiwani	70.22	55.	Fatehabad	59.38
22.	Jhajjar	69.86	56.	Rania	58.76
23.	Ganaur	69.72	57.	Dabwali	58.76
24.	Bawal	69.65	58.	Tohana	58.71
25.	Gohana	69.44	59.	Ellenabad	57.46
26.	Kharkhoda	69.39	60.	Taoru	57.36
27.	Dadri	69.38	61.	Guhla	57.11
28.	Narnaul	69.36	62.	Narwana	55.62
29.	Naraingarh	67.76	63.	Ratia	53.08
30.	Maham	67.65	64.	Hathin	45.61
31.	Indri	67.59	65.	Nuh	44.92
32.	Nilokheri	67.02	66.	Ferozepur Jhirka	40.00
33.	Jind	66.65	67.	Punahana	37.41

Source: Computed from, Census of India (2001), *Primary Census Abstract*, Haryana, Series 7, Tables A5-A8, Directorate of Census Operations, Haryana.

Note: Tehsils are arranged in descending order of literacy rate, 2001.

northern region consisting of Kalka (72.92 per cent), Panchkula (74.44 per cent), Ambala (78.33 per cent), Barara (72.38 per cent), Jagadhri (73.57 per cent), Shahbad (72.63 per cent), and Thanesar

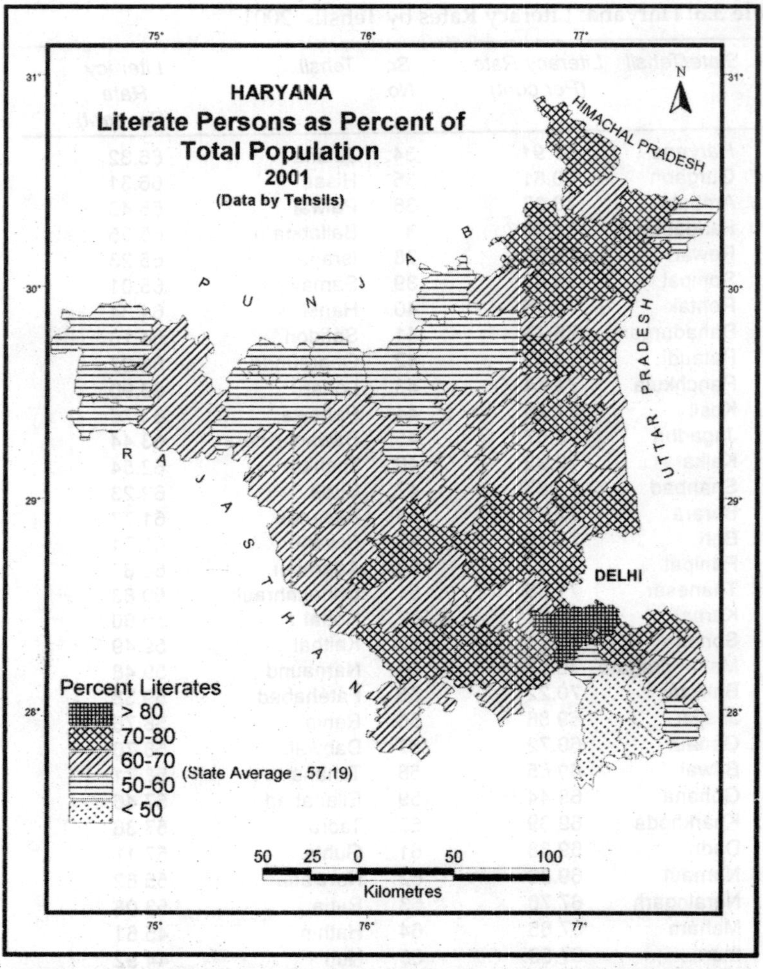

Map 3.1: Haryana: Literate Persons as Per cent of Total Population, 2001

(71.35 per cent) tehsils; eastern region comprising Karnal (71.01 per cent), Panipat (71.67 per cent), Sonipat (76.43 per cent), and Bahadurgarh (75.13 per cent) tehsils; central region comprising Rohtak (75.15 per cent), Beri (72.10 per cent) and Bhiwani (70.22 per cent) tehsils; and southern region consisting of Faridabad (77.98 per cent), Sohna (70.73 per cent), Pataudi (74.49 per cent), Rewari (76.56 per cent), Kosli (74.26 per cent), and Mahendragarh (70.57 per cent) tehsils.

Ambala, Panchkula, and Kalka towns comprise majority of persons belonging to service class. Their proximity to the union territory of Chandigarh has added a new dimension to the process of propagation of literacy and education in this area.

Jagadhri, Shahbad, Barara sub-region has a dominance of Industrial type of economy, Yamunanagar, and Jagadhri are two important trade centres. Yamunanagar being probably the biggest timber market in the entire northern India caters to the need of ammunition boxes to the Defence Department and Packing cases to tea and tobacco industries (Census of India, 1981). Jagadhri is famous for ferrous and non-ferrous metal utensils.

The large and medium scale industries of Rewari, Sonipat, Rohtak, Bahadurgarh, Pataudi, Kosli, Beri, Panipat, Karnal sub-regions are engaged in manufacturing cotton yarn, sanitary ware, plaster of paris, Sugar, Glass bottles, Steel pipes and tubes, ghee and milk powder, cattle feed, agricultural implements, cycles and brass utensils, etc. Mohan Spinning Mills, Haryana Co-operative Sugar Mills Limited, Hafed Cattle Feed Limited at Rohtak, National Fertilizers Ltd. at Panipat, The Atlas Cycle Industries Limited at Sonipat, Milk Dairy and Liberty Shoes factory in Karnal, Hindustan Sanitary Wares and Industries Limited and Bharat Udyog near Bahadurgarh, Aggarwal Metal Works Pvt. Limited and Rewari Textiles at Rewari are some such units.

So development of large and medium scale industries is one of the reasons for high level of literacy in these tehsils. Because higher the number of industries, higher the proportion of non-agricultural workers and higher the literacy rates as the requirements of the industrial based economy are such that acquisition of literacy skills becomes a functional prerequisite.

Besides, there are several other factors which are responsible for the higher level of literacy in these sub-regions. The proximity of Delhi, availability of educational institutions, degree of urbanization, standard of living, well developed means of transportation and communication are such factors. However, the availability of educational facilities within an easy access and within the reach of one's pocket works as a most positive factor in the propagation of literacy and education in these tehsils. Because Rohtak, Sonipat, Bhiwani and Rewari are leading education centres in Haryana, so there exists a positive correlation between the literacy rate and the degree of availability of educational institutions in these areas. Because, lower the number of people per educational institution, higher is the literacy rate.

3. Regions Having Moderate Literacy Rate (60 to 70 per cent)

This category covers 44.18 per cent area of the State and consists of a total of 29 tehsils. These are Naraingarh (67.76 per cent), and Pehowa (63.78 per cent) tehsils of northern region; Indri (67.59 per cent), Nilokheri (67.02 per cent), Gharaunda (64.07 per cent), Samalkha (65.01 per cent), Ganaur (69.72 per cent) and Kharkhoda (69.39 per cent) tehsils of eastern region; Assandh (61.77 per cent), Safidon (64.10 per cent), Jind (66.65 per cent), Julana (66.32 per cent), Gohana (69.44 per cent), Israna (65.23 per cent), Hansi (64.34 per cent), Meham (67.65 per cent), Bawani Khera (63.44 per cent), Dadri (69.38 per cent), and Jhajjar (69.86 per cent) tehsils of central region; Loharu (63.90 per cent), Tosham (62.54 per cent), Siwani (61.71 per cent), Hisar (66.31 per cent), Adampur (60.87 per cent), and Sirsa (62.23 per cent) tehsils of western region; Bawal (69.65 per cent), Narnaul (69.36 per cent), Palwal (65.43 per cent), and Ballabgarh (65.35 per cent) tehsils of southern region.

These areas have primarily agrarian economy and medium literacy rate can be ascribed to lack of industrial development, less educational facilities and socio-economic backwardness of the people.

4. Regions having Low Literacy Rate (50 to 60 per cent)

This category covers 21.57 per cent area of the State and comprises a total of 13 tehsils. These are Chhachhrauli (59.83 per cent), and Guhla (57.11 per cent) tehsils in the northern region; Kaithal (59.49 per cent), Narwana (55.62 per cent), and Narnaund (59.48 per cent) tehsils in the central region; Tohana (58.71 per cent), Ratia (53.08 per cent), Fatehabad (59.38 per cent), Ellenabad (57.46 per cent), Rania (58.76 per cent), and Dabwali (58.76 per cent) tehsils in western region; Taoru (57.36 per cent), and Hodal (59.60 per cent) tehsils in southern region. These sub-regions have low level of literacy. Almost all parts of this category are backward in agriculture as well as in industry. Here, industrial base has remained mainly agro-based. Most of the factories are engaged in manufacturing cotton textiles and food products. In addition to, some large and medium scale units of both public and private sectors are also found, such as Jindal Strips Limited and Nav Bharat Steels (Pvt.) Limited at Hisar, Milk Plant of Haryana Dairy Development Corporation and Cattle Feed Plant of Haryana Agro-Industries Corporation at Jind, etc.

Due to lack of industrialization in these tehsils, most of the people are engaged in agriculture. But agricultural operations are such that these do not have any demand of education resulting into the low level of literacy. The size of landholding is relatively large and with recent intensification of agriculture, demand for labour to work in the fields has increased. This keeps away many children especially those belonging to scheduled castes, from attending a school (Krishan and Chandna, 1974b). In addition to, the extremely poor families prefer their children to help them in making an earning rather than sparing them for schools. Hence, the low level of literacy in these parts of the State. Besides, lack of educational facilities, low level of income, less developed means of transportation and communication have also affected the literacy rates in these sub-regions.

5. *Regions having Very Low Literacy Rate (Below 50 per cent)*

This category of tehsils covers only 3.7 per cent area of the State and consists of four tehsils only in southern Haryana. Punhana tehsil has the lowest literacy rate (37.41 per cent) amongst the tehsils of Haryana. It is followed by the tehsils of Hathin (45.61 per cent), Nuh (44.92 per cent), and Ferozepur Jhirka (40.00 per cent). These tehsils have experienced very low literacy rate because these are industrially undeveloped and economically backward. Apart from this, the lowest literacy is also the outcome of social conservation of Muslim people who dominate the scene in these tehsils.

In Meo-Muslim society, equal status is not given to males and females and that is why suffers from low female literacy rates which affect adversely the total literacy rate. Not only this, but even the restrictions are imposed on the females' mobility and education resulting into the low female literacy and hence, low general literacy.

The other factors which affect the literacy rates of these regions to a great extent are (i) highly subsistence nature of agriculture which absorbs an overwhelming majority of the people, (ii) meagre urbanization, and (iii) lack of educational institutions. Although a number of schools have been opened by the government in Meo-Muslim inhabited tract of Nuh and Ferozepur tehsils but the response has been unmatching. Many Meos suggest that adoption of Urdu instead of Hindi as the medium of instruction in the schools located in this part of Haryana would facilitate the spread of literacy (Krishan and Chandna, 1974b).

3.5 Spatial Patterns of Urban-Rural Literacy

There is a reasonable gap between the literacy rates of rural (63.19 per cent) and urban (79.16 per cent) areas. The rural population lags far behind its urban counterparts in the literacy rates. Its reasons lie in the fact that in urban areas, living standard of people is high, economic conditions of people are good, more educational facilities are found, urban economy is diversified and more educated people come from rural areas to urban areas in search of job. Transportation and communication are developed in urban areas. There is no prejudice against female literacy. So literacy rate are always higher in urban areas than rural areas.

This disparity in literacy by residence is the product of five basic factors (Krishan and Chandna, 1974b):

1. The social life and economic patterns of urban places are such that the 'need to get educated is more in urban areas than in agricultural countryside';
2. Educational facilities are concentrated more in urban areas while these may be completely absent in certain rural areas;
3. Urban population is socially more awakened and economically more capable of imparting education to their children in comparison to the rural population;
4. Urban females enjoy relatively higher status in comparison to their rural compatriots and are not denied the opportunities of education as is the case in many rural areas;
5. Many educated ruralites migrate to urban places in search of jobs outside the agricultural sector particularly when there are no avenues in the countryside as a result of which

the number of literates in urban areas increases at the cost of rural areas.

3.5.1 Spatial Pattern of Urban Literacy

Urban areas experience very high literacy rates. However, spatial pattern of urban literacy show marked variation (Table 3.4).

On the basis of urban literacy rates as shown in Table 3.4, the tehsils of Haryana can be classified into five categories (Map 3.2):

1. Regions having Very High Urban Literacy Rate (Above 82 per cent)
2. Regions having High Urban Literacy Rate (77 to 82 per cent)
3. Regions having Moderate Urban Literacy Rate (72-77 per cent)
4. Regions having Low Urban Literacy Rate (67-72 per cent)
5. Regions having Very Low Urban Literacy Rate (Below 67 per cent)

1. Regions having Very High Urban Literacy Rate (Above 82 per cent)

About 9.23 per cent area of the State has recorded very high level of urban literacy and consists of only six tehsils. Gurgaon tehsil has the highest urban literacy rate (86.09 per cent) amongst 67 tehsils of Haryana and is followed by Ambala (85.68 per cent), Kalka (84.32 per cent), Rewari (82.78 per cent), Panchkula (82.33 per cent) and Karnal (82.08 per cent) tehsils. More than two-third of the population in these tehsils is literate. Reasons for high level of literacy are the availability of more educational facilities, high degree of urbanization and good economic condition.

2. Regions having High Urban Literacy Rate (77 to 82 per cent)

This category covers 38.19 per cent area of the State and comprises 21 tehsils. These are Chhachhrauli (79.70 per cent), Jagadhri (81.72 per cent), Naraingarh (81.54 per cent), Shahbad (81.35 per cent), Thanesar (81.11 per cent), and Pehowa (79.23 per cent) in northern part; Samalkha (78.93 per cent), Ganaur (79.09 per cent), Sonipat

Table 3.4: Haryana: Urban Literacy Rates by Tehsils, 2001

Sr. No.	State/Tehsil	Literacy Rate (Per cent)	Sr. No.	Tehsil	Literacy Rate (Per cent)
	Haryana	**79.16**	34.	Beri	75.98
1.	Gurgaon	86.09	35.	Palwal	75.91
2.	Ambala	85.68	36.	Fatehabad	75.88
3.	Kalka	84.32	37.	Safidon	75.74
4.	Rewari	82.78	38.	Sirsa	75.52
5.	Panchkula	82.33	39.	Sohna	75.22
6.	Karnal	82.08	40.	Kharkhoda	74.92
7.	Jagadhri	81.72	41.	Pataudi	74.55
8.	Sonipat	81.72	42.	Tosham	74.30
9.	Naraingarh	81.54	43.	Indri	74.16
10.	Rohtak	81.53	44.	Dabwali	73.94
11.	Shahbad	81.35	45.	Kaithal	73.21
12.	Thanesar	81.11	46.	Julana	72.77
13.	Jhajjar	80.13	47.	Tohana	72.40
14.	Chhachhrauli	79.70	48.	Assandh	71.90
15.	Dadri	79.65	49.	Hathin	71.51
16.	Bahadurgarh	79.62	50.	Narwana	71.16
17.	Faridabad	79.62	51.	Ratia	70.85
18.	Pehowa	79.23	52.	Guhla	68.20
19.	Ganaur	79.09	53.	Ellenabad	68.04
20.	Taoru	79.07	54.	Siwani	67.87
21.	Samalkha	78.93	55.	Hodal	67.70
22.	Gohana	78.69	56.	Nuh	67.14
23.	Hisar	78.55	57.	Bawani Khera	66.73
24.	Jind	78.42	58.	Loharu	66.56
25.	Bhiwani	78.37	59.	Punahana	66.16
26.	Mahendragarh	78.22	60.	Narnaund	66.06
27.	Narnaul	78.17	61.	Rania	63.68
28.	Hansi	76.87	62.	Ferozepur Jhirka	62.98
29.	Gharaunda	76.82	63.	Ballabgarh	Totally Rural
30.	Nilokheri	76.80	64.	Adampur	Totally Rural
31.	Bawal	76.63	65.	Kosli	Totally Rural
32.	Maham	76.51	66.	Israna	Totally Rural
33.	Panipat	76.01	67.	Barara	Totally Rural

Source: Computed from Census of India (2001), *Primary Census Abstract*, Haryana, Series 7, Tables A5-A8, Directorate of Census Operations, Haryana.

Note: Tehsils are arranged in descending order of literacy rate, 2001.

(81.72 per cent), and Bahadurgarh (79.62 per cent) in eastern part; Jhajjar (80.13 per cent), Dadri (79.65 per cent), Bhiwani (78.37 per cent), Rohtak (81.53 per cent), Gohana (78.69 per cent), and Jind (78.42 per cent) in central part; Mahendragarh (78.22 per cent),

Narnaul (78.17 per cent), Faridabad (79.62 per cent), and Taoru (79.07 per cent) in southern part; and Hisar (78.55 per cent) in western part. Reasons for high level of literacy are the availability of more educational facilities, high degree of urbanization and good economic conditions.

3. Regions having Moderate Urban Literacy Rates (72 to 77 per cent)

About 30.65 per cent area of the State has recorded moderate level of literacy and consists of a total of 20 tehsils. These are Indri (74.16 per cent), Nilokheri (76.80 per cent), Gharaunda (76.82 per cent), Panipat (76.01 per cent), and Kharkhoda (74.92 per cent) in eastern part; Kaithal (73.21 per cent), Safidon (75.74 per cent), Julana (72.77 per cent), Hansi (76.87 per cent), Meham (76.51 per cent), and Beri (75.98 per cent) in central part; Tosham (74.30 per cent), Tohana (72.40 per cent), Fatehabad (75.88 per cent), Sirsa (75.52 per cent), and Dabwali (73.94 per cent) in western part; Bawal (76.63 per cent), Pataudi (74.55 per cent), Sohna (75.22 per cent), and Palwal (75.91 per cent) in southern part. These tehsils are less urbanized and have low infrastructure and educational development.

4. Regions having Low Urban Literacy Rate (67 to 72 per cent)

A total of nine tehsils are characterized by low urban literacy rate. These are Guhla (68.20 per cent) of Kaithal district in northern Haryana; Assandh (71.90 per cent) of Karnal district, and Narwana (71.16 per cent) of Jind district in central Haryana; Ellenabad (68.04 per cent) of Sirsa district, Ratia (70.85 per cent) of Fatehabad district, and Siwani (67.87 per cent) of Bhiwani district in western Haryana; Nuh (67.14 per cent) of Gurgaon district, Hathin (71.51 per cent), and Hodal (67.70 per cent) of Faridabad district in southern Haryana. These tehsils also have low level of urbanization because still these are lacking in the development of big cities.

5. Regions having Very Low Urban Literacy Rates (Below 67 per cent)

This category covers 6.54 per cent area of the State and consists of only six tehsils. Ferozepur Jhirka tehsil has lowest urban literacy rate (62.98 per cent) amongst the tehsils of Haryana. It is followed by the tehsils of Bawani Khera (66.73 per cent), and Loharu (66.56 per cent) in Bhiwani district; Punahana (66.16 per cent) of Gurgaon

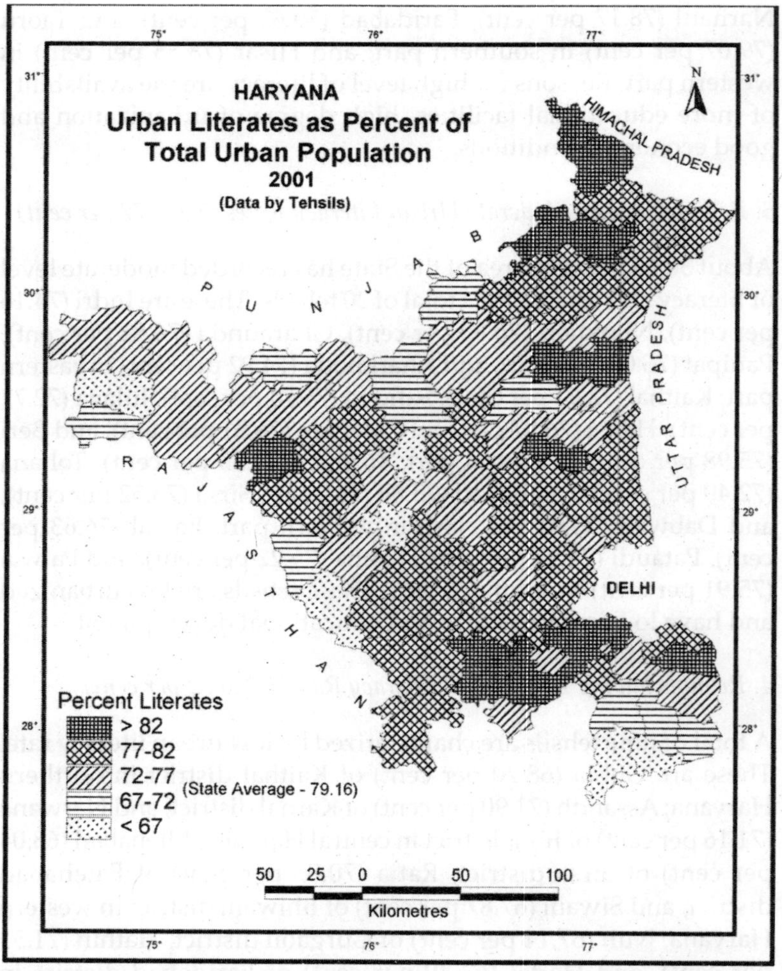

Map 3.2: Haryana: Urban Literates as Per cent of Total Urban Population, 2001

district; Narnaund (66.06 per cent) of Hisar district; and Rania (63.68 per cent) of Sirsa district. The reasons may be lack of educational facilities and low level of urbanization alongwith the dominance of Muslim population in certain tehsils.

3.5.2 *Spatial Patterns of Rural Literacy*

The rural literacy patterns present a wide difference between the highest and the lowest rates of literacy. In Haryana, rural literacy is found to be very low in most of tehsils as compared to urban literacy (Table 3.5).

On the basis of rural literacy rates as shown in Table 3.5, the tehsils of Haryana can be classified into five categories (Map 3.3):

1. Regions having Very High Rural Literacy Rate (Above 74 per cent);
2. Regions having High Rural Literacy Rate (64 to 74 per cent);
3. Regions having Moderate Rural Literacy Rate (54 to 64 per cent);
4. Regions having Low Rural Literacy Rate (44 to 54 per cent); and
5. Regions having Very Low Rural Literacy Rate (Below 44 per cent).

1. Regions having Very High Rural Literacy Rate (Above 74 per cent)

Only four tehsils of southern Haryana, viz., Gurgaon (77.28 per cent), Rewari (74.68 per cent), Pataudi (74.45 per cent) and Kosli (74.26 per cent) are attributed with very high rural literacy rate. Gurgaon tehsil has the highest rural literacy rate (77.28 per cent) amongst the total tehsils of the State. Very high rural literacy in this region is mainly due to its peripheral location to union territory of Delhi, the availability of sufficient educational facilities, and the prevailing social awareness among rural masses.

2. Regions having High Rural Literacy Rate (64 to 74 per cent)

This category covers about 39.28 per cent area of the State and comprises a total of 28 tehsils. These are Panchkula (67.97 per cent), Ambala (70.23 per cent), Barara (72.38 per cent), Shahbad (69.69 per cent), Thanesar (67.10 per cent), Jagadhri (67.23 per cent), and Naraingarh (66.40 per cent) in northern Haryana; Indri (66.85 per cent), Nilokheri (64.38 per cent), Panipat (64.81 per cent), Ganaur (67.83 per cent), Sonipat (73.19 per cent), Kharkhoda (68.67 per cent), and Bahadurgarh 72.29 per cent) in eastern Haryana; Jhajjar (68.68 per cent), Beri (71.56 per cent), Dadri (68.22 per cent), Bhiwani (65.55 per cent), Rohtak (70.58 per cent), Meham (66.66 per cent), Julana (65.38 per cent), Gohana (67.89 per cent), and Israna (65.23 per cent) in central Haryana; Mahendragarh (69.73 per cent), Narnaul

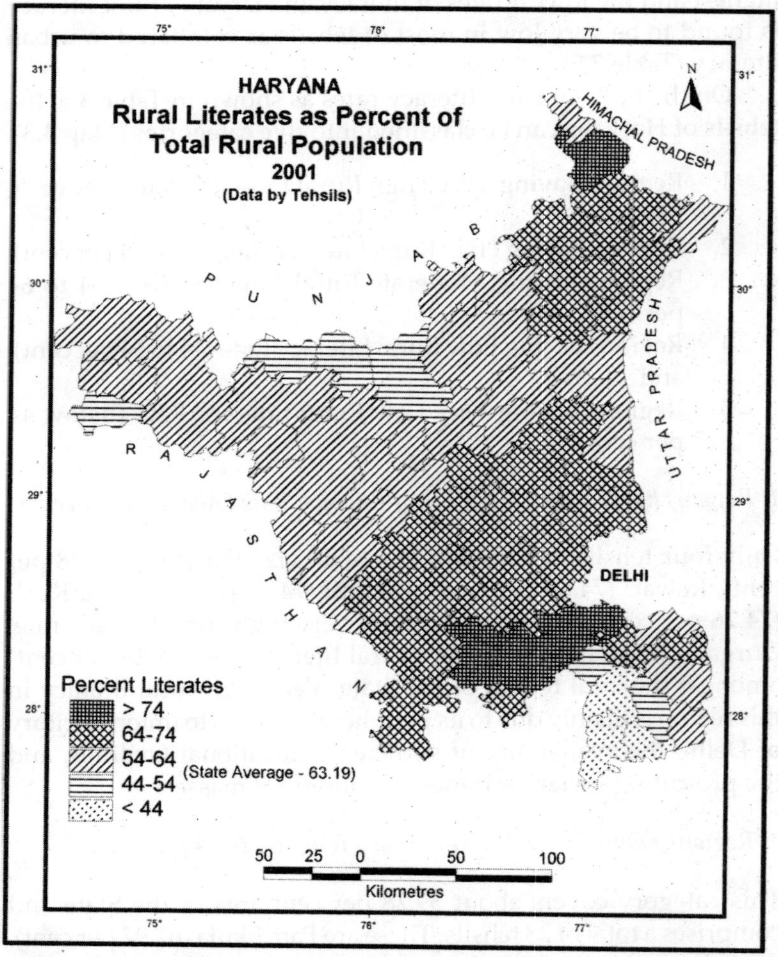

Map 3.3: Haryana: Rural Literates as Per cent of Total Rural Population, 2001

(67.61 per cent), Bawal (68.78 per cent), Sohna (69.61 per cent), and Ballabgarh (65.35 per cent) of southern Haryana. All these sub-regions have good transport network and educational infrastructure which reduce the isolation of rural areas.

3. *Regions having Moderate Rural Literacy Rate (54 to 64 per cent)*

This category covers 45.03 per cent area of the State and consists of a total of 26 tehsils. These are Loharu (63.66 per cent), Tosham (61.65 per cent), Siwani (60.31 per cent), Hisar (60.07 per cent), Adampur (60.87 per cent), Fatehabad (56.58 per cent), Sirsa (56.37 per cent), Rania (57.97 per cent), and Dabwali (54.16 per cent) in western region; Bawani Khera (62.84 per cent), Hansi (60.68 per cent), Narnaund (58.58 per cent), Jind (60.94 per cent), Kaithal (56.04 per cent), Assandh (60.37 per cent), and Safidon (62.47 per cent) in central region; Faridabad (62.05 per cent), Palwal (61.79 per cent), and Hodal (57.34 per cent) in southern region; Samalkha (63.04 per cent), Gharaunda (61.42 per cent), and Karnal (63.31 per cent) in eastern region; Guhla (54.75 per cent), Pehowa (60.34 per cent), Chhachhrauli (58.40 per cent), and Kalka (63.22 per cent) in northern region. The western and central regions have primarily agrarian economy, lacking in industrial development, educational facilities and are characterized with socio-economic backwardness of the people. The effect of Muslim population, in rural areas, above the State average (3.96 per cent) in some of the tehsils like Chhachhrauli (26.27 per cent), Samalkha (9.67 per cent), Hodal (9.07 per cent), Kalka (5.43 per cent), Palwal (5.47 per cent), and Gharaunda (4.86 per cent) cannot be ignored in reducing the rural literacy rate to moderate level.

4. *Regions having Low Rural Literacy Rate (44 to 54 per cent)*

This category covers 7.44 per cent area of the State and consists of six tehsils. These are Tohana (53.95 per cent), and Ratia (49.77 per cent) of Fatehabad district; Ellenabad (53.09 per cent) of Sirsa district; Narwana (52.86 per cent) of Jind district; Taoru (53.57 per cent) of Gurgaon district; and Hathin (44.05 per cent) of Faridabad district. Low level of rural literacy in the western part of Haryana is mainly due to involvement of rural people in agricultural activities, high proportion of scheduled castes population, availability of poor educational facilities and lack of industrial development. In addition to other causes, the dominance of Muslim population in the tehsils of Taoru (55.71 per cent) and Hathin (56.48 per cent) is the primary cause of low rural literacy. Both the tehsils are fourth and fifth ranking amongst 67 tehsils of the State in terms of the size of Muslim population.

Table 3.5: Haryana: Rural Literacy Rates by Tehsils, 2001

Sr. No.	*State/Tehsil*	*Literacy Rate (Per cent)*	*Sr. No.*	*Tehsil*	*Literacy Rate (Per cent)*
	Haryana	**63.19**	34.	Karnal	63.31
1.	Gurgaon	77.28	35.	Kalka	63.22
2.	Rewari	74.68	36.	Samalkha	63.04
3.	Pataudi	74.45	37.	Bawani Khera	62.84
4.	Kosli	74.26	38.	Safidon	62.47
5.	Sonipat	73.19	39.	Faridabad	62.05
6.	Barara	72.38	40.	Palwal	61.79
7.	Bahadurgarh	72.29	41.	Tosham	61.65
8.	Beri	71.56	42.	Gharaunda	61.42
9.	Rohtak	70.58	43.	Jind	60.94
10.	Ambala	70.23	44.	Adampur	60.87
11.	Mahendragarh	69.73	45.	Hansi	60.68
12.	Shahbad	69.69	46.	Assandh	60.37
13.	Sohna	69.61	47.	Pehowa	60.34
14.	Bawal	68.78	48.	Siwani	60.31
15.	Jhajjar	68.68	49.	Hisar	60.07
16.	Kharkhoda	68.67	50.	Narnaund	58.58
17.	Dadri	68.22	51.	Chhachhrauli	58.40
18.	Panchkula	67.97	52.	Rania	57.97
19.	Gohana	67.89	53.	Hodal	57.34
20.	Ganaur	67.83	54.	Fatehabad	56.58
21.	Narnaul	67.61	55.	Sirsa	56.37
22.	Jagadhri	67.23	56.	Kaithal	56.04
23.	Thanesar	67.10	57.	Guhla	54.75
24.	Indri	66.85	58.	Dabwali	54.16
25.	Maham	66.66	59.	Tohana	53.95
26.	Naraingarh	66.40	60.	Taoru	53.57
27.	Bhiwani	65.55	61.	Ellenabad	53.09
28.	Julana	65.38	62.	Narwana	52.86
29.	Ballabgarh	65.35	63.	Ratia	49.77
30.	Israna	65.23	64.	Hathin	44.05
31.	Panipat	64.81	65.	Nuh	43.62
32.	Nilokheri	64.38	66.	Ferozepur Jhirka	38.05
33.	Loharu	63.66	67.	Punahana	35.33

Source: Computed from Census of India (2001), *Primary Census Abstract*, Haryana, Series 7, Tables A5-A8, Directorate of Census Operations, Haryana.

Note: Tehsils are arranged in descending order of literacy rate, 2001.

5. Regions having Very Low Rural Literacy Rate (Below 44 per cent)

This category covers about 2.89 per cent area of the State and comprises only three tehsils of Nuh, Ferozepur Jhirka and Punahana in southern Haryana. Punahana has the lowest rural literacy rate (35.33 per cent) amongst the tehsils of Haryana and is followed by Ferozepur Jhirka (38.05 per cent) and Nuh (43.62 per cent) tehsils. One of the most important causes of low rural literacy rate is the dominance of Meo-Muslim population in these areas. Amongst the tehsils of Haryana, Ferozepur Jhirka (86.92 per cent) is the first ranking tehsil in terms of the size of Muslim population and is followed by Punahana (88.55 per cent) and Nuh (72.95 per cent) tehsils.

3.6 Spatial Patterns of Male-Female Literacy

There exists a great disparity between male (78.49 per cent) and female (55.73 per cent) literacy rates in Haryana. This wide disparity in the male-female literacy rates is the product of a variety of social and economic factors (Chandna, 2008).

Socially, the prejudices against the females' mobility and education, the low status granted to the females, lack of educational institutions for females, lack of female teachers, prevalence of early marriage and movement of girls from their parents' place of residence to the residence of their spouses at the time of marriage are the factors responsible for low female literacy. Economically, the appalling poverty and low degree of occupational participation among females are the factors responsible for wide disparity in the literacy rates of both the sexes.

3.6.1 Spatial Patterns of Male Literacy

The spatial patterns of male literacy in Haryana show marked variations (Table 3.6).

On the basis of male literacy rates as shown in Table 3.6, the tehsils of Haryana can be classified into five categories (Map 3.4):

1. Regions having Very High Male Literacy Rate (Above 88 per cent);
2. Regions having High Male Literacy Rate (80 to 88 per cent);
3. Regions having Moderate Male Literacy Rate (72 to 80 per cent);
4. Regions having Low Male Literacy Rate (64 to 72 per cent); and
5. Regions having Very Low Male Literacy Rate (Below 64 per cent).

Table 3.6: Haryana: Male Literacy Rates by Tehsils, 2001

Sr. No.	*State/Tehsil*	*Literacy Rate (Per cent)*	*Sr. No.*	*Tehsil*	*Literacy Rate (Per cent)*
	Haryana	**78.49**	34.	Jind	78.06
1.	Rewari	89.13	35.	Israna	77.62
2.	Gurgaon	89.12	36.	Hisar	77.43
3.	Kosli	88.60	37.	Indri	76.85
4.	Pataudi	86.44	38.	Tosham	76.63
5.	Faridabad	85.92	39.	Naraingarh	76.39
6.	Sonipat	85.74	40.	Bawani Khera	76.33
7.	Bawal	84.85	41.	Hansi	76.24
8.	Narnaul	84.75	42.	Samalkha	76.23
9.	Mahendragarh	84.70	43.	Hodal	75.99
10.	Bahadurgarh	84.49	44.	Siwani	75.91
11.	Beri	84.46	45.	Nilokheri	75.65
12.	Ambala	84.46	46.	Safidon	75.05
13.	Rohtak	84.18	47.	Adampur	75.01
14.	Sohna	83.59	48.	Gharaunda	74.73
15.	Dadri	82.90	49.	Taoru	73.06
16.	Jhajjar	81.64	50.	Narnaund	72.72
17.	Ganaur	81.30	51.	Pehowa	72.22
18.	Panchkula	81.02	52.	Sirsa	71.67
19.	Bhiwani	80.92	53.	Assandh	70.85
20.	Barara	80.82	54.	Fatehabad	70.82
21.	Gohana	80.57	55.	Kaithal	70.01
22.	Kalka	80.46	56.	Rania	68.76
23.	Jagadhri	80.46	57.	Chhachhrauli	68.75
24.	Shahbad	80.46	58.	Tohana	68.07
25.	Palwal	80.39	59.	Dabwali	67.76
26.	Ballabgarh	79.96	60.	Narwana	67.75
27.	Kharkhoda	79.94	61.	Ellenabad	67.66
28.	Panipat	79.59	62.	Guhla	65.57
29.	Thanesar	79.54	63.	Hathin	62.94
30.	Loharu	79.39	64.	Nuh	62.71
31.	Maham	79.22	65.	Ratia	61.31
32.	Julana	78.79	66.	Ferozepur Jhirka	58.20
33.	Karnal	78.54	67.	Punahana	55.43

Source: Computed from Census of India (2001), *Primary Census Abstract*, Haryana, Series 7, Tables A5-A8, Directorate of Census Operations, Haryana.

Note: Tehsils are arranged in descending order of literacy rate, 2001.

1. Regions having Very High Male Literacy Rate (Above 88 per cent)

These regions cover 4.52 per cent area of the State and comprise only three tehsils. The highest male literacy rate is found in Rewari tehsil (89.13 per cent), and is followed by Gurgaon (89.12 per cent) and Kosli (88.60 per cent) tehsils. Very high male literacy in this region is mainly due to its peripheral location to New Delhi, the National capital of India, availability of sufficient educational facilities, and the prevailing socio-economic awareness among people.

2. Regions having High Male Literacy Rate (80 to 88 per cent)

Regions having high male literacy rates cover 35.33 per cent area of the State and consist of a total of 22 tehsils. These are Faridabad (85.92 per cent), Palwal (80.39 per cent) Sohna (83.59 per cent), Pataudi (86.44 per cent), Bawal (84.85 per cent), Narnaul (84.75 per cent), and Mahendragarh (84.70 per cent) tehsils in southern region; Dadri (82.90 per cent), Bhiwani (80.92 per cent), Jhajjar (81.64 per cent), Beri (84.46 per cent), Rohtak (84.18 per cent), and Gohana (80.57 per cent) tehsils in central region; Sonipat (85.74 per cent), Bahadurgarh (84.49 per cent), and Ganaur (81.30 per cent) tehsils in eastern region; Ambala (84.46 per cent), Panchkula (81.02 per cent), Barara (80.82 per cent), Kalka (80.46 per cent), Jagadhri (80.46 per cent), and Shahbad (80.46 per cent) tehsils in the northern region. These tehsils have more educational institutes and well developed transportation system. Moreover, peripheral location of these regions to capital cities of New Delhi and Chandigarh is also one of the important causes responsible for high male literacy.

3. Regions having Moderate Male Literacy Rate (72 to 80 per cent)

These regions include 33.46 per cent area of the State and comprise a total of 26 tehsils. Moderate male literacy rates are recorded in the tehsils of Thanesar (79.54 per cent), Naraingarh (76.39 per cent) and Pehowa (72.22 per cent) tehsils in northern Haryana; Kharkhoda (79.94 per cent), Panipat (79.59 per cent), Karnal (78.54 per cent), Israna (77.62 per cent), Indri (76.85 per cent), Samalkha (76.23 per cent), Nilokheri (75.65 per cent) and Gharaunda

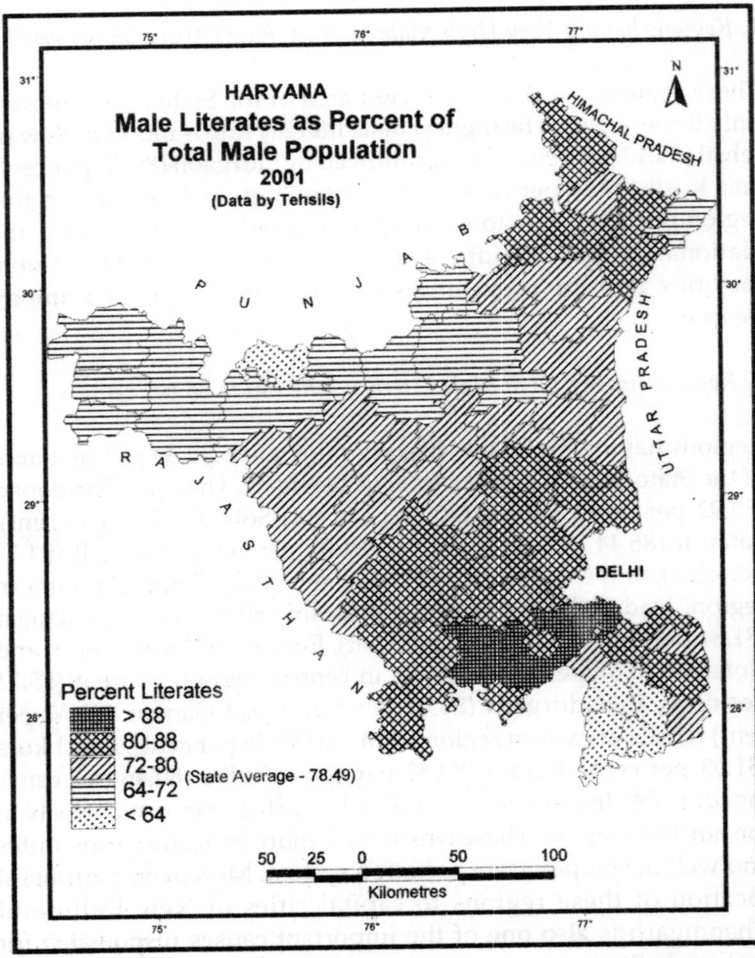

Map 3.4: Haryana: Male Literates as Per cent of Total Male Population, 2001

(74.73 per cent) tehsils in the eastern part,; in central part, Meham (79.22 per cent), Julana (78.79 per cent), Jind (78.06 per cent), and Safidon (75.05 per cent) tehsils and in the western part Loharu (79.39 per cent), Hisar (77.43 per cent), Tosham (76.63 per cent), Bawani Khera (76.33 per cent), Hansi (76.24 per cent), Siwani (75.91 per cent), Adampur (75.01 per cent) and Narnaund (72.72 per cent) tehsils; and in the south, Ballabgarh (79.96 per cent), Hodal (75.99 per cent) and Taoru (73.06 per cent) tehsils. In these tehsils, male population is mainly engaged in primary activities and transportation network is well developed.

4. Regions having Low Male Literacy Rates (64 to 72 per cent)

This category includes 21.78 per cent area of the State and consist of a total of 11 tehsils. Low levels of male literacy are recorded in the tehsils of Dabwali (67.76 per cent), Rania (68.76 per cent), Ellenabad (67.66 per cent), Sirsa (71.67 per cent), Fatehabad (70.82 per cent), and Tohana (68.07 per cent) in the western part; Kaithal (70.01 per cent), Narwana (67.75 per cent), and Assandh (70.85 per cent) in central part; Guhla (65.57 per cent), and Chhachhrauli (68.75 per cent) in northern part.

Low level of male literacy in these parts, especially in western part of Haryana is mainly due to involvement of people in agricultural activities, high proportion of scheduled castes population, availability of poor educational facilities, less developed means of transportation and communication and lack of industrial development. Here, industrial base has remained mainly agro-based. Most of the factories are engaged in manufacturing cotton textiles and food products. Agricultural operations are such that these do not have any demand of education resulting into the low level of literacy. In addition to, the extremely poor families prefer their children to help them in making an earning rather than sparing them for schools. Hence, the low level of literacy in these parts of the State.

In addition, the sizeable number of scheduled castes (21.61 per cent) and Muslim (24.93 per cent) population is the primary cause of low rural literacy in Chhachhrauli tehsil.

5. Regions having Very Low Male Literacy Rates (Below 64 per cent)

This category covers 4.91 per cent area of the State and consists of only five tehsils. The lowest male literacy rates are found in southern part of Haryana, where dominance of Muslim population is always considered as the main cause of low literacy among males. Punahana (55.43 per cent) tehsil has the lowest male literacy rate amongst the 67 tehsils of Haryana. It is followed by Ferozepur Jhirka (58.20 per cent), Nuh (62.71 per cent), and Hathin (62.94

per cent). Amongst the tehsils of Haryana, Punahana (84.96 per cent) is the first ranking tehsil in terms of the size of male Muslim population and is followed by Ferozepur Jhirka (82.31 per cent), Nuh (70.59 per cent) and Hathin (53.92 per cent) tehsils.

Ratia is the only tehsil in western Haryana which is characterized by very low male literacy rate (61.31 per cent). It is third ranking tehsil, after Punahana and Ferozepur Jhirka, in terms of lowest level of male literacy.

This tehsil has experienced very low literacy rate because it is industrially undeveloped and economically backward. Apart from this, Ratia tehsil has the highest concentration of scheduled castes population (36.69 per cent) in Haryana. The other factors which affect the male literacy rate, here, to a great extent are (i) highly subsistence nature of agriculture which absorbs an overwhelming majority of the people, (ii) meagre urbanization, and (iii) lack of educational institutions.

In nutshell, we can say that highest male literacy rates have been recorded in southern and northern parts of the State (as shown in Map 3.4) because of their bordering location with union territories of Delhi and Chandigarh respectively.

3.6.2 Spatial Patterns of Female Literacy

The female literacy patterns present a wide difference between the highest and the lowest rates of literacy. In Haryana, female literacy is found to be very low in most of the tehsils as compared to male literacy (Table 3.7).

On the basis of female literacy rates as shown in Table 3.7, the tehsils of Haryana can be classified into five categories (Map 3.5):

1. Regions having Very High Female Literacy Rate (Above 64 per cent);
2. Regions having High Female Literacy Rate (56 to 64 per cent);
3. Regions having Moderate Female Literacy Rate (48 to 56 per cent);
4. Regions having Low Female Literacy Rate (40 to 48 per cent); and
5. Regions having Very Low Female Literacy Rate (Below 40 per cent).

1. Regions having Very High Female Literacy (above 64 per cent)

These regions cover 13.12 per cent area of the State and consist of eight tehsils only. Ambala tehsil has the highest female literacy (71.30 per cent) amongst the total tehsils of Haryana. It is followed by Gurgaon (70.97 per cent), Faridabad (68.26 per cent), Panchkula (66.29 per cent), Jagadhri (65.65 per cent), Sonipat (65.32 per cent), Rohtak (64.61 per cent) and Kalka (64.13 per cent) tehsils. Here factor of prejudice against females' education is less powerful. People are broad-minded and are well aware about the utility of education in society. Development of educational facilities in abundance and peripheral location of these tehsils to the capital cities of either New Delhi or Chandigarh are the other causes responsible for very high female literacy rate in these tehsils.

2. Regions having High Female Literacy Rate (56 to 64 Per Cent)

These regions cover 22.96 per cent area of the State and comprise 19 tehsils. These are Shahbad (63.94 per cent), Thanesar (61.97 per cent), Barara (63.15 per cent), and Naraingarh (58.07 per cent) tehsils of northern region; Indri (57.11 per cent), Nilokheri (57.23 per cent), Karnal (62.35 per cent), Panipat (62.06 per cent), Ganaur (56.11 per cent), Kharkhoda (56.88 per cent), and Bahadurgarh (63.78 per cent) tehsils of eastern region; Sohna (56.12 per cent), Pataudi (61.46 per cent), Rewari (62.69 per cent), and Kosli (59.45 per cent) tehsils of southern region; Jhajjar (56.44 per cent), Beri (57.98 per cent), Bhiwani (57.87 per cent), and Gohana (56.62 per cent) tehsils of central region. The high female literacy rate in these tehsils is related to the increasing educational facilities along with availability of female teachers in abundance particularly in rural areas, increasing value of female education for matrimony, increasing degree of socio-economic awareness, and the waning social taboos and prejudices against females' education.

3. Regions having Moderate Female Literacy Rate (48 to 56 per cent)

This category covers 38.28 per cent area of the State and comprises a total of 22 tehsils. These are Mahendragarh (55.45 per cent), Narnaul (53.02 per cent), Bawal (52.99 per cent), Ballabgarh (48.25 per cent), and Palwal (48.13 per cent) tehsils of southern Haryana; Dadri

Table 3.7: Haryana: Female Literacy Rates by Tehsils, 2001

Sr. No.	State/Tehsil	Literacy Rate (Per cent)	Sr. No.	Tehsil	Literacy Rate (Per cent)
	Haryana	**55.73**	34.	Narnaul	53.02
1.	Ambala	71.30	35.	Bawal	52.99
2.	Gurgaon	70.97	36.	Julana	51.88
3.	Faridabad	68.26	37.	Gharaunda	51.77
4.	Panchkula	66.29	38.	Sirsa	51.64
5.	Jagadhri	65.65	39.	Samalkha	51.62
6.	Sonipat	65.32	40.	Assandh	51.52
7.	Rohtak	64.61	41.	Safidon	51.34
8.	Kalka	64.13	42.	Israna	50.90
9.	Shahbad	63.94	43.	Hansi	50.54
10.	Bahadurgarh	63.78	44.	Chhachhrauli	49.64
11.	Barara	63.15	45.	Bawani Khera	48.82
12.	Rewari	62.69	46.	Dabwali	48.81
13.	Karnal	62.35	47.	Ballabgarh	48.25
14.	Panipat	62.06	48.	Tohana	48.23
15.	Thanesar	61.97	49.	Palwal	48.13
16.	Pataudi	61.46	50.	Guhla	47.56
17.	Kosli	59.45	51.	Rania	47.55
18.	Naraingarh	58.07	52.	Kaithal	47.25
19.	Beri	57.98	53.	Loharu	46.91
20.	Bhiwani	57.87	54.	Tosham	46.55
21.	Nilokheri	57.23	55.	Fatehabad	46.53
22.	Indri	57.11	56.	Ellenabad	46.05
23.	Kharkhoda	56.88	57.	Siwani	45.89
24.	Gohana	56.62	58.	Adampur	44.79
25.	Jhajjar	56.44	59.	Narnaund	44.07
26.	Sohna	56.12	60.	Ratia	44.06
27.	Ganaur	56.11	61.	Narwana	41.63
28.	Mahendragarh	55.45	62.	Hodal	40.47
29.	Dadri	54.38	63.	Taoru	39.56
30.	Pehowa	54.35	64.	Hathin	25.64
31.	Maham	53.99	65.	Nuh	24.98
32.	Jind	53.24	66.	Ferozepur Jhirka	19.95
33.	Hisar	53.17	67.	Punahana	17.67

Source: Computed from Census of India (2001), *Primary Census Abstract*, Haryana, Series 7, Tables A5-A8, Directorate of Census Operations, Haryana.

Note: Tehsils are arranged in descending order of literacy rate, 2001.

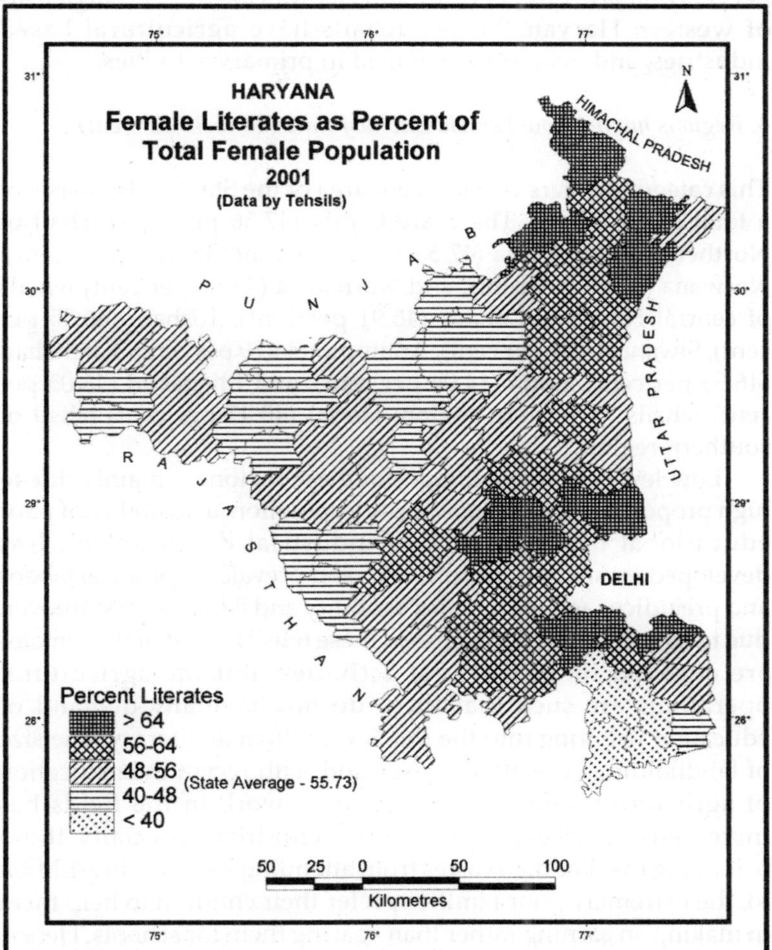

Map 3.5: Haryana: Female Literates as Per cent of Total Female Population, 2001

(54.38 per cent), Meham (53.99 per cent), Bawani Khera (48.82 per cent), Hansi (50.54 per cent), Julana (51.88 per cent), Jind (53.24 per cent), Safidon (51.34 per cent), Assandh (51.52 per cent), and Israna (50.90 per cent) tehsils of central Haryana; Samalkha (51.62 per cent), and Gharaunda (51.77 per cent) tehsils of eastern Haryana; Pehowa (54.35 per cent), and Chhachhauli (49.64 per cent) tehsils of northern Haryana; Hisar (53.17 per cent), Tohana (48.23

per cent), Sirsa (51.64 per cent), and Dabwali (48.81 per cent) tehsils of western Haryana. These tehsils have agricultural based industries, and people are engaged in primary activities.

4. Regions having Low Female Literacy Rate (40 to 48 per cent)

This category covers 24.8 per cent area of the State and consists of a total of 13 tehsils. These are Guhla (47.56 per cent) tehsil of Northern region; Rania (47.55 per cent), Kaithal (47.25 per cent), Narwana (41.63 per cent), and Narnaund (44.07 per cent) tehsils of central Haryana; Loharu (46.91 per cent), Tosham (46.55 per cent), Siwani (45.89 per cent), Adampur (44.79 per cent), Fatehabad (46.53 per cent), Ratia (44.06 per cent), and Ellenabad (46.05 per cent) tehsils of western region; Hodal (40.47 per cent) tehsil of southern region.

Low level of female literacy in these regions is mainly due to high proportion of scheduled caste population, availability of poor educational facilities, lack of industrial development, less developed means of transportation, and prevalence of social taboos and prejudices against females' mobility and education. Moreover, due to lack of industrialization in these tehsils, most of the females are engaged in agricultural activities. But the agricultural operations are such that these do not have any demand of education resulting into the low level of female literacy. The size of landholding is relatively large and with recent intensification of agriculture, demand for labour to work in the fields has increased. This keeps away many children especially those belonging to scheduled castes from attending a school. In addition to, the extremely poor families prefer their children to help them in making an earning rather than sparing them for schools. Hence, the low level of female literacy in these parts of the State.

5. Regions having Very Low Female Literacy Rate (Below 40 per cent)

These tehsils cover 4.26 per cent area of the State. Very low level of female literacy has been observed in only four tehsils of southern Haryana. Amongst these, the lowest female literacy is found in Taoru (39.56 per cent) tehsil and is followed by Hathin (25.64 per cent), Nuh (24.98 per cent), Ferozepur Jhirka (19.95 per cent) and Punahana (17.67 per cent) tehsils.

These tehsils have experienced very low female literacy, because these are industrially undeveloped and economically backward. Apart from this, very low female literacy is also the outcome of social conservation of Muslim people who dominate the scene in these tehsils. In Meo-Muslim society, equal status is not given to males and females and that is why suffers from low female literacy rates Not only this, but even the restrictions are imposed on the females' mobility and education resulting into the low female literacy. The other factors which affect the female literacy in these regions to a great extent are (i) highly subsistence nature of agriculture which absorbs an overwhelming majority of the people, (ii) meagre urbanization, and (iii) lack of educational institutions for females alongwith the poor availability of female teachers especially in rural areas.

In nutshell, the northern and eastern parts have recorded high female literacy rates (as shown in Map 3.5) than the western, central and the southern parts.

Conclusions

The spatial pattern of literacy in Haryana is bimodal, with literacy peaks characteristic of the zone peripheral to the union territory of Delhi and of Chandigarh. Literacy rates go on declining as one moves away from these two areas. The north-western quadrant of Haryana is the most extensive tract with low literacy though the lowest literacy rates are characteristic of the Meo-Muslim inhabited tract in southern part of the State.

There are striking spatial disparities in literacy rates within Haryana ranging from only 37.41 per cent in Punahana tehsil in Gurgaon district to 80.81 per cent in Gurgaon tehsil. It means both the highest and lowest literacy rates are found in the district of Gurgaon. This tehsil has experienced very high literacy rate because this is industrially developed, economically sound and also has the favourable impact of big town like New Delhi as National capital of India.

Thus, being an industrial based region, several other factors have also helped in the growth of its literacy rate, e.g., high job opportunities, high standard of living and well developed means of transportation and communications. The development of transportation and communication network has increased the degree of spatial interaction resulting into the breaking up of rural isolation.

On the other hand, the lowest level of literacy has been observed in the tehsil of Punhana (37.41 per cent) and is followed by Ferozepur Jhirka (40.00 per cent), Nuh (44.92 per cent), and Hathin (45.60 per cent) tehsils. These areas have experienced very low literacy rate because these are industrially undeveloped and economically backward and are characterized with meagre urbanization. Apart from this, the lowest literacy is also the outcome of social conservation of the people as in Meo-Muslim society who dominate in Punahana (85.23 per cent), Ferozepur Jhirka (82.54 per cent), Nuh (71.14 per cent), and Taoru (49.11 per cent), tehsils of Gurgaon district and Hathin (54.34 per cent) and tehsil of Faridabad district.

In Meo-Muslim society, equal status is not given to males and females and that is why suffers from low female literacy rates which affect adversely the total literacy rate. Not only this, but even the restrictions are imposed on the females' mobility and education resulting into the low female literacy and hence, low general literacy.

There is a wide disparity between the literacy rates of rural (63.19 per cent) and urban (79.16 per cent) areas. This disparity in literacy by residence is the product of five basic factors: (i) need to get education is more in urban areas than in agricultural countryside, (ii) educational facilities are concentrated more in urban areas while these may be completely absent in certain rural areas, (iii) urban population is socially more awakened and economically more capable of imparting education to their children in comparison to the rural counterpart, (iv) urban females enjoy relatively high status in comparison to their rural compatriots and are not denied the opportunities of educations as is the case in many rural areas, (v) many educated ruralites migrate to urban places in search of jobs outside the agricultural sector particularly when there are no avenues in the countryside as a result of which the number of literates in urban areas increase at the cost of rural areas.

The spatial patterns of both urban as well as rural literacy show marked variation. Highest urban literacy is found in Thanesar tehsil (89.11 per cent) and is followed by the tehsils of Gurgaon (86.09 per cent), Ambala (85.68 per cent), Kalka (84.32 per cent), and

Rewari (82.78 per cent). Reasons for high level of literacy are the availability of more educational facilities, high degree of urbanization and good economic condition.

At the other end of the scale, the very low level of urban literacy is found in Ferozepur Jhirka tehsil (62.98 per cent) followed by Rania (63.68 per cent), Narnaund (66.06 per cent), Punahana (66.16 per cent), and Loharu (66.56 per cent) tehsils. The reasons may be lack of educational facilities and low level of urbanization alongwith the dominance of Muslim population.

By comparison, highest rates of rural literacy are found in Gurgaon tehsil (77.28 per cent) and is followed by Hodal (75.34 per cent), Rewari (74.68 per cent), Pataudi (74.45 per cent), and Kosli (74.26 per cent) tehsils. Very high rural literacy in Gurgaon may be due to its peripheral location to union territory of Delhi and tradition in army service is strong in Rewari and Kosli tehsils alongwith the availability of sufficient educational facilities.

At the other end of the scale, the tehsil of Punahana (35.33 per cent) is characterized by lowest level of rural literacy, followed by Ferozepur Jhirka (38.05 per cent), Nuh (43.62 per cent), Hathin (44.05 per cent), Ratia (49.77 per cent), and Narwana (52.86 per cent) tehsils. One of the most important causes of low rural literacy rate is the dominance of Meo-Muslim population in the tehsils of Punahana, Ferozepur Jhirka, Nuh, and Hathin.

Thus, urban literacy rates are high in big administrative, commercial and industrial towns with more educational institutions and good economic condition. By comparison, rural literacy rates are high where (i) degree of urban influence is great, (ii) proportion of non-agricultural workers is comparatively large, and (iii) tradition in army service is strong such as in Rewari and Kosli tehsils.

The analysis about literacy rates of Haryana in terms of males and females reveals the picture which is generally true for the whole India, i.e., the male literacy is higher than female literacy and the difference between two is 22.76 per cent. It means, there exists a great disparity between male (78.49 per cent) and female (55.73 per cent) literacy rates in Haryana. This wide disparity in the male-female literacy rates is the product of a variety of social and economic factors.

Socially, the prejudices against the females' mobility and education, the low status granted to the females, lack of educational institutions for females, lack of female teachers, prevalence of early marriage and movement of girls from their parents' place of residence to the residence of their spouses at the time of marriage are the factors responsible for low female literacy. In addition to, poor people instead of educating their daughters prefer to educate their sons, because earning by sons will become helpful for parents adding to their income. Whereas about daughters a feeling is there that they will have to go to others' houses ultimately. It means daughters are always considered as *Praya Dhan*. Economically, the appalling poverty and low degree of occupational participation among females are the factors responsible for wide disparity in the literacy rates of both the sexes.

Not only this, but the levels of literacy for both males and females vary widely within Haryana. Highest male literacy has been recorded in Rewari tehsil (89.13 per cent) followed by Gurgaon (89.12 per cent) and Kosli (88.60 per cent) tehsils. In nut shell, we can say that highest male literacy rates have been recorded in southern and northern parts of the State because of their bordering location with union territories of Delhi and Chandigarh respectively.

At the other extreme, the lowest literacy rate for males is found in the tehsils of Punahana (55.43 per cent) followed by Ferozepur Jhirka (58.20 per cent) in the southern part and Ratia (61.31 per cent) in the western part. These tehsils are not economically sound. Hence, it is considered as the main reason for low literacy. Moreover, dominance of Muslim population in the aforesaid southern tehsils of Haryana and the highest concentration of scheduled castes population (36.69 per cent) in Ratia tehsil are also considered as the main causes of low literacy among males.

On the other hand, highest female literacy rates are found in the tehsil of Ambala (71.30 per cent) and is followed by Gurgaon (70.97 per cent), Faridabad (68.26 per cent), Panchkula (66.29 per cent) and Jagadhary (65.65 per cent) tehsils. Here, factor of prejudice against females' education is less powerful. People are broad minded and are aware about the utility of education in society, so female literacy rate is high in these tehsils.

At the other end of the scale, the lowest female literacy is the characteristic of Punahana (17.67 per cent) tehsil followed by Ferozepur Jhirka (19.95 per cent), Nuh (24.98 per cent), Hathin (25.64 per cent), and Taoru (39.56 per cent) tehsils. These tehsils have experienced very low female literacy, because these are industrially undeveloped and economically backward. Apart from this, very low female literacy is also the outcome of social conservation of Muslim people who dominate the scene in these tehsils.

In every tehsil, male literacy is higher than female literacy in both rural and urban populations and urban male and female populations always have a higher level of literacy than their respective rural counterpart in the same tehsil. It means the disparity in literacy by sex is larger in rural areas than in urban areas.

To sum up, the northern and eastern parts have recorded high female literacy rates than the western and the southern parts.

4 Male-Female Disparity in Literacy

In the preceding chapter, spatial variations in literacy were analysed. The present chapter attempts to analyse the spatial pattern of male-female disparity in literacy.

4.1 Male-Female Disparity in Literacy

The male-female disparity in literacy was very high in the beginning of present century due to very low female literacy. The colonial period in Indian literacy transition represented the black period in which literacy was primarily meant for male population. The British administration of pre-Independence days spent very little amount (1.70 per cent) of the total budget on education that was accessible only to a limited number of wealthy persons of the country (Petrov, 1985). Before Independence, the educational institutions were few and far between and the socio-economic conditions were not too conducive to the growth of education, particularly for females. Undoubtedly, after Independence, the female literacy improved a lot, yet it was far behind the male literacy. The low level of female literacy in the country was the product of prevalence of prejudices against the females' education, mobility and employment, inadequate schools for females, dearth of female teachers particularly in rural areas; early engagement/marriage of the females and household responsibilities of the females. Besides, the appalling general poverty and the low degree of participation of females in work were the other factors responsible for wide male-female disparity in literacy (Chandna, 1986).

The disparities in male and female literacy occur both in rural and urban areas. However such disparities are sharper in rural areas in comparison to urban areas. In urban areas, the female literacy does not lag far behind male literacy. The relatively low differential in urban male-female literacy may be attributed to the relatively better status of the women; availability of educational institutions equally for males and females, relatively better standard of living; increasing value of female education for matrimonial and employment purposes and increasing degree of socio-economic awakening among urbanites (Sagar, 1984).

The male-female disparity index had been declining gradually due to the increase in female literacy in the country. The relatively high rate of increase in female literacy was related to the increasing educational facilities, increase in the standard of living, increasing participation of females in economically gainful activities, increasing value of female education for matrimony (Chandna, 1986), increasing female mobility as a result of waning prejudices against their mobility, increasing availability of female teachers in rural areas and increasing degree of socio-economic awareness.

Similar to India, Haryana is marked not only by a low level of literacy rates but also by wide disparity in literacy by sex, residence and area. The disparity which has been narrowing down since independence, reflect the necessity, propensity and opportunity of various degrees for getting literate among different population groups.

4.2 Spatial Patterns of Male-Female Disparity in Literacy

Haryana experiences a great disparity between male and female literacy rates ranging between 0.5972 in Punahana tehsil and 0.1203 in Ambala tehsil as disparity index values (Table 4.1). This wide disparity in the male-female literacy rates is the product of a variety of social and economic factors (Chandna,2008), such as prejudices against the female mobility and education, low status granted to the females, prevalence of early marriage, appalling poverty and low degree of occupational participation among females. The male-female disparity in literacy was inversely associated with per capita income, male literacy, general literacy, female literacy, percentage of non-agricultural workers or urban population, and it was positively correlated with the percentage of scheduled caste population. These apart, a strong negative association between the disparity index and the level of socio-economic development could also be observed. In other words, as the general literacy decreases, the disparity index increases. But since the general literacy usually gets depressed in areas of low female literacy, the disparity index in such areas becomes high. Both the general literacy and female literacy are normally low in less developed areas where the disparity index becomes high. Thus, the male-female disparity index in literacy is low in relatively prosperous areas and high in socially and economically backward areas. After taking into account these above mentioned factors responsible for wide disparity in the literacy rates of both the sexes, the patterns of regional variation among male-female disparity in the levels of literacy will be discussed for the following segments of population :

1. Male-Female (Total)
2. Male-Female (Rural)
3. Male-Female (Urban)

On the basis of disparity indices for various segments of population as shown in Table 4.1, the tehsils of Haryana can be classified into five categories (Map 4.1) as:

1. Areas of Very High Disparity
2. Areas of High Disparity
3. Areas of Moderate Disparity
4. Areas of Low Disparity
5. Areas of Very Low Disparity

1. Areas of Very High Disparity

In all, there are 6 tehsils where the male-female literacy disparity index was more than 0.3401. Very high disparity index is the rule of those tehsils which are either least urbanized or dominated by Muslim population. The tehsil of Punahana has the highest disparity (0.5972) between male-female literacy which is followed by the tehsils of Ferozepur Jhirka (0.5687), Nuh (0.5052), Hathin (0.4945), Hodal (0.3831), and Taoru (0.3681) (Table 4.1 and Map 4.1).

Table 4.1: Haryana: Male-Female Disparity Indices of Literacy by Tehsils, 2001

Sr. No.	State/Tehsil	Disparity index	Sr. No.	Tehsil	Disparity Index
	Haryana	**0.2233**	34.	Kaithal	0.2408
1.	Punahana	0.5972	35.	Safidon	0.2404
2.	Ferozepur Jhirka	0.5687	36.	Pataudi	0.2345
3.	Nuh	0.5052	37.	Ellenabad	0.2327
4.	Hathin	0.4945	38.	Gohana	0.2326
5.	Hodal	0.3831	39.	Gharaunda	0.2325
6.	Taoru	0.3681	40.	Rania	0.2252
7.	Loharu	0.3321	41.	Kharkhoda	0.2241
8.	Palwal	0.3265	42.	Bhiwani	0.2225
9.	Ballabgarh	0.3211	43.	Tohana	0.2105
10.	Adampur	0.3180	44.	Sirsa	0.2054
11.	Siwani	0.3126	45.	Dabwali	0.2006
12.	Tosham	0.3112	46.	Chhachhrauli	0.2005
13.	Bawal	0.3105	47.	Assandh	0.1990
14.	Narnaul	0.3093	48.	Ratia	0.1944
15.	Narnaund	0.3057	49.	Guhla	0.1941
16.	Narwana	0.2897	50.	Bahadurgarh	0.1938
17.	Mahendragarh	0.2821	51.	Indri	0.1935
18.	Bawani Khera	0.2813	52.	Sonipat	0.1896
19.	Dadri	0.2778	53.	Rohtak	0.1828
20.	Kosli	0.2742	54.	Nilokheri	0.1812
21.	Israna	0.2689	55.	Pehowa	0.1802
22.	Julana	0.2685	56.	Naraingarh	0.1791
23.	Sohna	0.2650	57.	Thanesar	0.1675
24.	Hansi	0.2606	58.	Barara	0.1672
25.	Fatehabad	0.2572	59.	Panipat	0.1671
26.	Beri	0.2530	60.	Gurgaon	0.1648
27.	Maham	0.2489	61.	Faridabad	0.1625
28.	Samalkha	0.2480	62.	Shahbad	0.1561
29.	Jind	0.2467	63.	Karnal	0.1547
30.	Rewari	0.2458	64.	Kalka	0.1542
31.	Ganaur	0.2446	65.	Jagadhari	0.1391
32.	Jhajjar	0.2442	66.	Panchkula	0.1379
33.	Hisar	0.2416	67.	Ambala	0.1203

Source: Computed from Census of India (2001), *Primary Census Abstract*, Haryana, Series 7, Tables A5-A8, Directorate of Census Operations, Haryana.

Note: Tehsils are arranged in descending order of disparity index, 2001.

These tehsils are least urbanized, whereas Meo-Muslim population dominates in all the tehsils, except Hodal. Highest sex disparity in Meo-Muslims society is mainly due to lowest female

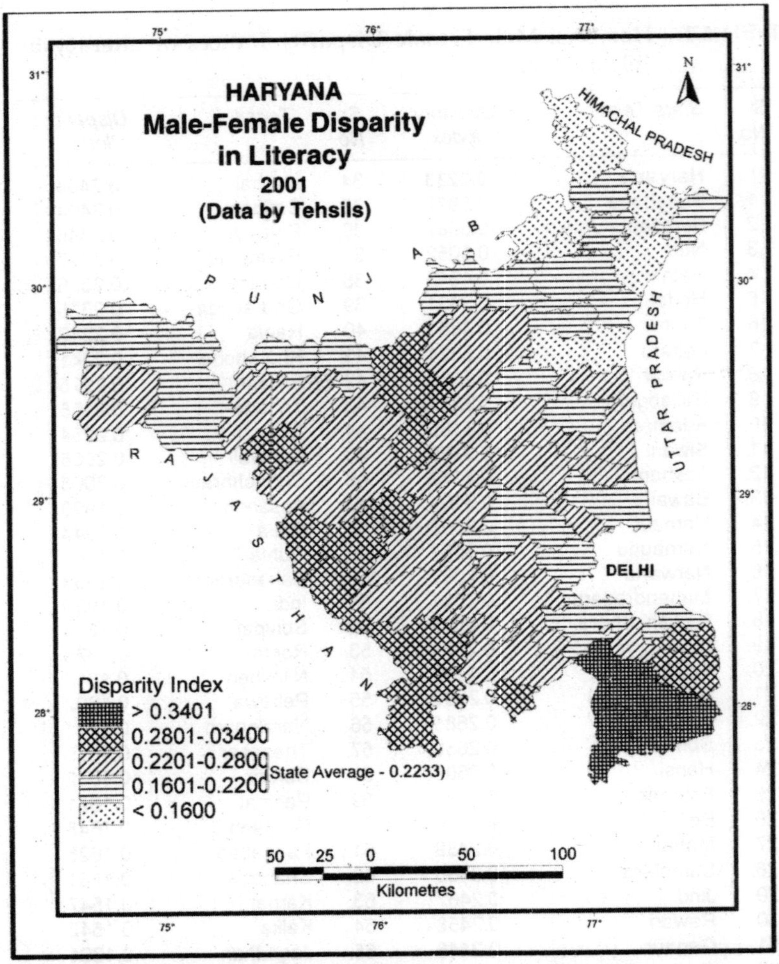

Map 4.1: Haryana: Male-Female Disparity in Literacy, 2001

literacy which is the outcome of social conservation of these people, unequal status given to males and females and even the restriction imposed on females' mobility and education.

Male-female disparity in rural areas is also highest in the tehsils of Punhana (0.6473), Ferozepur Jhirka (0.6174), Nuh (0.5318), Hathin (0.5199), Hodal (0.4279), Taoru (0.4172) and Palwal (0.3938), all in southern Haryana (Table 4.2 and Map 4.2). This is mainly because of the reasons mentioned above in case of total male-female disparity in literacy.

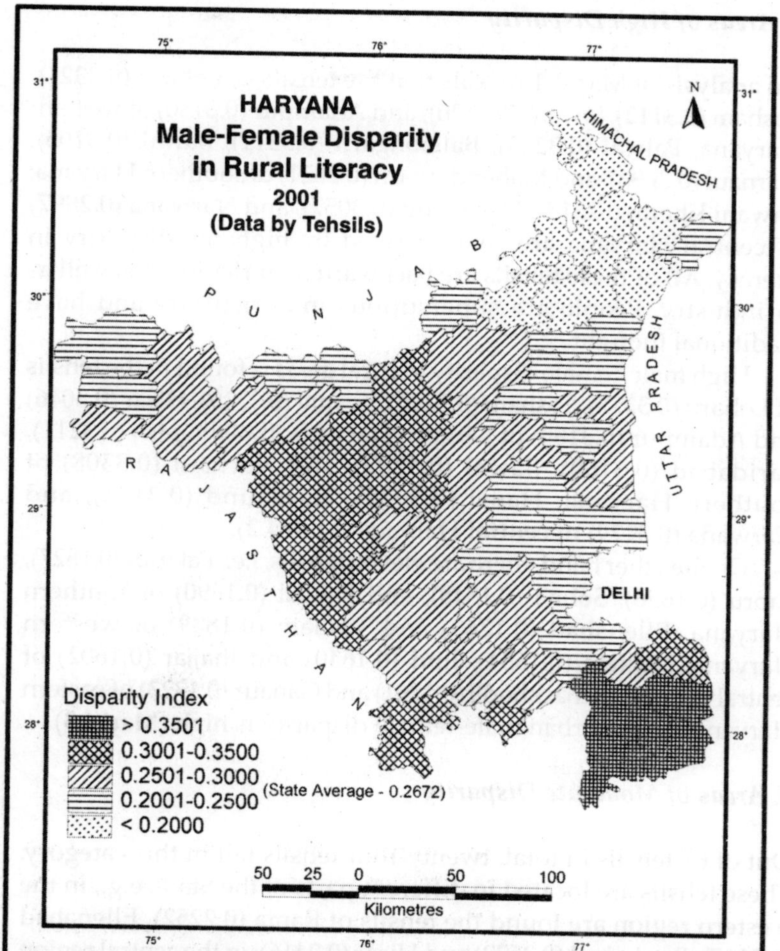

Map 4.2: Haryana: Male-Female Disparity in Rural Literacy, 2001

Whereas in urban areas, sex disparity is very high in Punahana (0.2909), Loharu (0.2710), Ferozepur Jhirka (0.2667) and is followed by Narnaund (0.2639), Bawani Khera (0.2550), Hodal (0.2498), Hathin (0.2461), Siwani (0.2348), Bawal (0.2319), Nuh (0.2294), Beri (0.2189), Narnaul (0.2073), Mahendragarh (0.2049), Julana (0.1998) and Narwana (0.1952) tehsils (Table 4.3 and Map 4.3). All these tehsils are least unbanished and the people are very prejudiced against the females' education.

2. *Areas of High Disparity*

An analysis of Map 4.1 reveals that the tehsils of Loharu (0.3321), Tosham (0.3112), Siwani (0.3126), and Adampur (0.3180) of western Haryana; Palwal (0.3265), Ballabhgarh (0.3211), Bawal (0.3105), Narnaul (0.3093), and Mahendragarh (0.2821) of southern Haryana; Bawani Khera (0.2813). Narnaund (0.3057), and Narwana (0.2897) of central Haryana are characterized by high sex disparity in literacy. All of these tehsils are backward in agriculture as well as in industry. People are superstitious in agriculture and have traditional thought.

High male-female disparity in rural areas is found in the tehsils of Loharu (0.3377), Tosham (0.3225), Siwani (0.3319), Hisar (0.3046) and Adampur (0.3180) of western Haryana; Ballabhgarh (0.3211), Faridabad (0.3160), Bawal (0.3207), and Narnaul (0.3308) of southern Haryana; Hansi (0.3070), Narnaund (0.3121), and Narwana (0.3129) of central Haryana (Map 4.2).

On the other hand, there are eleven tehsils, i.e., Pataudi (0.1827), Taoru (0.1696), Sohna (0.1848), and Palwal (0.1690) of southern Haryana; Ellenabad (0.1763) and Tosham (0.1839) of western Haryana; Maham (0.1654), Jind (0.1640) and Jhajjar (0.1602) of central Haryana; Kharkhoda (0.1761) and Ganaur (0.1723) of eastern Haryana, where urban male-female disparity is high (Map 4.3).

3. *Areas of Moderate Disparity*

Out of 67 tehsils in total, twenty-four tehsils fall in this category. These tehsils are located in different parts of the State, e.g., in the western region are found the tehsils of Rania (0.2252), Ellenabad (0.2327), Fatehabad (0.2572) and Hisar (0.2416); in the central region are the tehsils of Dadri (0.2778), Bhiwani (0.2225), Julana (0.2685), Jind (0.2467), Safidon (0.2404), Hansi (0.2606), Kaithal (0.2408), Israna (0.2689), Beri (0.2530), Jhajjar (0.2442), Maham (0.2489) and Gohana (0.2326); in the southern region are Kosli (0.2742), Rewari (0.2458), Pataudi (0.2345), and Sohna (0.2650); and in eastern region are Kharkhoda (0.2241)), Ganaur (0.2446), Samalkha (0.2480) and Gharaunda (0.2325) tehsils (Map 4.1). These regions have primarily agrarian economy and moderate sex differential can be ascribed to lack of industrial development, less educational facilities and socio-economic backwardness of the people.

Table 4.2: Haryana: Male-Female Disparity Indices of Rural Literacy by Tehsils, 2001

Sr. No.	*State/Tahsil*	*Disparity Index*	*Sr. No.*	*Tehsil*	*Disparity Index*
	Haryana	**0.2672**	34.	Maham	0.2408
1.	Punahana	0.6473	35.	Pataudi	0.2404
2.	Ferozepur Jhirka	0.6174	36.	Ellenabad	0.2345
3.	Nuh	0.5318	37.	Beri	0.2327
4.	Hathin	0.5199	38.	Safidon	0.2326
5.	Hodal	0.4279	39.	Jhajjar	0.2325
6.	Taoru	0.4172	40.	Gharaunda	0.2252
7.	Palwal	0.3938	41.	Sirsa	0.2241
8.	Loharu	0.3377	42.	Gohana	0.2225
9.	Siwani	0.3319	43.	Tohana	0.2105
10.	Narnaul	0.3308	44.	Panipat	0.2054
11.	Tosham	0.3225	45.	Rohtak	0.2006
12.	Ballabgarh	0.3211	46.	Rania	0.2005
13.	Bawal	0.3207	47.	Sonipat	0.1990
14.	Adampur	0.3180	48.	Kharkhoda	0.1944
15.	Faridabad	0.3160	49.	Dabwali	0.1941
16.	Narwana	0.3129	50.	Bahadurgarh	0.1938
17.	Narnaund	0.3121	51.	Ratia	0.1935
18.	Hansi	0.3070	52.	Chhachhrauli	0.1896
19.	Hisar	0.3046	53.	Gurgaon	0.1828
20.	Jind	0.2981	54.	Assandh	0.1812
21.	Dadri	0.2933	55.	Karnal	0.1802
22.	Mahendragarh	0.2910	56.	Nilokheri	0.1791
23.	Bawani Khera	0.2863	57.	Guhla	0.1675
24.	Sohna	0.2862	58.	Indri	0.1672
25.	Fatehabad	0.2853	59.	Kalka	0.1671
26.	Julana	0.2799	60.	Pehowa	0.1648
27.	Rewari	0.2761	61.	Panchkula	0.1625
28.	Kosli	0.2742	62.	Thanesar	0.1561
29.	Kaithal	0.2709	63.	Naraingarh	0.1547
30.	Israna	0.2689	64.	Jagadhari	0.1542
31.	Bhiwani	0.2679	65.	Shahbad	0.1391
32.	Samalkha	0.2656	66.	Barara	0.1379
33.	Ganaur	0.2615	67.	Ambala	0.1203

Source: Computed from Census of India (2001), *Primary Census Abstract*, Haryana, Series 7, Tables A5-A8, Directorate of Census Operations, Haryana.

Note: Tehsils are arranged in descending order of disparity index, 2001.

Twenty-one tehsils are characterized by moderate sex disparity in literacy rates among the rural population. The tehsils which fall under this category are Mahendragarh (0.2910), Kosli (0.2742),

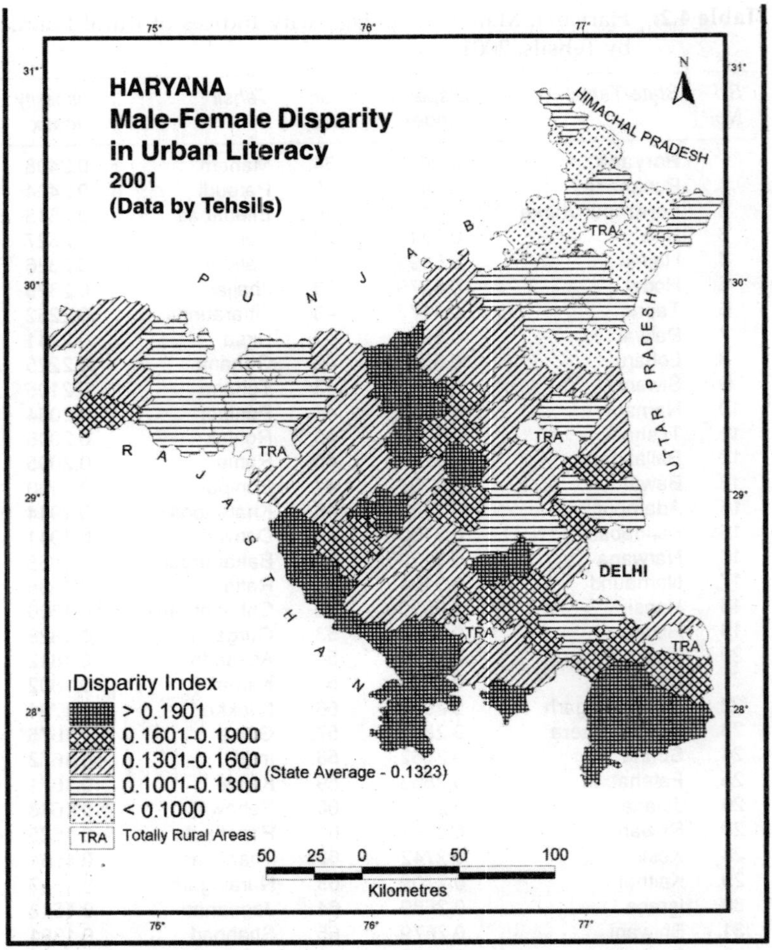

Map 4.3: Haryana: Male-Female Disparity in Urban Literacy, 2001

Rewari (0.2761), Pataudi (0.2404), and Sohna (0.2862) in southern Haryana; Fatehabad (0.2853), and Ellenabad (0.2345) in western Haryana; Jhajjar (0.2325), Beri (0.2327), Dadri (0.2933), Bhiwani (0.2679), Bawani Khera (0.2863), Maham (0.2408), Julana (0.2799), Jind (0.2981), Kaithal (0.2709), Safidon (0.2326), and Israna (0.2689) in central Haryana; Samalkha (0.2656), and Ganaur (0.2615) of eastern Haryana (Table 4.2 and Map 4.2). People of these tehsils are mainly engaged in the primary activities.

A total of 17 tehsils have moderate sex disparity in literacy rates among the urban population. These are Gharaunda (0.1560), Samalkha (0.1449), and Bahadurgarh (0.1467) of eastern Haryana; Faridabad (0.1479), and Rewari (0.1470) of southern Haryana; Dadri (0.1521), Bhiwani (0.1511), Hansi (0.1326), Guhla (0.1499), Kaithal (0.1496), Asandh (0.1359), Safidon (0.1483), and Gohana (0.1559) of central Haryana; Dabwali (0.1318), Rania (0.1519), Hisar (0.1412), and Tohana (0.1372) tehsils of western Haryana (Table 4.3 and Map 4.3). These tehsils are less urbanized as compared to the other tehsils of Haryana.

4. *Areas of Low Disparity*

This category comprises nineteen tehsils in all. The tehsils of Dabwali (0.2006), Sirsa (0.2054), Ratia (0.1944), and Tohana (0.2105) are in the western part; Guhla (0.1941), Naraingarh (0.1791), Barara (0.1672), Chhachhrauli (0.2005), Thanesar (0.1675), and Pehowa (0.1802) in the northern part; Indri (0.1935), Nilokheri (0.1812), Panipat (0.1671), Sonipat (0.1896), and Bahadurgarh (0.1938) in the eastern part; Assandh (0.1990), and Rohtak (0.1828) in the central part; Gurgaon (0.1648) and Faridabad (0.1625) in the southern part of the State (Map 4.1).

These are the areas which are either industrially and educationally developed or have the impact of proximity to big cities like Chandigarh and Delhi. However, in the western part of the State, the literacy rate for both males and females is low resulting into low male-female disparity in literacy.

Rural male-female disparity is low in eighteen tehsils of the State. These tehsils are located in different parts of the State, e.g., the tehsils of Indri (0.1672), Nilokheri (0.1791), Karnal (0.1802), Panipat (0.2054), Sonipat (0.1990), Kharkhoda (0.1944), and Bahadurgarh (0.1938) in the eastern part; Guhla (0.1675), and Chhachhrauli (0.1896), in the northern part; Gurgaon (0.1828) in the southern part; Dabwali (0.1941), Rania (0.2005), Sirsa (0.2498), Ratia (0.1935), and Tohana (0.2105) in the western part; Assandh (0.1812), Gohana (0.2476), and Rohtak (0.2006) in the central part of the State (Map 4.2).

On the other hand, urban male-female disparity is low among fourteen tehsils of the State. These are Kalka (0.1112), Naraingarh (0.1249), Chhchhrauli (0.1113), Thanesar (0.1083), and Pehowa

(0.1124) in northern Haryana; Indri (0.1295), Nilokheri (0.1039), Panipat (0.1230), and Sonipat (0.1256) in eastern Haryana; Rohtak (0.1119) in central Haryana; Gurgaon (0.1018) in southern Haryana; Fatehabad (0.1278), Ratia (0.1209), and Sirsa (0.1248) in western Haryana (Table 4.3 and Map 4.3). Except the tehsils located in western Haryana, these tehsils have better educational facilities, more general awareness to be educated among both the segments of population resulting into low male-female disparity in literacy.

5. *Areas of Very Low Disparity*

There are only six tehsils which come under this category. Ambala tehsil has the lowest male-female disparity (0.1203) followed by Panchkula (0.1379), Jagadhri (0.1391), Kalka (0.1542), Karnal (0.1547) and Shahbad (0.1561) (Table 4.1 and Map 4.1). All these tehsils are located in northern and north-eastern region of the State. Kalka, Panchkula, Ambala, Jagadhri, and Shahbad are in northern part; whereas Karnal comes in north-eastern part of the State. These are the areas which are industrially and educationally well-developed and have proximity to the capital city of Chandigarh. Their proximity to Chandigarh has added a new dimension to the process of propagation of literacy and education in these areas, hence characterized by very low literacy disparity among males and females.

There are nine tehsils which have very low literacy disparity by sex in rural areas. Ambala tehsil has the lowest male-female disparity in literacy (0.1663) and is followed by Barara (0.1672), Shahbad (0.1788), Jagadhri (0.1823), Naraingarh (0.1857), Thanesar (0.1945), Panchkula (0.1982), Pehwoa (0.1987) and Kalka (0.1999) (Table 4.2 and Map 4.2). All these tehsils are located in northern part of the State.

But as far as urban male-female disparity in literacy is concerned, it is also the lowest in Ambala tehsil (0.0799), followed by Panchkula (0.0825), Jagadhri (0.0885), Karnal (0.0919) and Shahbad (0.0958) tehsils (Table 4.3 and Map 4.3). Again, all these tehsils, except Karnal which is part of north-eastern Haryana, are located in northern part of the State and have the impact of the development of industrial and educational facilities as well as the proximity of Chandigarh.

Table 4.3: Haryana: Male-Female Disparity Indices of Urban Literacy by Tehsils, 2001

Sr. No.	*State/Tehsil*	*Disparity index*	*Sr. No.*	*Tehsil*	*Disparity Index*
	Haryana	**0.1323**	34.	Safidon	0.1483
1.	Punahana	0.2909	35.	Faridabad	0.1479
2.	Loharu	0.2710	36.	Rewari	0.1470
3.	Ferozepur Jhirka	0.2667	37.	Bahadurgarh	0.1467
4.	Narnaund	0.2639	38.	Samalkha	0.1449
5.	Bawani Khera	0.2550	39.	Hisar	0.1412
6.	Hodal	0.2498	40.	Tohana	0.1372
7.	Hathin	0.2461	41.	Assandh	0.1359
8.	Siwani	0.2348	42.	Hansi	0.1326
9.	Bawal	0.2319	43.	Dabwali	0.1318
10.	Nuh	0.2294	44.	Indri	0.1295
11.	Beri	0.2189	45.	Fatehabad	0.1278
12.	Narnaul	0.2073	46.	Sonipat	0.1256
13.	Mahendragarh	0.2049	47.	Naraingarh	0.1249
14.	Julana	0.1998	48.	Sirsa	0.1248
15.	Narwana	0.1952	49.	Panipat	0.1230
16.	Sohna	0.1848	50.	Ratia	0.1209
17.	Tosham	0.1839	51.	Pehowa	0.1124
18.	Pataudi	0.1827	52.	Rohtak	0.1119
19.	Ellenabad	0.1763	53.	Chhachhrauli	0.1113
20.	Kharkhoda	0.1761	54.	Kalka	0.1112
21.	Ganaur	0.1723	55.	Thanesar	0.1083
22.	Taoru	0.1696	56.	Nilokheri	0.1039
23.	Palwal	0.1690	57.	Gurgaon	0.1018
24.	Maham	0.1654	58.	Shahbad	0.0958
25.	Jind	0.1640	59.	Karnal	0.0919
26.	Jhajjar	0.1602	60.	Jagadhari	0.0885
27.	Gharaunda	0.1560	61.	Panchkula	0.0825
28.	Gohana	0.1559	62.	Ambala	0.0799
29.	Dadri	0.1521	63.	Barara	Totally Rural
30.	Rania	0.1519	64.	Israna	Totally Rural
31.	Bhiwani	0.1511	65.	Adampur	Totally Rural
32.	Guhla	0.1499	66.	Kosli	Totally Rural
33.	Kaithal	0.1496	67.	Ballabgarh	Totally Rural

Source: Computed from Census of India (2001), *Primary Census Abstract*, Haryana, Series 7, Tables A5-A8, Directorate of Census Operations, Haryana.

Note: Tehsils are arranged in descending order of disparity index, 2001.

It is apparent from the above discussion that the lowest male-female disparity in literacy rates for both rural and urban areas is the characteristic of those regions surrounding the industrial centres of Ambala and Jagadhri and also have proximity to Chandigarh. So, the least disparity in literacy rates is due to high degree of industrialization and urbanization of this part of the State and also due to the influence of capital city of Chandigarh. Apart from this, the existing disparity between male and female literacy rates in urban areas is because of better educational facilities and general awareness towards education among both the sexes.

Thus, the disparity index was low in the tehsils with high general and female literacy, good infrastructure of educational facilities, high proportion of urban population and of non-agricultural workers.

Conclusions

The sex disparity in Indian education was not of recent origin but was more marked in the medieval period. Till Independence, the country had to pass through different phases of colonial rule in which little attention was paid to the propagation of females' education and the literacy was mainly male literacy. Female literacy was practically non-existent during this period. The male-female disparity in literacy was very high in the beginning of present century due to very low female literacy. Before Independence, the educational institutions were few and far between and the socio-economic conditions were not too conducive to the growth of education, particularly for females. Undoubtedly, after Independence, the female literacy improved a lot, yet it was far behind the male literacy.

The low level of female literacy in the country was the product of prevalence of prejudices against the females' education, mobility and employment, inadequate schools for females, dearth of female teachers particularly in rural areas; early engagement/marriage of the females and household responsibilities of the females. Besides, the appalling general poverty and the low degree of participation of females in work were the other factors responsible for wide male-female disparity in literacy.

Like India, Haryana also has high sex disparity in literacy rate. This large disparity between the male and female literacy was the product of heavy backlog of illiterate females population; slow and haphazard growth of educational institutions especially for females, non-availability of female teachers particularly in the countryside, prevalence of traditional prejudices against females' education and their mobility; strong adherence to the tradition of early marriage; low level of urbanization and general poverty.

The male-female disparity index has been declining gradually due to the increase in female literacy in the State The disparity which has been narrowing down since independence, reflect the necessity, propensity and opportunity of various degrees for getting literate among different population groups.

The male-female disparity in literacy was inversely associated with per capita income, male literacy, general literacy, female literacy, percentage of non-agricultural workers or urban population, and it was positively correlated with the percentage of scheduled caste population.

These apart, a strong negative association between the disparity index and the level of socio-economic development could also be observed. In other words, as the general literacy decreases, the disparity index increases. But since the general literacy usually gets depressed in areas of low female literacy, the disparity index in such areas becomes high. Both the general literacy and female literacy are normally low in less developed areas, where the disparity index becomes high. Thus, the male-female disparity index in literacy is low in relatively prosperous areas and high in socially and economically backward areas.

Spatially, there were wide regional variations in the male-female disparity index. Broadly speaking, the northern and eastern Haryana recorded low literacy disparity in comparison to the southern and central parts of the State. Haryana experiences a wide disparity between male and female literacy rates which was 0.2233 as per 2001 census This wide disparity in the male-female literacy rates is the product of a variety of social and economic factors, such as prejudices against the female's mobility and education, low status granted to the females, prevalence of early marriage, appalling poverty and low degree of occupational participation among females.

In all, there are 6 tehsils where the male-female disparity in literacy is very high and the disparity index value was more than 0.3401. Very high differential index is the rule of those tehsils which are either least urbanized or dominated by Muslim population. The tehsil of Punahana has the highest disparity (0.5972) between male-female literacy which is followed by the tehsils of Ferozepur Jhirka (0.5687), Nuh (0.5052), Hathin (0.4945), Hodal (0.3831), and Taoru (0.3681). These tehsils are least urbanized, whereas Meo-Muslim population dominates in Ferozepur Jhirka and Nuh tehsils. Highest sex disparity in Meo-Muslims society is mainly due to lowest female literacy which is the outcome of social conservation of these people, unequal status given to males and females and even the restriction imposed on females' mobility and education.

The male-female disparity index in literacy contrasted sharply in both urban and rural areas. The index in urban areas (0.1323) was almost half of that in rural areas (0.2672). The relatively low literacy disparity in urban areas was associated with availability of educational facilities for both males and females, relatively high social status of women, and education being considered matrimonial necessity in case of females. These apart, better standard of living and high degree of socio-economic awakening among urban dwellers were the other factors responsible for low male-female disparity.

Male-female disparity in rural areas is also the highest in the tehsils of Punhana (0.6473), Ferozepur Jhirka (0.6174), Nuh (0.5318), Hathin (0.5199), Hodal (0.4279), Taoru (0.4172) and Palwal (0.3938). This is mainly because of the reasons mentioned above in case of total male-female disparity in literacy.

Whereas in urban areas, sex disparity is very high in Punahana (0.2909), Loharu (0.2710), Ferozepur Jhirka (0.2667) and is followed by Narnaund (0.2639), Bawani Khera (0.2550), Hodal (0.2498), Hathin (0.2461), Siwani (0.2348), Bawal (0.2319), Nuh (0.2294), Beri (0.2189), Narnaul (0.2073), Mahendragarh (0.2049), Julana (0.1998) and Narwana (0.1952) tehsils (Table 4.3). All these tehsils are least unbanished and the people are very prejudiced against the females' mobility and education.

On the other hand, very low male-female disparity is also experienced in six tehsils of the State. Ambala has the lowest sex disparity (0.1203) followed by Panchkula (0.1379), Jagadhri (0.1391), Kalka (0.1542), Karnal (0.1547) and Shahbad (0.1561). These are the areas which are industrially and educationally developed and have proximity to the capital city of Chandigarh. Their proximity to Chandigarh has added a new dimension to the process of propagation of literacy and education in these areas, hence characterized by very low disparity among males and females.

There are nine tehsils which have very low literacy disparity by sex in rural areas. Ambala tehsil has the lowest male-female disparity in literacy (0.1663) and is followed by Barara (0.1672), Shahbad (0.1788), Jagadhri (0.1823), Naraingarh (0.1857), Thanesar (0.1945), Panchkula (0.1982), Pehwoa (0.1987) and Kalka (0.1999) tehsils.

But as far as urban male-female disparity in literacy is concerned, it is also the lowest in Ambala tehsil (0.0799), followed by Panchkula (0.0825), Jagadhri (0.0885), Karnal (0.0919) and Shahbad (0.0958) tehsils. Again, all these tehsils, except Karnal which is part of north-eastern Haryana, are located in northern part of the State and have the impact of the development of industrial and educational facilities as well as the proximity of Chandigarh.

In nutshell, the lowest male-female disparity in literacy rates for both rural and urban areas is the characteristic of those regions surrounding the industrial centres of Ambala and Jagadhri and also have proximity to Chandigarh. So, the least disparity in literacy rates is due to high degree of industrialization and urbanization of this part of the State and also due to the influence of capital city of Chandigarh. Apart from this, the existing disparity between male and female literacy rates in urban areas is because of better educational facilities and general awareness towards education among both the sexes.

Thus, the disparity index was low in the tehsils with high general and female literacy, good infrastructure of educational facilities, high proportion of urban population and of non-agricultural workers.

5 Urban-Rural Disparity in Literacy

Apart from wide disparities in male and female literacy, there is notable disparity in the literacy rates of the urban and rural areas. These disparities are essentially a function of socio-cultural and economic diversity between the two areas. Hoselitz (1960) rightly observes that the cultural difference between the city and the countryside is the product of sharp resistance from the native culture of rural areas to the alien culture of urban areas and the social change can take place only by enhancing the interaction between them. The urban society that is comparatively more heterogeneous and more hierarchically structured is also enriched more with a number of modern traits of life. Among these traits, literacy being a qualitative attribute of modernization diffuses subsequently into the countryside (Krishan and Shyam, 1978). The diffusion of literacy from urban areas depends upon the degree of interaction, the adoptive behaviour, the favourable outlook and the progressive attitude of rural population towards education. Generally, the lack of educational facilities in the countryside in the Third World countries, like India, has been responsible for the large differences in the literacy rate of urban and rural population. The present chapter examines these urban-rural disparity in literacy in detail.

5.1 Urban-Rural Disparity in Literacy

In 2001, while 79.16 per cent of urban population in Haryana was literate, the corresponding figure for rural population was only

63.19 per cent, implying wide disparity in urban and rural literacy rates (Table 5.1).

Table 5.1: Haryana: Literacy Rates by Urban-Rural Residence, 2001

Person/Male/Female	*Literacy Rate (%)*			*Urban-Rural Disparity*
	Total	*Urban*	*Rural*	
Persons	67.91	79.16	63.19	15.97
Males	78.49	85.83	75.37	10.46
Females	55.73	71.34	49.26	22.08

Source: Census of India (2001), *Primary Census Abstract*, Haryana, CD2, Office of the Registrar General and Census Commissioner, India, New Delhi, Table 7.

This urban-rural disparity was sharper among females than among males. The female literacy in rural areas of Haryana was only 49.26 per cent, while in urban areas 71.34 per cent of the females were literate. By comparison, the male literacy rates in rural and urban areas were 75.37 per cent and 85.83 per cent, respectively.

These urban-rural differentials in literacy rates are associated with a number of factors. Firstly, the urban occupations require greater skills and, hence, need literate persons. Secondly, urban places are far better equipped with educational facilities. Thirdly, the need to be educated is more in urban areas than in the countryside. Fourthly, urban people are socially more awakened and economically more capable of imparting education to their children. Fifthly, females are not denied the opportunities of education in urban places as is generally the case in many rural areas. Lastly, many literate rural persons migrate to urban places in search of jobs as a result of which the number of literates in urban areas increases at the cost of rural areas (Krishan and Chandna, 1974b).

5.2 Trends in Urban-Rural Disparity in Literacy, 1961-2001

Since the analysis of literacy differentials by urban-rural residence has not been possible for the pre-Independence period because of the non-availability of census data for this period, hence, the data on growth of literacy have been provided for the post-Independence period from 1961 to 2001 (Table 5.2).

Table 5.2 reveals that the literacy rate improved from 19.9 per cent in 1961 to 36.14 per cent in 1981 and increased further to 67.91 per cent in 2001. Similarly, the literacy rate for urban areas which was 44.7 per cent in 1961 rose to 56.9 per cent in 1981 and then increased further to 79.16 per cent in 2001. In rural areas, the literacy rate which was only 14.8 per cent in 1961 increased to 30.3 per cent in 1981 and further improved to 63.19 per cent in 2001.

The urban-rural disparity ratio is decreasing continuously over the time since 1961, when it was sharper (3.02 : 1), as there was only one rural literate for every three urban literates. This disparity ratio declined from 3.02 : 1 in 1961 to 1.25 : 1 in 2001. The rural literacy had registered an increase of more than four times from 14.8 per cent in 1961 to 63.19 per cent in 2001 and the differential index narrowed down gradually from 0.5169 in 1951 to 0.3013 in 1991.

The narrowing down of the urban-rural disparity index as well as disparity ratio was associated with increasing degree of rural-urban interaction, increasing socio-economic functional value of education in the countryside, improving standards of living, increasing facilities for schooling in the countryside and the waning social taboos and prejudices against females' education particularly in rural areas.

This disparity was more pronounced in the pre-Independence period when both the village improvement and their educational development were the last in the priority list of administration (Ojha, 1966) that wanted to create an elite class of limited number of educated persons only from the urban areas (Naik, 1978). Thus, prior to 1951, the literacy was a rare privilege in rural areas. By comparison, the urban literacy rates were relatively high; and towns and cities stood as islands in the oceans of illiteracy in the Indian sub-continent (Gosal, 1967). After the Independence, the improving standards of living; improvement in technology and means of communication; diversification of economy; constructive policies for the uplift of the down trodden; increasing degree of rural-urban interaction and increasing social and economic functional value of education in rural areas were responsible for narrowing down the urban-rural disparity index, significantly in the State.

As per 2001 Census, the urban-rural disparity index in literacy in Haryana is 0.1518. From among various districts, the disparity

Table 5.2: Haryana: Literacy Rate and Disparity Ratio by Urban-Rural Residence, 1961-2001

Census Year	*Literacy Rate (Per cent)*			*Urban-Rural Disparity*	*Urban-Rural Disparity Ratio*
	Total	*Urban*	*Rural*		
1961*	19.9	44.7	14.8	29.9	3.02 : 1
1971*	26.89	51.0	21.7	29.3	2.35 : 1
1981*	36.14	56.9	30.3	26.5	1.88 : 1
1981**	43.88	66.83	37.26	29.57	1.79 : 1
1991**	55.85	73.66	49.85	23.81	1.48 : 1
2001**	67.91	79.16	63.19	15.97	1.25 : 1

Sources: Adopted and Computed from:

(i) Sharma, O.P. and Retherford, R.D. (1987), *Recent Literacy Trends in India,* Occasional Paper No. 1 of 1987, Office of the Registrar General and Census Commissioner, India, Government of India, New Delhi, Statements 8, 13 and 15, pp. 17-27.

(ii) *Census of India (1991),* Final Population Totals: Brief Analysis of Primary Census Abstract, *Paper 2 of 1992,* Office of the Registrar General and Census Commissioner, India, Ministry of Home Affairs, Government of India, New Delhi, Statement 19, p. 61.

(iii) Census of India (2001), *Primary Census Abstract,* Haryana, CD2, Office of the Registrar General and Census Commissioner, India, New Delhi, Table 7.

* Literacy rates for 1961, 1971 and 1981 censuses relate to the population aged five years and above.

** Literacy rates for 1981, 1991 and 2001 relate to the population aged seven years and above.

index was the highest in Gurgaon (0.2378) and the lowest in Rewari (0.0781). At the tehsil level, Punahana tehsil has the highest urban-rural disparity index in literacy (0.3626), while it is the lowest in Pataudi (0.0009) (Table 5.3). In Punahana tehsil, the disparity index had stood on high because of the subsistence nature of agricultural economy; low degree of urbanization, strong prejudices against females' education and their mobility and the high ratio of the socially and economically backward sections of scheduled castes in rural areas. By contrast, in Pataudi tehsil, the lowest disparity index was attributable to early start of education, highly diversified nature of rural economy, and high proportion of non-agricultural workers.

5.3 Spatial Patterns of Urban-Rural Disparity in Literacy

Apart from a large disparity in literacy rates of males and females, there is a wide gap between the literacy rates of rural and urban areas. The patterns of regional variations among urban-rural disparity in the level of literacy will be discussed for the following segments of population:

1. Urban-Rural (Total)
2. Urban-Rural (Male)
3. Urban-Rural (Female)

On the basis of disparity indices for various segments of population, the tehsils of Haryana can be classified into six categories as:

1. Areas of Very High Disparity
2. Areas of High Disparity
3. Areas of Moderate Disparity
4. Areas of Low Disparity
5. Areas of Very Low Disparity
6. Totally Rural Areas

1. Areas of Very High Disparity

There are five tehsils where the disparity index values are 0.2401 and above. Out of these five tehsils, four tehsils namely Punahana (0.3626), Ferozepur Jhirka (0.2915), Nuh (0.2581) and Taoru (0.2521) belong to Gurgaon district and the tehsil of Hathin (0.2945) to Faridabad district in the extreme south-east of Haryana and are characterized with very high urban-rural disparity index values (Map 5.1). These are the tehsils which are dominated by Muslim population, especially in rural areas. Hence, all the Muslim dominated tehsils are attributed with very high urban-rural disparity in literacy rates.

Gurgaon district with subsistence nature of agricultural economy, low degree of urbanization (22.28 per cent), strong prejudices against females' education (with second lowest female literacy rate—39.79 per cent—for rural population) and their mobility outside home, dominance of Muslim population

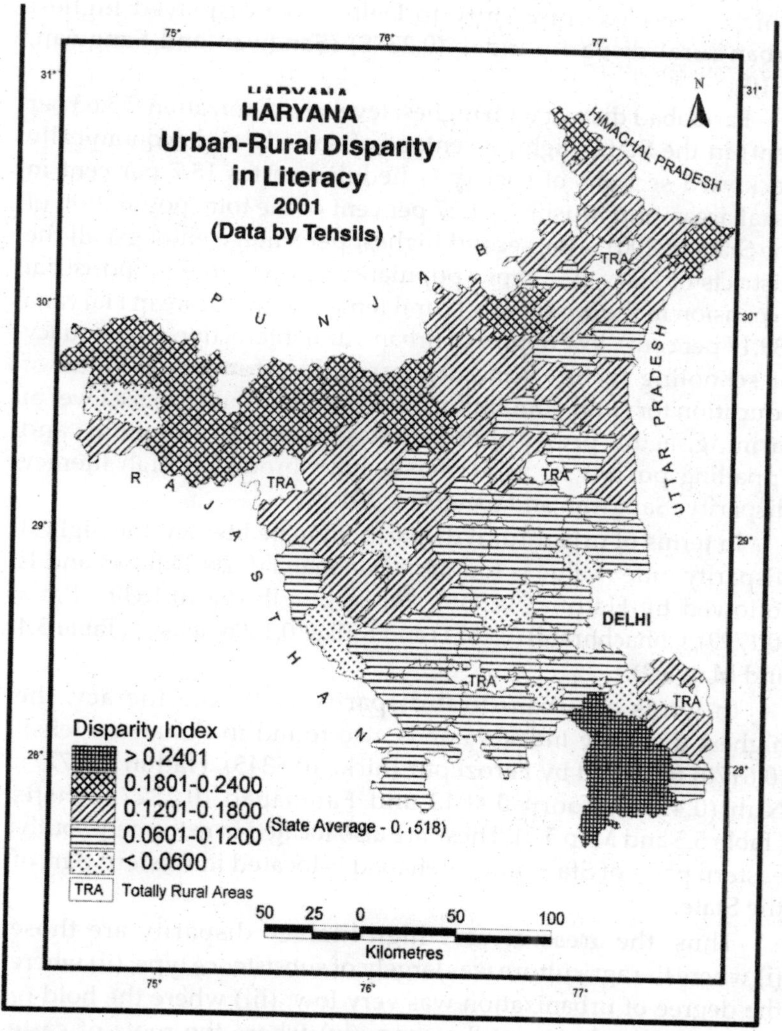

Map 5.1: Haryana: Urban-Rural Disparity in Literacy, 2001

(37.22 per cent of the total population of the State in 2001—the highest percentage amongst all the districts of Haryana), low incidence of rural-urban interaction, inadequate educational infrastructure and late start of education in rural areas, rapid population growth due to industrial expansion in the area and also because of relatively faster growth of Gurgaon Urban Estate which is in close proximity to Delhi have displayed highest urban-rural disparity index (0.2378) (Sangwan and Sangwan, 2010).

Faridabad district with highest level of urbanization (55.63 per cent) in the State, high percentage of socially and economically backward sections of society (scheduled castes 18.7 per cent in rural areas; and Muslims 11.27 per cent of the total population of the State in 2001—the second highest percentage amongst all the districts of Haryana), rapid population growth due to industrial expansion in the area, lowest rural female literacy rate in Haryana (39.17 per cent), low degree of urban-rural interaction, inadequacy of schooling facilities in rural areas, low functional value of education for rural population, backward and subsistence level of farming, acute pressure of population on the farmland, and appalling poverty of rural masses have produced high literacy disparity (Sangwan and Sangwan, 2010).

In terms of urban-rural disparity in male literacy, the highest disparity index value is found in Punahana (0.2607) tehsil and is followed by Hathin (0.2038), Ferozepur Jhirka (0.1839), Ratia (0.1799), Chhachhrauli (0.1671) and Kalka (0.1606) tehsils (Table 5.4 and Map 5.2).

In terms of urban-rural disparity in female literacy, the highest disparity index value is also found in Punahana tehsil (0.6170) followed by Ferozepur Jhirka (0.5345), Hathin (0.4777), Nuh (0.4581), Taoru 0.4043 and Fatehabad (0.2827) tehsils (Table 5.5 and Map 5.3). These are also located in extremely south-eastern parts of State and Fatehabad is located in western part of the State.

Thus, the areas of very high literacy disparity are those (i) where the agriculture was largely of subsistence type; (ii) where the degree of urbanization was very low; (iii) where the hold of feudal landlords was still strong; (iv) where the roots of caste system are deep and strong; (v) where the proportion of scheduled caste population had increased through recent immigration (Sangwan and Sangwan, 2010).

In nutshell, the maximum urban-rural disparity in literacy rates is the rule of those areas which are either highly urbanized but dominated by Muslim population or least urbanized with high concentration of scheduled castes population in rural areas.

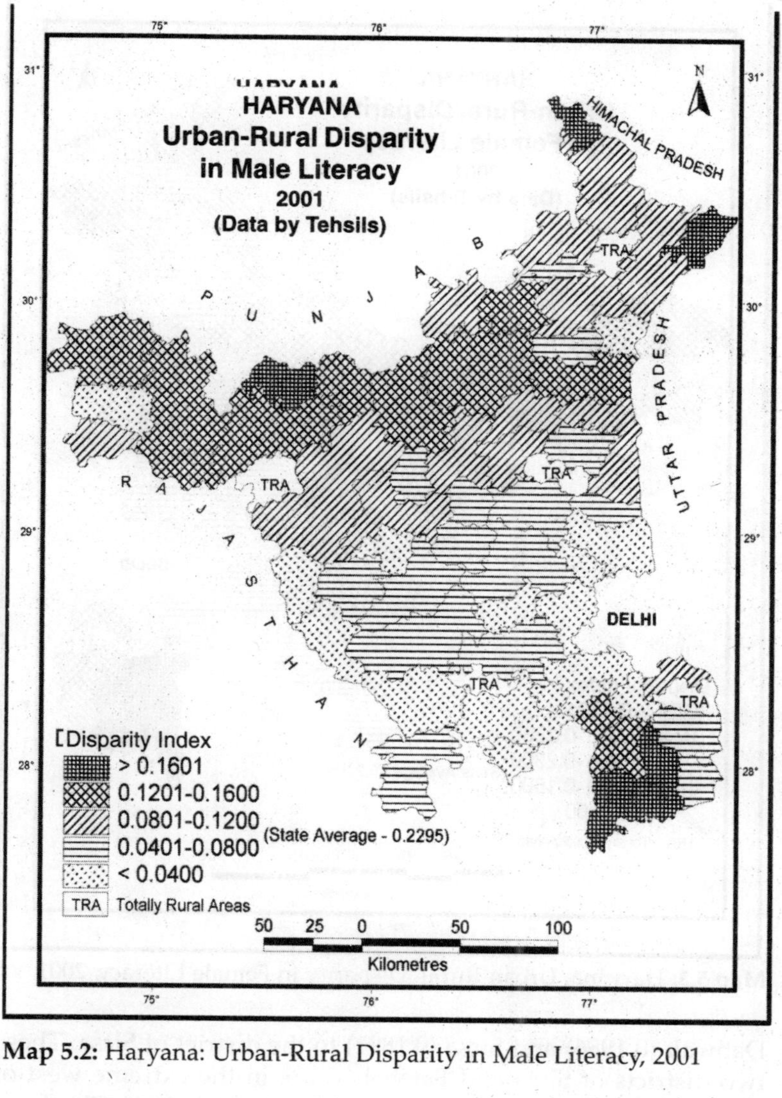

Map 5.2: Haryana: Urban-Rural Disparity in Male Literacy, 2001

2. *Areas of High Disparity*

Out of the total of 67 tehsils, nine tehsils are characterized by high urban-rural disparity in literacy (Table 5.3 and Map 5.1). The three tehsils, namely Ratia (0.2190), Fatehabad (0.1902), and Tohana (0.1864), belong to Fatehabad district and two tehsils, namely

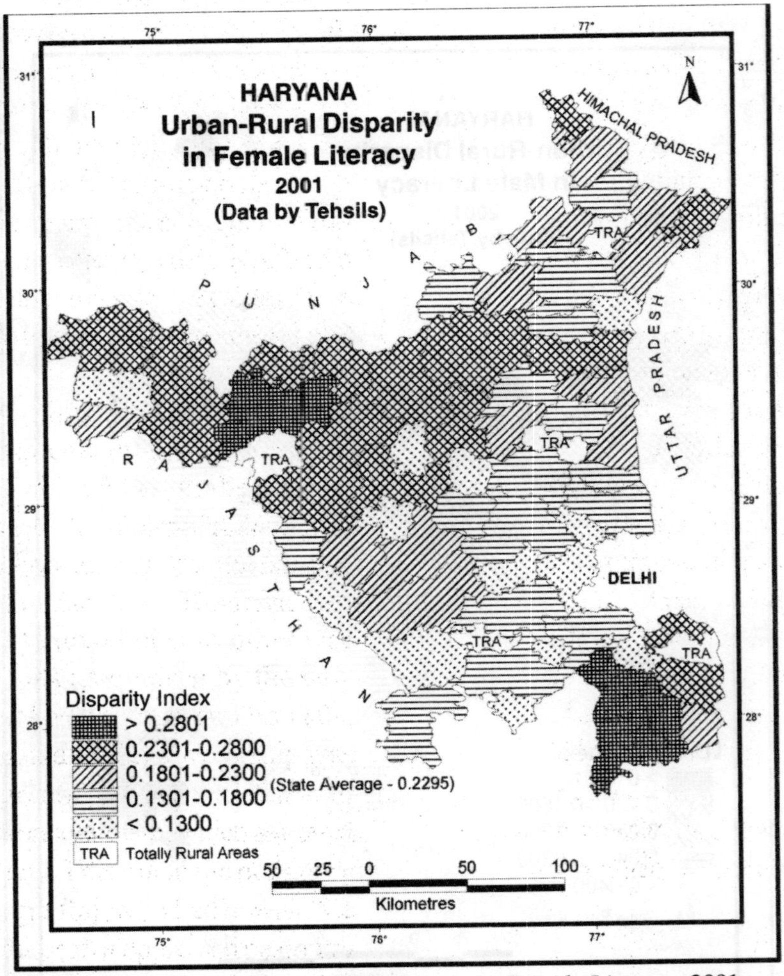

Map 5.3: Haryana: Urban-Rural Disparity in Female Literacy, 2001

Dabwali (0.1986) and Sirsa (0.1891) to the district of Sirsa. These two districts of Sirsa and Fatehabad are in the extreme west of Haryana along the Rajasthan and Punjab borders. The high disparity in urban-rural literacy is attributable to a variety of factors like low level of urbanization especially in Fatehabad district which ranks second after Mahendragarh (13.46 per cent) in terms of lowest level of urbanization (17.63 per cent) in Haryana, meagre industrialization, highly restricted females' mobility in rural areas, low functional value of education for rural population, strong social taboos against females' education (with third lowest female literacy rate—42.43 per cent—for rural population being in Fatehabad and 44.09 per cent in Sirsa), low incidence of rural-urban interaction, and high concentration of scheduled castes population in rural areas (29.0 per cent in Fatehabad with third ranking and 28.2 per cent in Sirsa with fourth ranking in the State after Yamunanagar 31.5 per cent and Ambala 31.1 per cent, being the first and second respectively).

The other four tehsils with high urban-rural disparity in literacy are that of Chhachhrauli (0.2058) in Yamunanagar district, Kalka (0.1979) in Panchkula district, Narwana (0.1868) in Jind district, and Pehowa (0.1814) in Kurukshetra district.

The high urban-rural disparity in male literacy is the characteristic of 10 tehsils located in different parts of the State. These are Dabwali (0.1586), Sirsa (0.1365), Fatehabad (0.1252), and Tohana (0.1427) in western part; Narwana (0.1431), and Kaithal (0.1238) in north-central part; Pehowa (0.1441) in northern part; Karnal (0.1275) in eastern part; and Taoru (0.1566) and Nuh (0.1556) in southern part of the State (Table 5.4 and Map 5.2).

The urban-rural disparity in female literacy is high in 15 tehsils of the State. These are Hisar (0.2756), Tohana (0.2495), Ratia (0.2711), Sirsa (0.2616), and Dabwali (0.2558) in western part; Hansi (0.2606), Jind (0.2500), Narwana (0.2609), and Kaithal (0.2451) in north-central part; Kalka (0.2493), Chhachhrauli (0.2662), and Pehowa (0.2304) in northern part; Karnal (0.2427) in eastern part; Palwal (0.2739), Faridabad (0.2640) in southern part of the State (Table 5.5 and Map 5.3). The high literacy disparity is characteristic of areas of low urbanization, more proportion of agricultural workers, low literacy rate of population and less development of means of transportation and communication.

3. *Areas of Moderate Disparity*

This category comprises 19 tehsils located mainly in the northern, eastern and central parts of the State (Table 5.3 and Map 5.1).

Among these tehsils, 7 tehsils namely, Hisar (0.1780) and Hansi (0.1564) tehsils of Hisar district, Karnal tehsil (0.1769) of Karnal district, Kaithal tehsil (0.1712) of Kaithal district, Jind tehsil (0.1678) of Jind district, Faridabad tehsil (0.1675) of Faridabad district and

Table 5.3: Haryana: Urban-Rural Disparity Indices of Literacy by Tehsils, 2001

Sr. No.	*State/Tehsil*	*Disparity Index*	*Sr. No.*	*Tehsil*	*Disparity Index*
	Haryana	**0.1518**	34.	Nilokheri	0.1183
1.	Punahana	0.3626	35.	Assandh	0.1134
2.	Hathin	0.2945	36.	Shahbad	0.1079
3.	Ferozepur Jhirka	0.2915	37.	Panipat	0.1069
4.	Nuh	0.2581	38.	Dadri	0.1067
5.	Taoru	0.2521	39.	Jhajjar	0.1066
6.	Ratia	0.2190	40.	Ganaur	0.1053
7.	Chhachhrauli	0.2058	41.	Hodal	0.1048
8.	Dabwali	0.1986	42.	Gohana	0.1012
9.	Kalka	0.1979	43.	Rohtak	0.1011
10.	Fatehabad	0.1902	44.	Narnaul	0.0991
11.	Sirsa	0.1891	45.	Maham	0.0932
12.	Narwana	0.1868	46.	Gurgaon	0.0792
13.	Tohana	0.1864	47.	Mahendragarh	0.0791
14.	Pehowa	0.1814	48.	Sonipat	0.0781
15.	Hisar	0.1780	49.	Narnaund	0.0758
16.	Karnal	0.1769	50.	Siwani	0.0755
17.	Kaithal	0.1712	51.	Rewari	0.0738
18.	Jind	0.1678	52.	Bawal	0.0738
19.	Faridabad	0.1675	53.	Julana	0.0710
20.	Hansi	0.1564	54.	Indri	0.0696
21.	Ellenabad	0.1544	55.	Bahadurgarh	0.0677
22.	Samalkha	0.1512	56.	Kharkhoda	0.0590
23.	Gharaunda	0.1483	57.	Rania	0.0586
24.	Naraingarh	0.1415	58.	Sohna	0.0527
25.	Ambala	0.1414	59.	Beri	0.0412
26.	Guhla	0.1375	60.	Bawani Khera	0.0386
27.	Palwal	0.1363	61.	Loharu	0.0287
28.	Jagadhari	0.1350	62.	Pataudi	0.0009
29.	Panchkula	0.1333	63.	Barara	Totally Rural
30.	Thanesar	0.1307	64.	Israna	Totally Rural
31.	Safidon	0.1278	65.	Adampur	Totally Rural
32.	Tosham	0.1227	66.	Kosli	Totally Rural
33.	Bhiwani	0.1211	67.	Ballabgarh	Totally Rural

Source: Computed from Census of India (2001), *Primary Census Abstract,* Haryana, Series 7, Tables A5-A8, Directorate of Census Operations, Haryana.

Note: Tehsils are arranged in descending order of disparity index, 2001.

Ellenabad tehsil of Sirsa district are characterized with literacy disparity above the State average (0.1518).

On the other hand, 12 tehsils, viz., Samalkha tehsil (0.1512) of

Panipat district, Gharaunda tehsil (0.1483) of Karnal district, Naraingarh (0.1415) and Ambala (0.1414) tehsils of Ambala district, Gulha tehsil (0.1375) of Kaithal district, Palwal tehsil (0.1363) of Faridabad district, Jagadhari tehsil (0.1350) of Yamunanagar district, Panchkula tehsil (0.1333) of Panchkula district, Thanesar tehsil (0.1307) of Kurukshetra district, Safidon tehsil (0.1278) of Jind district, and Tosham (0.1227) and Bhiwani (0.1211) tehsils of Bhiwani district are characterized with literacy disparity below the State average (0.1518),

The impact of the capital city of Chandigarh can be visualized on the adjoining tehsils of Panchkula district which is one of the most urbanized districts of Haryana with second highest level of urbanization (44.47 per cent) in the State. Panchkula district is also characterized with rapid growth of population as high increase in population is associated with the faster development of Panchkula Urban Estate which is in close proximity to Chandigarh.

Yamunanagar district is ranked fourth in the level of urbanization (40 per cent) and is relatively more industrialized. The district is also credited with the distinction of having the highest concentration of scheduled castes population in rural areas (31.5 per cent). Hence, Jagadhari tehsil (0.1350) of Yamunanagar district is characterized with literacy disparity below the State average (0.1518),

The tehsils of Hisar, Jind, Kaithal and Karnal districts have moderate urban-rural disparity in literacy mainly because of diversified rural economy, speedy increase in the level of urbanization, increasing degree of rural-urban interaction, increasing awareness about literacy among rural people. The means of transportation also made educational institutions accessible to rural people to a great extent. The urban-rural disparity in literacy would have been still lower but for late start in education, in urban-industrial growth and in rural mobility and inheritance of rural mass illiteracy.

The impact of the capital city of Chandigarh can also be visualized on the adjoining tehsils of Ambala district, where literacy differentials are moderate and the schooling facilities are expanded to almost all the rural areas. The district is also characterised with rapidly growing urbanization (35.19 per cent) and the second highest percentage of scheduled castes population in rural areas (31.1 per cent).

The Thanesar tehsil of Kurukshetra district, the pious land of *Mahabharata,* is also characterized with the moderate urban-rural disparity in literacy mainly because of increasing awareness among rural masses, high rural female literacy rate (56.61 per cent), and low proportion of scheduled castes population in rural areas (23.46 per cent).

Panipat district is the third most urbanized (40.51 per cent) district of Haryana. Here, Samalkha tehsil is characterised with high rural female literacy rate (48.98 per cent) due to increasing awareness among rural masses resulting into moderate urban-rural disparity in literacy.

Hence, the moderate urban-rural disparity in literacy was found in those areas where there are moderate literacy rates of general population. The rural-urban interaction is increasing with the help of improvement in transportation system which increased accessibility between rural and urban areas. The differential is moderate in areas of rapidly growing urbanization and where the rural economy is more diversified. The areas where rural population is socio-economically more aware about benefits of literacy are also having moderate disparity.

The urban-rural disparity in male literacy has comparatively low value of disparity indices ranging between –0.0347 to 0.2607. The areas having disparity index values between 0.0801 to 0.1200 for urban-rural males have been considered in this category. There are 15 tehsils, viz., Ellenabad (0.1189), and Hisar (0.1122) in western region; Hansi (0.0863), Jind (0.1159), Safidon (0.0847), Assandh (0.0826) in north-central region; Guhla (0.1132), Thanesar (0.0918), Jagadhari (0.0935), Ambala (0.1018), Naraingarh (0.1161), Panchkula (0.0890) in northern region; Gharaunda (0.1087), and Samalkha (0.1025) in eastern region; and Faridabad (0.0959) in southern region of the State (Table 5.4 and Map 5.2).

On the contrary, eleven tehsils of Haryana have been characterized by the moderate level of urban-rural disparity in female literacy. Such a phenomenon is found in the tehsils of Samalkha (0.2233), and Gharaunda (0.2039) in eastern Haryana; Tosham (0.2054), and Ellenabad (0.2021) in western Haryana; Bhiwani (0.1883), Dadri (0.1864), and Safidon (0.1924) in central Haryana; Panchkula (0.2046), Ambala (0.1882), and Jagadhri (0.1873) in northern Haryana; and Hodal (0.2190) in southern Haryana (Table 5.5 and Map 5.3). Some of these tehsils have the impact of educationally and industrially developed centres within them, while others have agrarian economy.

4. *Areas of Low Disparity*

Urban-rural disparity index values in literacy are low in as much as 22 tehsils of the State. These are Shahbad (0.1079) in the north; Indri (0.0696), Nilokheri (0.1183), Panipat (0.1069), Ganaur (0.1053), Sonipat (0.0781), Bahadurgarh (0.0677) in the east; Assandh (0.1134), Narnaud (0.0758), Julana (0.0710), Gohana (0.1012), Rohtak (0.1011), Maham (0.0932), Jhajjar (0.1066), and Dadri (0.1067) in the centre; Siwani (0.0755) in the west; Mahendragarh (0.0791), Narnaul (0.0991), Bawal (0.0738), Rewari (0.0738), Gurgaon (0.0792), and Hodal (0.1048) in the south (Table 5.3 and Map 5.1).

In the tehsil of Rewari, tradition of joining Army service is strong resulting into high level of rural literacy (74.68 per cent), hence, low urban-rural disparity in literacy. Bahadurgarh, Sonipat and Gurgaon tehsils fall in the zone peripheral to the union territory of Delhi. So, their proximity to Delhi has the impact on the overall literacy rates in these areas resulting into low urban-rural disparity.

The urban-rural disparity in male literacy is low in 17 tehsils of the State. These are Shahbad (0.0711) in northern region; Nilokheri (0.0746), Panipat (0.0565), and Ganaur (0.0701) in eastern region; Gohana (0.0641), Maham (0.0564), Rohtak (0.0476), Jhajjar (0.0663), Dadri (0.0453), Bhiwani (0.0714), Julana (0.0405), and Narnaund (0.0581) in central region; Tosham (0.0667) in western region; Mahendragarh (0.0404), Narnaul (0.0435), Palwal (0.0491), and Hodal (0.0409) in southern region of the State (Table 5.4 and Map 5.2).

Urban-rural disparity in female literacy is low in 17 tehsils of the State. These are Naraingarh (0.1769), Shahbad (0.1541), Thanesar (0.1780), and Guhla (0.1673) in northern Haryana; Nilokheri (0.1757), Panipat (0.1771), Ganaur (0.1593), Sonipat (0.1404) in eastern Haryana; Assandh (0.1558), Gohana (0.1558), Maham (0.1508), Rohtak (0.1759), and Jhajjar (0.1610) in central Haryana; Siwani (0.1327) in western Haryana; Narnaul (0.1669), Rewari (0.1428) and Gurgaon (0.1416) in southern Haryana (Table 5.5 and Map 5.3).

Table 5.4: Haryana: Urban-Rural Disparity Indices of Male Literacy by Tehsils, 2001

Sr. No.	State/Tehsil	Disparity Index	Sr. No.	Tehsil	Disparity Index
	Haryana	**0.0945**	34.	Shahbad	0.0711
1.	Punahana	0.2607	35.	Ganaur	0.0701
2.	Hathin	0.2038	36.	Tosham	0.0667
3.	Ferozepur Jhirka	0.1839	37.	Jhajjar	0.0663
4.	Ratia	0.1799	38.	Gohana	0.0641
5.	Chhachhrauli	0.1671	39.	Narnaund	0.0581
6.	Kalka	0.1606	40.	Panipat	0.0565
7.	Dabwali	0.1586	41.	Maham	0.0564
8.	Taoru	0.1566	42.	Palwal	0.0491
9.	Nuh	0.1556	43.	Rohtak	0.0476
10.	Pehowa	0.1441	44.	Dadri	0.0453
11.	Narwana	0.1431	45.	Narnaul	0.0435
12.	Tohana	0.1427	46.	Hodal	0.0409
13.	Sirsa	0.1365	47.	Julana	0.0405
14.	Karnal	0.1275	48.	Mahendragarh	0.0404
15.	Fatehabad	0.1252	49.	Indri	0.0389
16.	Kaithal	0.1238	50.	Kharkhoda	0.0389
17.	Ellenabad	0.1189	51.	Siwani	0.0355
18.	Naraingarh	0.1161	52.	Bawal	0.0341
19.	Jind	0.1159	53.	Bahadurgarh	0.0340
20.	Guhla	0.1132	54.	Sonipat	0.0337
21.	Hisar	0.1122	55.	Gurgaon	0.0330
22.	Gharaunda	0.1087	56.	Bawani Khera	0.0260
23.	Samalkha	0.1025	57.	Beri	0.0240
24.	Ambala	0.1018	58.	Rania	0.0231
25.	Faridabad	0.0959	59.	Rewari	0.0136
26.	Jagadhari	0.0935	60.	Sohna	0.0105
27.	Thanesar	0.0918	61.	Loharu	0.0015
28.	Panchkula	0.0890	62.	Pataudi	–0.0347
29.	Hansi	0.0863	63.	Barara	Totally Rural
30.	Safidon	0.0847	64.	Israna	Totally Rural
31.	Assandh	0.0826	65.	Adampur	Totally Rural
32.	Nilokheri	0.0746	66.	Kosli	Totally Rural
33.	Bhiwani	0.0714	67.	Ballabgarh	Totally Rural

Source: Computed from, Census of India (2001), *Primary Census Abstract*, Haryana, Series 7, Tables A5-A8, Directorate of Census Operations, Haryana.

Note: Tehsils are arranged in descending order of disparity index, 2001.

Thus, areas of low urban-rural disparity in aggregate levels are those which are either least urbanized or have the impact of big urban, educational or industrial centres on rural areas.

5. *Areas of Very Low Disparity (0.0600 and Below)*

There are only seven tehsils, which are characterized by very low urban-rural disparity in literacy. Pataudi has the lowest urban-rural disparity in literacy (0.0009) and is followed by the tehsils of Loharu (0.0287), Bawani Khera (0.0386), Beri (0.0412), Sohna (0.0527), Rania (0.0586) and Kharkhoda (0.0590) (Table 5.3 and Map 5.1).

Out of these seven tehsils, two tehsils namely Bawani Khera (0.0386) and Loharu (0.0287) are located in Bhiwani district, two tehsils, viz., Sohna (0.0527) and Pataudi (0.0009) in Gurgaon district; and the remaining three tehsils are that of Kharkhoda (0.0590) in Sonipat district, Rania (0.0586) in Sirsa district, and Beri (0.0412) in Jhajjar district and are characterized with very low urban-rural disparity index values (Table 5.3) (Map 5.1).

The tehsils of Pataudi (74.45 per cent), Beri (71.56 per cent), Sohna (69.61 per cent) and Kharkhoda (68.67 per cent) are characterized with rural literacy rates above the State average (63.19 per cent) and the urban literacy rates below the State average (79.16 per cent) resulting into very low urban-rural disparity in literacy. In case of remaining tehsils of Loharu, Bawani Khera and Rania, both the rural and urban literacy rates are below the State's averages (63.19 per cent and 79.16 per cent respectively), but very near to each other. Hence, very low urban-rural disparity in literacy, because they are also characterized with meagre urbanization.

Very low urban-rural disparity in male literacy is found in 14 tehsils of the State. These are Indri (0.0389), Sonipat (0.0337), Kharkhoda (0.0389), and Bahadurgarh (0.0340) in eastern region; Beri (0.0240) in central region; Loharu (0.0015), Siwani (0.0355), Bawani Kheri (0.0260) and Rania (0.0231) in western region; Bawal (0.0341), Rewari (0.0136), Gurgaon (0.0330), Sohna (0.0105), and Pataudi (–0.0347) in southern region of the State (Table 5.4 and Map 5.2). Pataudi is the only tehsil in Haryana which is characterised with the negative value of urban-rural disparity in male literacy (–0.0347), because in Pataudi, male literacy rate (87.73 per cent) in rural areas is more than the male literacy rate (83.82 per cent) in urban areas.

Very low urban-rural disparity in female literacy is found in 13 tehsils of the State. These are Indri (0.1106), Kharkhoda (0.0941), and Bahadurgarh (0.1118) in eastern Haryana; Beri (0.0628), Julana (0.1206) and Bawani Khera (0.0572) in the central Haryana; Rania

(0.1093), Narnaund (0.1064), and Loharu (0.0682) in western Haryana; Mahendragarh (0.1265), Bawal (0.1229), Pataudi (0.0423) and Sohna (0.1119) in southern Haryana (Table 5.5 and Map 5.3).

Table 5.5: Haryana: Urban-Rural Disparity Indices of Female Literacy by Tehsils, 2001

Sr. No.	*State/Tehsil*	*Disparity Index*	*Sr. No.*	*Tehsil*	*Disparity Index*
	Haryana	**0.2295**	34.	Panipat	0.1771
1.	Punahana	0.6170	35.	Naraingarh	0.1769
2.	Ferozepur Jhirka	0.5345	36.	Rohtak	0.1759
3.	Hathin	0.4777	37.	Nilokheri	0.1757
4.	Nuh	0.4581	38.	Guhla	0.1673
5.	Taoru	0.4043	39.	Narnaul	0.1669
6.	Fatehabad	0.2827	40.	Jhajjar	0.1610
7.	Hisar	0.2756	41.	Ganaur	0.1593
8.	Palwal	0.2739	42.	Assandh	0.1558
9.	Ratia	0.2711	43.	Gohana	0.1558
10.	Chhachhrauli	0.2662	44.	Shahbad	0.1541
11.	Faridabad	0.2640	45.	Maham	0.1508
12.	Sirsa	0.2616	46.	Rewari	0.1428
13.	Narwana	0.2609	47.	Gurgaon	0.1416
14.	Hansi	0.2606	48.	Sonipat	0.1404
15.	Dabwali	0.2558	49.	Siwani	0.1327
16.	Jind	0.2500	50.	Mahendragarh	0.1265
17.	Tohana	0.2495	51.	Bawal	0.1229
18.	Kalka	0.2493	52.	Julana	0.1206
19.	Kaithal	0.2451	53.	Sohna	0.1119
20.	Karnal	0.2427	54.	Bahadurgarh	0.1118
21.	Pehowa	0.2304	55.	Indri	0.1106
22.	Samalkha	0.2233	56.	Rania	0.1093
23.	Hodal	0.2190	57.	Narnaund	0.1064
24.	Tosham	0.2054	58.	Kharkhoda	0.0941
25.	Panchkula	0.2046	59.	Loharu	0.0682
26.	Gharaunda	0.2039	60.	Beri	0.0628
27.	Ellenabad	0.2021	61.	Bawani Khera	0.0572
28.	Safidon	0.1924	62.	Pataudi	0.0423
29.	Bhiwani	0.1883	63.	Barara	Totally Rural
30.	Ambala	0.1882	64.	Israna	Totally Rural
31.	Jagadhari	0.1873	65.	Adampur	Totally Rural
32.	Dadri	0.1864	66.	Kosli	Totally Rural
33.	Thanesar	0.1780	67.	Ballabgarh	Totally Rural

Source: Computed from Census of India (2001), *Primary Census Abstract*, Haryana, Series 7, Tables A5-A8, Directorate of Census Operations, Haryana.

Note: Tehsils are arranged in descending order of disparity index, 2001.

Reasons for very low disparity in literacy rates are the availability of more educational facilities, high degree of urbanization and good economic conditions. The areas are also characterized with the peripheral locations to union territories of Delhi and Chandigarh.

6. Totally Rural Areas

There are five tehsils, namely Barara of Ambala district, Israna of Panipat district, Adampur of Hisar district, Kosli of Rewari district and Ballabgarh of Faridabad district which are totally rural in character. Hence, no urban-rural disparity exists in literacy.

Conclusions

1. During the post-Independence period from the Census of 1961 onwards and especially since its formation as a separate State in 1966, Haryana has experienced a continuous increase in literacy rate during the span of 50 years which increased from 19.9 per cent in 1961 to 67.91 per cent in 2001—an increase of more than three times.
2. The same trend has been observed in case of both male and female literacy rates. However, in case of female literacy rate, a remarkable increase of more than six times (from 9.2 per cent in 1961 to 55.73 per cent in 2001) has been observed.

   The relatively high rate of increase in female literacy is related to the increasing educational facilities along with availability of female teachers in abundance particularly in rural areas, increasing value of female education for matrimony, increasing degree of socio-economic awareness, and the waning social taboos and prejudices against females' education.
3. The total literacy rate (67.91 per cent) in Haryana is more than that of the country as a whole (64.8 per cent) in 2001. It is also true in case of male literacy rate (State average—78.49 per cent and national average—75.2 per cent) and female literacy rate (State average—55.73 per cent and national average—53.6 per cent). Thus, more than three-fourth of the male and more than half of the female

population aged seven years and above are literate in the State today.

4. The urban literacy rate which was 44.7 per cent in 1961 increased to 79.16 per cent in 2001. Similarly, the rural literacy rate which was only 14.8 per cent in 1961 improved to 63.19 per cent in 2001.

   In other words, in 2001, while 79.16 per cent of urban population in Haryana was literate, the corresponding figure for rural population was only 63.19 per cent, implying the narrowing down of wide disparity in rural and urban literacy rates.

5. The narrowing down of the urban-rural disparity in literacy was associated with increasing degree of rural-urban interaction, increasing socio-economic functional value of education in the countryside, improving standards of living, increasing facilities for schooling in the countryside and the waning social taboos and prejudices against females' education particularly in rural areas.

6. In regional perspective, the maximum urban-rural disparity in literacy rates is the rule of those areas which are either highly urbanized but dominated by Muslim population or least urbanized with high concentration of scheduled castes population in rural areas. There are five tehsils which are characterized with very high urban-rural disparity index values (0.2401 and above). Out of these five tehsils, four tehsils namely Punahana (0.3626), Ferozepur, Jhirka (0.2915), Nuh (0.2581) and Taoru (0.2521) belong to Gurgaon district and the tehsil of Hathin (0.2945) to Faridabad district in the extreme south-east of Haryana.

7. By comparison, the low urban-rural disparity in literacy is found in both the less developed areas and rapidly developing areas. In the former case, both urban and rural literacy rates are low and resultant disparity is low. In the latter case, both the urban and rural literacy rates are high and the resultant disparity is also low.

   There are only seven tehsils, which are characterized by very low urban-rural differential in literacy. The tehsils of Pataudi (74.45 per cent), Beri (71.56 per cent), Sohna (69.61 per cent) and Kharkhoda (68.67 per cent) are characterized by rural literacy rates above the State average (63.19 per cent) and the urban literacy rates below the State average (79.16 per cent) resulting into very low urban-rural disparity in literacy. In case of remaining tehsils of Loharu, Bawani Khera and Rania, both the rural and urban literacy rates are below the State's averages (63.19 per cent and 79.16 per cent respectively). Hence, very low urban-rural disparity in literacy.

8. In the areas of high literacy (both urban and rural), early start of education, diversification of rural economy and relatively high degree of urbanization have their strong impact. In rural areas, commercialization of agriculture, opening of more schools, the long tradition of military service, and the waning social taboos and prejudices against females' education particularly in rural areas have played a vital role in the increase of literacy rates, thereby decreasing urban-rural gap.

6 Literacy Disparity between Scheduled Castes and Non-Scheduled Castes

Article 341 of the Constitution provides that the President may, with respect to any State or Union territory, specify the castes, races or tribes or parts of or groups within castes, races or tribes which shall for the purposes of the Constitution be deemed to be Scheduled Castes in relation to that State or Union Territory. In pursuance of these provisions, the list of scheduled castes are notified for each State and Union territory and are valid only within the jurisdiction of that State or Union Territory and not outside.

It is important to mention here that under the Constitution (scheduled castes) Order 1950, no person who professed a religion different from Hinduism was deemed to be a member of a scheduled caste in addition to every member of the Ramdasi, Kabirpanthi, Majhabi or Sikligar caste resident in Punjab or Patiala and East Punjab States Union were in relation to that State whether they professed the Hindu or the Sikh religion.

Subsequently, in September 1956, by an amendment, the Presidential Order of 1950 and in all subsequent Presidential Orders relating to scheduled castes, the population professing the Hindu and the Sikh religions were placed on the same footing with regard to their inclusion as scheduled castes.

Later on, as per the amendment made in the Constitution (Scheduled Castes) Order 1990, the Hindu, the Sikh and the Buddhist professing population were placed on the same footing with regard to the recognition of the scheduled castes.

For finalizing the list of scheduled castes/scheduled tribes notified in each State/Union Territory, all the constitutional amendments that have taken place prior to the conduct of 2001 Census were taken into account. Since there is no scheduled castes list for the State of Nagaland and the Union Territories of Andaman and Nicobar Islands and Lakshadweep; and no scheduled tribes list for the States of Delhi, Haryana and Punjab and the Union Territories of Chandigarh and Pondicherry, the scheduled castes and scheduled tribes population figures are furnished for only the relevant category in respect of these States and Union territories.

The instructions to the enumerators for recording the individual responses on religion and the scheduled castes and the scheduled tribes were more or less the same as in the past censuses. Each enumerator was provided with a notified list of scheduled castes and scheduled tribes in respect of his/her State/Union Territory. The religion for each individual was first of all determined. Then it was ascertained from the respondent for each individual whether she or he belonged to a scheduled caste or a scheduled tribe through Question No. 8 and 9 of the Household Schedule. If in reply to either of this question, the answer was in the affirmative, the name of caste/tribe to which the individual belonged was ascertained. If the name of caste/tribe returned by the respondent appeared in the approved list for the State, the enumerator was expected to treat the individual, as belonging to scheduled caste or scheduled tribe and record the appropriate entry (Census of India, 2001).

In Haryana, the proportion of the scheduled castes to total population is higher at 19.35 per cent in comparison of National average of 16.2 per cent in 2001 Census. The proportion of scheduled castes population has decreased slightly in the State from 19.7 per cent in 1991 to 19.3 per cent in 2001 Census.

In terms of literacy and education, the scheduled castes population, comprising of about one-sixth of the country's total population (16.20 per cent) lags behind the rest of population. The Census of India (2001) revealed only 54.69 per cent of the scheduled castes population as literate. The relatively low rates of literacy among the scheduled castes population have been the outcome of their age old association with menial jobs, long history of their neglect, deprivation, social injustice, long spells of social and economic segregation in terms of residence, worship, education and occupation, poverty, lack of awareness, superstitions, long duration of cultural apathy towards their piousness, spiritual purity and cleanliness, adverse attitude of princely states towards their welfare and the age old tradition of physical and residential isolation.

In Haryana, as per Census of India (2001), there exists a wide gap in the literacy rates of the scheduled castes and the non-scheduled castes population (Table 6.1).

Table 6.1: Haryana: Literacy Rates of Scheduled Castes and Non-Scheduled Castes and the Disparity Index, 2001

Population	*Per cent Literates*		*Disparity Index*
	Non-Scheduled Castes Population	*Scheduled Castes Population*	
Total			
Persons	70.81	55.40	0.1550
Males	81.18	66.93	0.1331
Females	58.87	42.26	0.1923
Rural			
Persons	65.60	54.13	0.1190
Males	77.90	65.88	0.1136
Females	51.56	40.64	0.1341
Urban			
Persons	82.22	60.19	0.2099
Males	88.26	70.67	0.1600
Females	75.12	48.11	0.2786

Source: Computed from Census of India (2001), *Primary Census Abstract*, Haryana Series 7, Table A5-A8, Directorate of Census Operations, Haryana.

6.1 Literacy among Scheduled Castes

The Census of India 2001 reveals that Haryana has only 55.43 per cent of the Scheduled Castes population as literate. The literacy rate among Scheduled Castes population was very low in comparison to general population. There are many reasons such as social injustice, lack of awareness, association with menial jobs and restriction to participate in economically gainful activities. Mahendragarh district (68.7 per cent) has highest literacy rate among Scheduled Castes population and Fatehabad district (41.0 per cent) has lowest literacy rate among scheduled castes population. But in case of tehsils, Gurgaon has the highest literacy rate among scheduled castes and Ratia tehsil of Sirsa district has the lowest literacy rate (Table 6.2).

Table 6.2: Haryana: Literacy Rates of Scheduled Castes by Tehsils, 2001

Sr. No.	*State/Tehsil*	*Literacy Rate (%)*	*Sr. No.*	*Tehsil*	*Literacy Rate (%)*
	Haryana	**55.43**	34.	Julana	55.72
1.	Gurgaon	69.35	35.	Indri	55.61
2.	Rewari	69.32	36.	Palwal	55.50
3.	Pataudi	68.03	37.	Israna	55.36
4.	Kosli	67.69	38.	Karnal	55.29
5.	Kalka	67.30	39.	Gharaunda	55.20
6.	Bawal	66.51	40.	Nilokheri	54.86
7.	Sonipat	65.41	41.	Loharu	54.29
8.	Sohna	64.38	42.	Jind	53.34
9.	Taoru	64.24	43.	Tosham	53.15
10.	Barara	63.92	44.	Bawani Khera	52.68
11.	Mahendragarh	63.89	45.	Nuh	52.58
12.	Jagadhri	63.66	46.	Siwani	52.29
13.	Ambala	63.59	47.	Safidon	52.05
14.	Bahadurgarh	63.55	48.	Hathin	51.19
15.	Narnaul	63.44	49.	Ferozepur Jhirka	51.12
16.	Beri	62.40	50.	Hansi	51.07
17.	Jhajjar	61.68	51.	Pehowa	50.56
18.	Kharkhoda	61.54	52.	Hisar	50.04
19.	Naraingarh	61.47	53.	Hodal	49.09
20.	Ganaur	61.07	54.	Narnaund	47.81
21.	Panchkula	61.00	55.	Adampur	46.45
22.	Rohtak	60.25	56.	Asandh	46.20
23.	Dadri	59.78	57.	Kaithal	45.76
24.	Thanesar	59.50	58.	Punahana	44.40
25.	Samalkha	59.43	59.	Tohana	43.34
26.	Ballabgarh	58.80	60.	Fatehabad	43.05
27.	Faridabad	58.67	61.	Sirsa	42.23
28.	Gohana	58.51	62.	Narwana	42.03
29.	Chhachhrauli	57.50	63.	Guhla	41.02
30.	Bhiwani	57.18	64.	Dabwali	41.01
31.	Shahbad	56.97	65.	Ellenabad	40.30
32.	Maham	56.43	66.	Rania	39.57
33.	Panipat	55.92	67.	Ratia	34.74

Source: Computed from Census of India (2001), *Primary Census Abstract*, Haryana, Series 7, Tables A5-A8, Directorate of Census Operations, Haryana.

Note: Tehsils are arranged in descending order of literacy rate, 2001.

On the basis of total scheduled castes literacy, the tehsils of Haryana can be divided into five categories (Map 6.1). These are as under:

1. Areas of Very High Scheduled Castes Literacy Rate (> 66 per cent);
2. Areas of High Scheduled Castes Literacy Rate (58–66 per cent);
3. Areas of Moderate Scheduled Castes Literacy Rate (50–58 per cent);
4. Areas of Low Scheduled Castes Literacy Rate (42–50 per cent); and
5. Areas of Very Low Scheduled Castes Literacy Rate (< 42 per cent).

1. *Areas of Very High Scheduled Castes Literacy Rate (66 per cent and above)*

Six tehsils come under this category and cover only 5.88 per cent area of the State. Gurgaon tehsil has highest scheduled castes literacy rate (69.35 per cent) and is followed by the tehsils of Rewari (69.32 per cent), Pataudi (68.03 per cent), Kosli (67.69 per cent), Kalka (67.30 per cent) and Bawal (66.51 per cent).

High scheduled castes literacy rate in these tehsils is because these are industrially developed, economically sound and also have the favourable impact of the peripheral location of the National and State capitals of New Delhi and Chandigarh respectively. In addition, early start of education, high job opportunities and well developed transportation network have also helped in the growth of literacy rate.

2. *Areas of High Scheduled Castes Literacy Rate (58–66 per cent)*

Twenty-two tehsils fall under this category and cover 32.89 per cent area of the State. These are Samalkha (59.43 per cent), Ganaur (61.07 per cent), Sonipat (65.41 per cent), Kharkhoda (61.54 per cent), and Bahadurgarh (63.55 per cent) tehsils in eastern region; Jhajjar (61.68 per cent), Dadri (59.78 per cent), Beri (62.40 per cent), Rohtak (60.25 per cent), and Gohana (58.51 per cent) tehsils in central region; Faridabad (58.67 per cent), Ballabgarh (58.80 per cent),

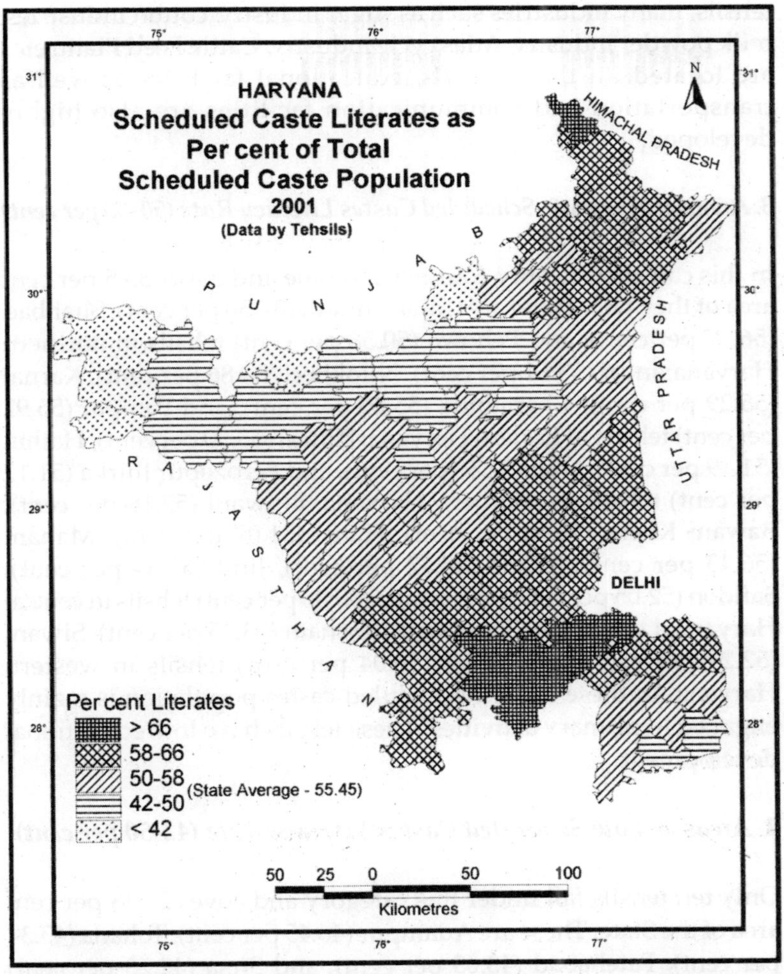

Map 6.1: Haryana: Scheduled Caste Literates as Per cent of Total Scheduled Castes Population, 2001

Sohna (64.38 per cent), Taoru (64.24 per cent), Narnaul (63.44 per cent), and Mahendragarh (63.89 per cent) tehsils in southern region; Thanesar (59.50 per cent), Jagadhri (63.66 per cent), Barara (63.92 per cent), Ambala (63.59 per cent), Naraingarh (61.47 per cent), and Panchkula (61.00 per cent) tehsils in northern region. These tehsils are economically sound and industrially developed. In these tehsils, many industries such as sugar industry, cotton industries, milk powder industry, Atlas cycle industry, Cattle Feed Plant, etc., are located. In these tehsils, educational facilities as well as transportation and communication facilities are also highly developed.

3. *Areas of Moderate Scheduled Castes Literacy Rate (50-58 per cent)*

In this category, twenty-four tehsils come and cover 33.5 per cent area of the State. These are Chhachhrauli (57.50 per cent), Shahbad (56.97 per cent), and Pehowa (50.56 per cent) tehsils in northern Haryana; Indri (55.61 per cent), Nilokheri (54.86 per cent), Karnal (55.29 per cent), Gharaunda (55.20 per cent), and Panipat (55.92 per cent) tehsils in Eastern Haryana; Palwal (55.50 per cent), Hathin (51.19 per cent), Nuh (52.58 per cent), and Ferozepur Jhirka (51.12 per cent) tehsils in southern Haryana; Bhiwani (57.18 per cent), Bawani Khera (52.68 per cent), Hansi (51.07 per cent), Maham (56.43 per cent), Julana (55.72 per cent), Jind (53.34 per cent), Safidon (52.05 per cent), and Israna (55.36 per cent) tehsils in central Haryana; Loharu (54.29 per cent), Tosham (53.15 per cent), Siwani (52.29 per cent), and Hisar (50.04 per cent) tehsils in western Haryana. In these tehsils, scheduled castes population is mainly engaged in primary activities. These tehsils have low educational development.

4. *Areas of Low Scheduled Castes Literacy Rate (42-50 per cent)*

Only ten tehsils fall under this category and cover 20.48 per cent area of the State. These are Adampur (46.45 per cent), Tohana (43.34 per cent), Fatehabad (43.05 per cent), and Sirsa (42.23 per cent) tehsils in western part; Narnaund (47.81 per cent), Narwana (42.03 per cent), Kaithal (45.76 per cent) and Assandh (46.20 per cent) tehsils in central part; Hodal (49.09 per cent), and Punahana (44.40 per cent) tehsils in southern part.

The low literacy rates in these tehsils are attributed to large concentration of scheduled castes population and their backwardness both socially and economically. Because, most of the scheduled castes people in these tehsils are agricultural labourers and they have no work during a major part of the year.

5. *Areas of Very Low Scheduled Castes Literacy Rate (42 per cent and below)*

Only five tehsils come under this category and cover only 7.25 per cent area of the State. Ratia tehsil of Fatehabad district has the lowest scheduled castes literacy rate (34.74 per cent) and is followed by Rania (39.57 per cent), Ellenabad (40.30 per cent), and Dabwali (41.01 per cent) tehsils of Sirsa district in western part; and Guhla (41.02 per cent) tehsil of Kaithal district in northern part of the State.

These tehsils are backward in agriculture as well as in industry. Due to lack of industrialization in these tehsils, most of the people are engaged in agriculture. But agricultural operations are such that these do not have any demand of education resulting into the low level of literacy. The size of land holding is relatively large and with recent intensification of agriculture, demand for labour to work in the fields has increased. This keeps away many children especially those belonging to scheduled castes, from attending a school (Krishan and Chandna, 1974b). In addition to, lack of awareness, association with menial jobs and restrictions to participate in economically gainful activities are the reasons of low scheduled castes literacy.

6.2 Literacy among Non-Scheduled Castes

In 2001 census, 70.81 per cent of the non-scheduled castes population was able to read and write (Table 6.3). Here both the male and female literacy rates were higher in comparison to scheduled castes population.

On the basis of total non-scheduled castes literacy rates, tehsils of the State can be divided into five categories (Map 6.2). These are:

1. Areas of Very High Non-Scheduled Castes Literacy Rate (82 per cent and above);
2. Areas of High Non-Scheduled Castes Literacy Rate (71-82 per cent);
3. Areas of Moderate Non-Scheduled Castes Literacy Rate (60-71 per cent); and
4. Areas of Low Non-Scheduled Castes Literacy Rate (49-60 per cent).

5. Areas of Very Low Non-Scheduled Castes Literacy Rate (49 per cent and below).

1. Areas of Very High Non-Scheduled Castes Literacy Rate (82 per cent and above)

Only two tehsils come under this category. Gurgaon (82.50 per cent) and Ambala (82.22 per cent) cover 3.27 per cent of area of the State. Both of these tehsils are highly urbanized and industrialized. The level of urbanization in Gurgaon and Ambala tehsils is 39.55 per cent and 51.69 per cent respectively as against the State average of 28.92 per cent in 2001. Gurgaon tehsil has the highest level of literacy (82.50 per cent), because this is industrially developed, economically sound and also has the favourable impact of National capital of New Delhi. The proximity of Ambala tehsil to the Union Territory of Chandigarh has added a new dimension to the process of propagation of literacy and education in this area.

Besides, there are several other factors which are responsible for the higher level of literacy in these sub-regions. The availability of educational institutions in large number, high job opportunities, high standard of living, and well developed means of transportation and communication are such factors.

2. Areas of High Non-Scheduled Castes Literacy Rate (71-82 per cent)

Twenty-five thesils come under this category and cover 36.61 per cent area of the State. These are Faridabad (80.01 per cent), Sohna (71.96 per cent), Pataudi (76.30 per cent), Rewari (78.21 per cent), Kosli (75.70 per cent), and Mahendragarh (71.88 per cent) tehsils in southern Haryana; Bahadurgarh (77.37 per cent), Kharkhoda (71.26 per cent), Sonipat (78.62 per cent), Ganaur (71.50 per cent), Panipat (74.43 per cent), and Karnal (74.45 per cent) tehsils in eastern Haryana; Pehowa (71.95 per cent), Thanesar (74.25 per cent), Shahbad (76.48 per cent), Barara (76.81 per cent), Jagadhri (76.77 per cent), Panchkula (76.44 per cent), and Kalka (74.34 per cent) tehsils in northern Haryana; Gohana (72.04 per cent), Rohtak (78.45 per cent), Beri (74.22 per cent), Jhajjar (71.70 per cent), Dadri (71.24 per cent) and Bhiwani (73.23 per cent) tehsils in central Haryana. Development in agriculture, industries, transportation and communication system is the main reason for high literacy in these tehsils.

Table 6.3: Haryana: Literacy Rates of Non-Scheduled Castes by Tehsils, 2001

Sr. No.	*State/Tehsil*	*Literacy Rate (Per cent)*	*Sr. No.*	*Tehsil*	*Literacy Rate (Per cent)*
	Haryana	**70.81**	34.	Naraingarh	70.26
1.	Gurgaon	82.50	35.	Jind	69.60
2.	Ambala	82.22	36.	Julana	68.96
3.	Faridabad	80.01	37.	Sirsa	68.78
4.	Sonipat	78.62	38.	Palwal	68.13
5.	Rohtak	78.45	39.	Hansi	68.02
6.	Rewari	78.21	40.	Bawani Khera	67.88
7.	Bahadurgarh	77.37	41.	Israna	67.50
8.	Barara	76.81	42.	Ballabgarh	66.94
9.	Jagadhri	76.77	43.	Safidon	66.87
10.	Shahbad	76.48	44.	Gharaunda	66.68
11.	Panchkula	76.44	45.	Assandh	66.31
12.	Pataudi	76.30	46.	Loharu	66.06
13.	Kosli	75.70	47.	Dabwali	66.01
14.	Karnal	74.45	48.	Samalkha	65.99
15.	Panipat	74.43	49.	Rania	65.82
16.	Kalka	74.34	50.	Hodal	65.52
17.	Thanesar	74.25	51.	Tohana	65.39
18.	Beri	74.22	52.	Tosham	65.12
19.	Bhiwani	73.23	53.	Siwani	64.11
20.	Gohana	72.04	54.	Adampur	63.96
21.	Sohna	71.96	55.	Fatehabad	63.66
22.	Pehowa	71.95	56.	Ratia	63.19
23.	Mahendragarh	71.88	57.	Kaithal	62.94
24.	Jhajjar	71.70	58.	Narnaund	62.67
25.	Ganaur	71.50	59.	Ellenabad	62.47
26.	Kharkhoda	71.26	60.	Guhla	62.32
27.	Dadri	71.24	61.	Chhachhrauli	60.47
28.	Hisar	70.80	62.	Narwana	59.12
29.	Indri	70.77	63.	Taoru	56.16
30.	Nilokheri	70.77	64.	Hathin	45.01
31.	Maham	70.46	65.	Nuh	44.33
32.	Narnaul	70.45	66.	Ferozepur Jhirka	39.20
33.	Bawal	70.36	67.	Punahana	37.00

Source: Computed from, Census of India (2001), *Primary Census Abstract*, Haryana, Series 7, Tables A5-A8, Directorate of Census Operations, Haryana.

Note: Tehsils are arranged in descending order of literacy rate, 2001.

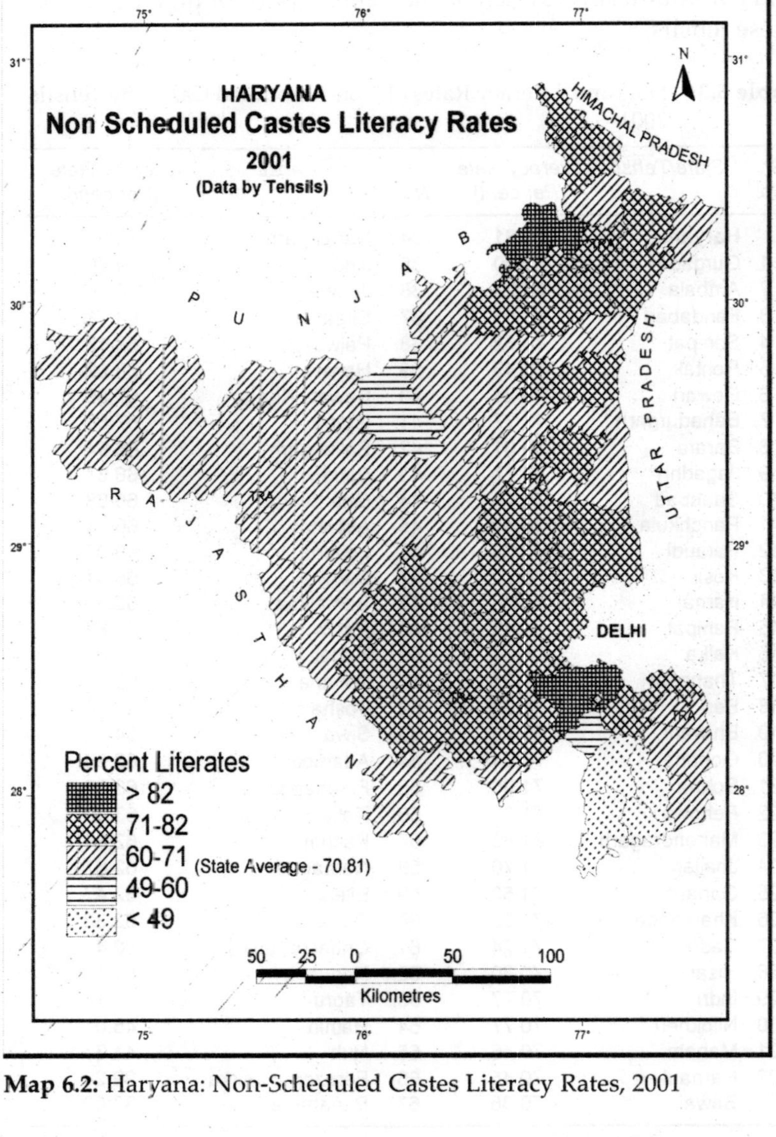

Map 6.2: Haryana: Non-Scheduled Castes Literacy Rates, 2001

3. *Areas of Moderate Non-Scheduled Castes Literacy Rate (60-71 per cent)*

Thirty-four tehsils come under this category and cover

53.25 per cent area of the State. These are Dabwali (66.01 per cent), Rania (65.82 per cent), Ellenabad (62.47 per cent), Sirsa (68.78 per cent), Fatehabad (63.66 per cent), Ratia (63.19 per cent), Tohana (65.39 per cent), Adampur (63.96 per cent), Hisar (70.80 per cent), Siwani (64.11 per cent), Tosham (65.12 per cent), and Loharu (66.06 per cent) tehsils in western part; Indri (70.77 per cent), Nilokheri (70.77 per cent), Gharaunda (66.68 per cent), and Samalkha (65.99 per cent) tehsils in eastern part; Naraingarh (70.26 per cent), Chhachhrauli (60.47 per cent), and Guhla (62.32 per cent) tehsils in northern part; Kaithal (62.94 per cent), Assandh (66.31 per cent), Safidon (66.87 per cent), Israna (67.50 per cent), Jind (69.60 per cent), Julana (68.96 per cent), Narnaund (62.67 per cent), Hansi (68.02 per cent), Bawani Khera (67.88 per cent), and Maham (70.46 per cent) tehsils in central part; Narnaul (70.45 per cent), Bawal (70.36 per cent), Palwal (68.13 per cent), Ballabgarh (66.94 per cent), and Hodal (65.52 per cent) tehsils in southern part of the State.

In all these tehsils, population is engaged in primary activities. Here, prejudices against the females' mobility and education, low degree of urbanization are other factors affecting the literacy among non-scheduled castes.

In addition to, the western and central regions have primarily agrarian economy, lacking in industrial development, educational facilities and are characterized with socio-economic backwardness of the people. The effect of Muslim population, in rural areas, above the State average (3.96 per cent) in some of the tehsils like Chhachhrauli (26.27 per cent), Samalkha (9.67 per cent), Hodal (9.07 per cent), Kalka (5.43 per cent), Palwal (5.47 per cent), and Gharaunda (4.86 per cent) cannot be ignored in reducing the non-scheduled castes literacy rate to moderate level, especially in rural areas.

4. *Areas of Low Non-Scheduled Castes Literacy Rate (49-61 per cent)*

Only two tehsils of Narwana (59.12 per cent) and Taoru (56.16 per cent) come under this category and cover only 3.11 per cent of area of the State. Both tehsils have also low general literacy rate and people are mainly engaged in primary activities and are characterized with low status of woman in society.

5. *Areas of Very Low Non-Scheduled Castes Literacy Rate (49 per cent and below)*

Only four tehsils of Hathin (45.01 per cent), Nuh (44.33 per cent), Ferozepur Jhirkha (39.20 per cent) and Punahana (37.00 per cent) are characterized with very low literacy rate among the non-scheduled castes population. These tehsils cover 3.76 per cent area of the State. Punahana tehsil has the lowest literacy rate amongst all tehsils of Haryana. All these tehsils are located in the southern part of the State. Very low literacy rates in these tehsils are mainly because of the dominance of Meo-Muslim population among non-scheduled castes and are also characterized with low levels of urbanization and industrialization alongwith poor development of educational institutions.

6.3 Literacy Disparity between Scheduled Castes and Non-Scheduled Castes

In 2001, the index of literacy disparity between non-scheduled castes and scheduled castes population is 0.1550. It is highest in Ratia tehsil (0.3419) and negative in Ferozepur Jhirka tehsil (–0.1488) (Table 6.4). The highest index in Ratia is due to low rates of general literacy, widespread poverty, prevalent socio-economc segregation, lack of employment opportunities and strong feeling of insecurity particularly among rural females. The negative index of Ferozepur Jhirka tehsil was associated with high concentration of Muslim population among non-scheduled castes.

6.3.1 Spatial Pattern

It is noticed wide regional variations in the index of literacy disparity between non-scheduled castes and scheduled castes population.

On the basis of State average, i.e., 0.1550, five types of areas can be classified (Map 6.3):

1. Areas of Very High Disparity in Literacy (0.2501 and above);
2. Areas of High Disparity in Literacy (0.1701-0.2500);
3. Areas of Moderate Disparity in Literacy (0.0901-0.1700);

Table 6.4: Haryana: Literacy Disparity between Non-Scheduled Castes and Scheduled Castes Population by Tehsils, 2001

Sr. No.	*State/Tehsil*	*Disparity Index*	*Sr. No.*	*Tehsil*	*Disparity Index*
	Haryana	**0.1550**	34.	Gohana	0.1340
1.	Ratia	0.3419	35.	Bahadurgarh	0.1319
2.	Rania	0.2985	36.	Palwal	0.1288
3.	Sirsa	0.2919	37.	Jagadhri	0.1253
4.	Dabwali	0.2811	38.	Tosham	0.1251
5.	Ellenabad	0.2552	39.	Sonipat	0.1248
6.	Tohana	0.2475	40.	Siwani	0.1248
7.	Guhla	0.2442	41.	Israna	0.1241
8.	Fatehabad	0.2310	42.	Barara	0.1230
9.	Asandh	0.2177	43.	Loharu	0.1217
10.	Hisar	0.2154	44.	Gurgaon	0.1215
11.	Faridabad	0.2058	45.	Gharaunda	0.1179
12.	Narwana	0.1979	46.	Beri	0.1143
13.	Shahbad	0.1916	47.	Dadri	0.1133
14.	Adampur	0.1916	48.	Ganaur	0.1024
15.	Karnal	0.1909	49.	Jhajjar	0.0980
16.	Kaithal	0.1896	50.	Kharkhoda	0.0953
17.	Panipat	0.1840	51.	Naraingarh	0.0866
18.	Hansi	0.1769	52.	Rewari	0.0830
19.	Ambala	0.1754	53.	Ballabgarh	0.0821
20.	Rohtak	0.1752	54.	Pataudi	0.0779
21.	Pehowa	0.1750	55.	Mahendragarh	0.0774
22.	Jind	0.1666	56.	Kosli	0.0757
23.	Narnaund	0.1621	57.	Sohna	0.0733
24.	Nilokheri	0.1610	58.	Narnaul	0.0685
25.	Bhiwani	0.1592	59.	Kalka	0.0669
26.	Bawani Khera	0.1574	60.	Samalkha	0.0663
27.	Safidon	0.1547	61.	Bawal	0.0372
28.	Indri	0.1529	62.	Chhachhrauli	0.0310
29.	Panchkula	0.1492	63.	Hathin	–0.0736
30.	Hodal	0.1455	64.	Taoru	–0.0835
31.	Thanesar	0.1444	65.	Nuh	–0.0978
32.	Maham	0.1411	66.	Punahana	–0.0994
33.	Julana	0.1344	67.	Ferozepur Jhirka	–0.1488

Source: Computed from Census of India (2001), *Primary Census Abstract*, Haryana, Series 7, Tables A5-A8, Directorate of Census Operations, Haryana.

Note: Tehsils are arranged in descending order of disparity index, 2001.

4. Areas of Low Disparity in Literacy (0.0100-0.0900); and
5. Areas of Negative Disparity in Literacy where the literacy among Non-Scheduled Castes was relatively lower than that among Scheduled Castes.

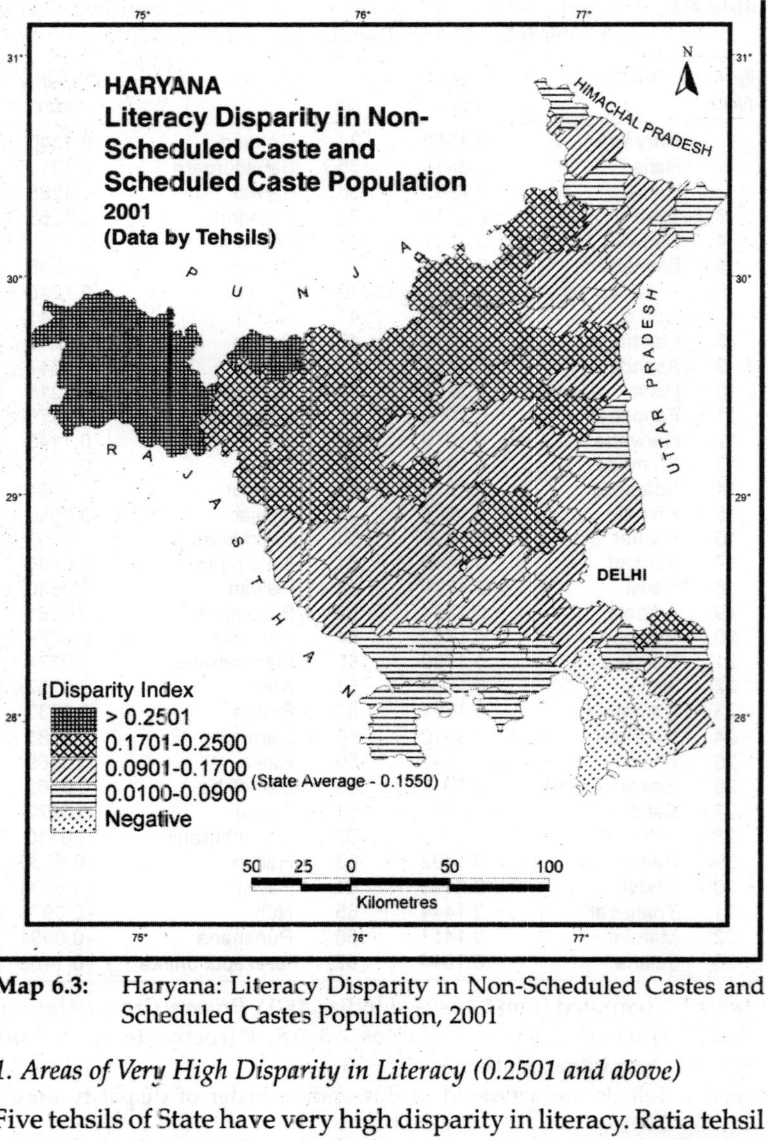

Map 6.3: Haryana: Literacy Disparity in Non-Scheduled Castes and Scheduled Castes Population, 2001

1. Areas of Very High Disparity in Literacy (0.2501 and above)

Five tehsils of State have very high disparity in literacy. Ratia tehsil of Fatehabad district has the highest disparity in literacy (0.3419), and is followed by Rania (0.2985), Sirsa (0.2919), Dabwali (0.2811), and Ellenabad (0.2552) tehsils, all are situated in the western part of the State. Very high disparity in literacy is mainly because of the high proportion of scheduled castes population in these tehsils.

This social group lags much behind in the race of socio-economic development. Very high literacy differential is also related to poverty, less developed agriculture, low standard of living, low per capita income, less educational facilities, less developed means of transportation and industrialization, and rigid caste system, subsistence farm economy, low degree of urbanization, involvement of large proportion of scheduled castes population as agricultural labour in construction activity and informal service sector.

2. *Areas of High Disparity in Literacy (0.1701-0.2500)*

Sixteen tehsils have experienced high disparity in literacy. These are Tohana (0.2475), Fatehabad (0.2310), Hisar (0.2154), and Adampur (0.1916) tehsils in western part; Guhla (0.2442), Kaithal (0.1896), Assandh (0.2177), Narwana (0.1979), Hansi (0.1769), and Rohtak (0.1752) tehsils in central part; Pehowa (0.1750), Shahbad (0.1916), and Ambala (0.1754) tehsils in northern part; Karnal (0.1909), and Panipat (0.1840) tehsils in eastern part; Faridabad (0.2058) tehsil in southern part of the State.

These areas of high disparity in literacy are the result of low degree of urbanization and industrialization, high proportion of scheduled castes population, and deep roots of caste system either by natural growth rate or by immigration.

3. *Areas of Moderate Disparity in Literacy (0.0901-0.1700)*

There are 29 tehsils which have moderate disparity in literacy. These include Jind (0.1666), Safidon (0.1547), Julana (0.1344), Narnund (0.1621), Bawani Khera (0.1574), Bhiwani (0.1592), Dadri (0.1133), Jhajjar (0.0980), Beri (0.1143), Maham (0.1411), Gohana (0.1340), and Israna (0.1241) tehsils in central part; Indri (0.1529), Nilokhera (0.1610), Gharaunda (0.1179), Ganaur (0.1024), Sonipat (0.1248), Kharkhoda (0.0953), and Bahadurgarh (0.1319) tehsils in eastern part; Panchkula (0.1492), Barara (0.1230), Jagadhri (0.1253), and Thanesar (0.1444) tehsils in northern part; Hodal (0.1455), Palwal (0.1288), and Gurgaon (0.1215) tehsils in southern part; Tosham (0.1251), Siwani (0.1248), and Loharu (0.1217) tehsils in western part of the State.

In these tehsils, increasing awareness among all the sections of society, development of means of transportation and industrialization, high proportion of workers engaged in non-agricultural activities, expansion of educational facilities, and increasing degree of urban-rural interaction had caused moderate disparity in literacy.

4. Areas of Low Disparity in Literacy (0.0100-0.0900)

Only twelve tehsils has low disparity in literacy. These include Kalka (0.0669), Naraingarh (0.0866), and Chhachhrauli (0.0310) tehsils in northern region; Narnaul (0.0685), Mahendragarh (0.0774), Kosli (0.0757), Rewari (0.0830), Bawal (0.0372), Pataudi (0.0779), Sohna (0.0733), and Ballabgarh (0.0821) tehsils in southern region; Samalkha (0.0663) tehsil in eastern region of the State.

The main reasons of low disparity in these tehsils are: high literacy rate among the scheduled castes, improved standard of living, commercialization of agriculture, expansion of employment opportunities, high mobility and awareness among people in rural areas and developed means of transportation.

5. Areas of Negative Disparity in Literacy

Only five tehsils of Hathin (–0.0736), Taoru (–0.0835), Nuh (–0.0978), Punahana (–0.0994), and Ferozepur Jhirka (-0.1488) have experienced negative disparity in literacy ranging from highest (–0.0736) in Hathin tehsil to lowest (–0.1488) in Ferozepur Jhirka tehsil. In all these tehsils, the scheduled castes literacy was higher than non-scheduled castes literacy because of the dominance of Muslims in non-scheduled castes population.

6.4 Scheduled Castes-Non-Scheduled Castes Literacy Disparity among Males

In 2001, the index of literacy disparity between male non-scheduled castes and male scheduled castes population is 0.1331. It is highest in Ratia tehsil (0.2924) and negative in Ferozepur Jhirka (–0.0917) tehsil. The highest index in Ratia is due to low rate of male literacy, lack of employment opportunities, agrarian based economy. The negative index in Ferozepur Jhirka is associated with the dominance of Muslim population among non-scheduled castes in which male literacy is less than the male literacy among the scheduled castes population, because of their more awareness about their rights.

6.4.1 Spatial Pattern

A wide regional variations have been noticed in the index of literacy disparity between male non-scheduled castes and male scheduled castes population. Ratia tehsil displayed the highest disparity index (0.2924), while Bawal tehsil has the lowest disparity index (0.0341).

On the basis of State average, i.e., 0.1331, five types of areas can be classified (Table 6.5 and Map 6.4):

1. Areas of Very High Disparity in Male Literacy, where the index value is more than 0.2201;
2. Areas of High Disparity in Male Literacy, where the index value is between 0.1501-0.2200;
3. Areas of Moderate Disparity in Male Literacy, where the index value is between 0.0801-0.1500;
4. Areas of Low Disparity in Male Literacy, where the index value is between 0.0100-0.0800; and
5. Areas of Negative Disparity in Male Literacy, where the literacy among Non-Scheduled Castes is relatively lower than that among Scheduled Castes.

1. Areas of Very High Disparity in Male Literacy (Above 0.2201)

Out of sixty-seven tehsils, only four tehsils are having literacy disparity among males above 0.2201. Ratia tehsil has the highest male literacy disparity (0.2924) and is followed by Dabwali (0.2726), Sirsa (0.2685), and Rania (0.2626) tehsils. The main causes for very high literacy disparity among males in these tehsils are of their agrarian economy, availability of less educational facilities, low level of urbanisation, and high proportion of scheduled castes population.

2. Areas of High Disparity in Male Literacy (0.1501-0.2200)

Thirteen tehsils are characterized by high disparity in literacy between male non-scheduled castes and male scheduled castes.

Table 6.5: Literacy Disparity among Male Non-Scheduled Castes and Male Scheduled Castes Population by Tehsils, 2001

Sr. No.	State/Tehsil	Disparity Index	Sr. No.	Tehsil	Disparity Index
	Haryana	**0.1331**	34.	Loharu	0.1256
1.	Ratia	0.2924	35.	Maham	0.1254
2.	Dabwali	0.2726	36.	Thanesar	0.1144
3.	Sirsa	0.2685	37.	Panchkula	0.1099
4.	Rania	0.2626	38.	Palwal	0.1090
5.	Tohana	0.2084	39.	Dadri	0.1088
6.	Fatehabad	0.2080	40.	Gohana	0.1083
7.	Ellenabad	0.2063	41.	Israna	0.1049
8.	Narwana	0.1954	42.	Bahadurgarh	0.1045
9.	Guhla	0.1951	43.	Beri	0.0952
10.	Adampur	0.1927	44.	Gharaunda	0.0929
11.	Assandh	0.1919	45.	Barara	0.0927
12.	Hisar	0.1879	46.	Sonipat	0.0925
13.	Kaithal	0.1760	47.	Jagadhri	0.0891
14.	Narnaund	0.1581	48.	Ganaur	0.0852
15.	Shahbad	0.1578	49.	Gurgaon	0.0751
16.	Karnal	0.1548	50.	Kharkhoda	0.0722
17.	Hansi	0.1516	51.	Ballabgarh	0.0702
18.	Faridabad	0.1498	52.	Mahendragarh	0.0668
19.	Jhajjar	0.1471	53.	Naraingarh	0.0659
20.	Jind	0.1471	54.	Kosli	0.0596
21.	Bawani Khera	0.1466	55.	Sohna	0.0546
22.	Pehowa	0.1458	56.	Narnaul	0.0530
23.	Rohtak	0.1430	57.	Rewari	0.0518
24.	Bhiwani	0.1415	58.	Pataudi	0.0511
25.	Nilokheri	0.1369	59.	Kalka	0.0476
26.	Ambala	0.1365	60.	Samalkha	0.0441
27.	Panipat	0.1339	61.	Chhachhrauli	0.0341
28.	Tosham	0.1339	62.	Bawal	0.0227
29.	Safidon	0.1313	63.	Nuh	–0.0424
30.	Siwani	0.1299	64.	Hathin	–0.0447
31.	Julana	0.1291	65.	Punahana	–0.0516
32.	Hodal	0.1287	66.	Taoru	–0.0601
33.	Indri	0.1285	67.	Ferozepur Jhirka	–0.0917

Source: Computed from, Census of India (2001), *Primary Census Abstract*, Haryana, Series 7, Tables A5-A8, Directorate of Census Operations, Haryana.

Note: Tehsils are arranged in descending order of disparity index, 2001.

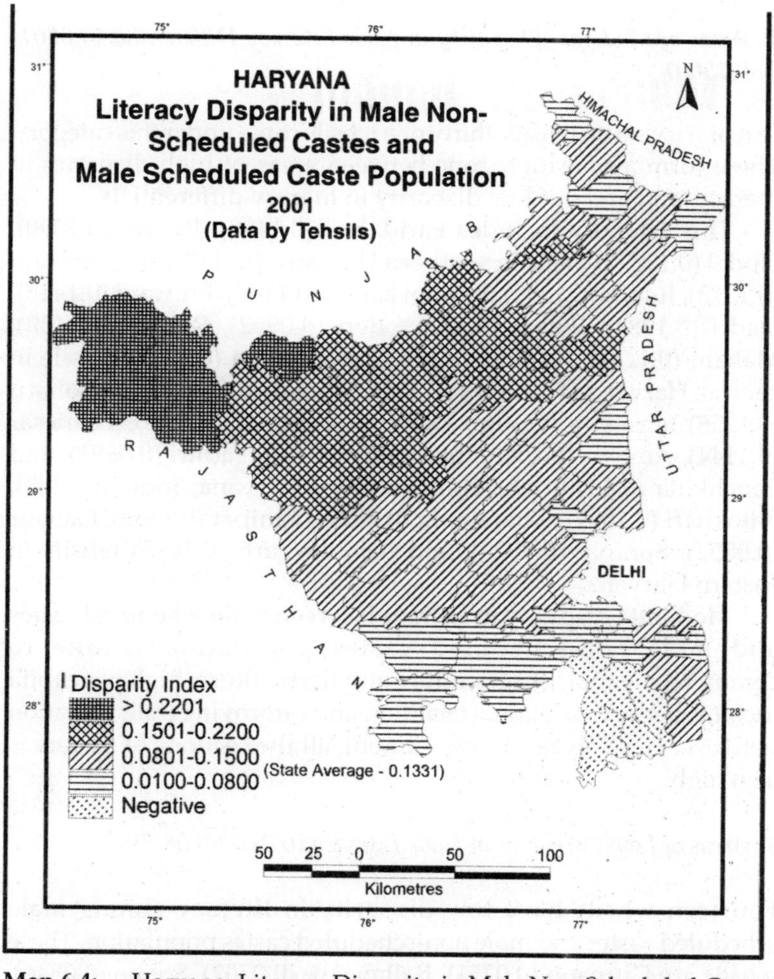

Map 6.4: Haryana: Literacy Disparity in Male Non-Scheduled Castes and Male Scheduled Castes Population, 2001

These are Tohana (0.2084), Fatehabad (0.2080), Adampur (0.1927), Hisar (0.1879), and Ellenabad (0.2063) tehsils in western part; Hansi (0.1516), Narnaund (0.1581), Narwana (0.1954), Kaithal (0.1760), and Assandh (0.1919) tehsils in central part; Guhla (0.1951), and Shahbad (0.1578) tehsils in northern part, Karnal (0.1548) tehsil in eastern part of the State. These tehsils also have agriculture based economy, and high proportion of scheduled castes population.

3. Areas of Moderate Disparity in Male Literacy Differential (0.0801-0.1500)

Out of sixty seven tehsils, thirty one tehsils come under this category. These form a transition zone between areas of high disparity in literacy and areas of low disparity in literacy differentials.

This category includes Faridabad (0.1498), Palwal (0.1090), Hodal (0.1287) tehsils in southern Haryana; Jind (0.1471), Safidon (0.1313), Julana (0.1291), Bawani Khera (0.1466), Bhiwani (0.1415), Dadri (0.1088), Jhajjar (0.1471), Beri (0.0952), Rohtak (0.1430), Maham (0.1254), Gohana (0.1083), and Israna (0.1049) tehsils in central Haryana; Tosham (0.1339), Siwani (0.1299), and Loharu (0.1256) tehsils in western Haryana; Pehowa (0.1458), Thanesar (0.1144), Ambala (0.1365), Barara (0.0927), Jagadhri (0.0891), and Panchkula (0.1099) tehsils in northern Haryana; Indri (0.1285), Nilokheri (0.1369), Gharaunda (0.0929), Panipat (0.1339), Ganaur (0.0852), Sonipat (0.0925), and Bahadurgarh (0.1045) tehsils in eastern Haryana.

Moderate disparity in literacy between male scheduled castes and male non-scheduled castes population is due to commercialization of agriculture and horticulture, high per capita income, better educational facilities, and improving transportation network. Here, the awareness among all the sections of society is also high.

4. Areas of Low Disparity in Male Literacy (0.0100-0.0800)

Fourteen tehsils have low disparity in literacy among male scheduled castes and male non-scheduled castes population. These tehsils are Gurgaon (0.0751), Ballabgarh (0.0702), Sohna (0.0546), Pataudi (0.0511) in south east; Kharkhoda (0.0722), Samalkha (0.0441) in east; Mahendragarh (0.0668), Kosli (0.0596), Narnaul (0.0530), Rewari (0.0518), Bawal (0.0227) in south; Naraingarh (0.0659), Kalka (0.0476), and Chhachhrauli (0.0341) in northern parts of the State.

All these tehsils are characterized by early start of education, and have better educational facilities. A more socio-economic awareness has also helped in reducing literacy disparity between male scheduled castes and male non-scheduled castes population.

5. Areas of Negative Disparity in Male Literacy

Only five tehsils have negative disparity in literacy where male scheduled castes literacy rate is more than the male non-scheduled castes literacy rate. Ferozepur Jhirka tehsil has the lowest negative disparity in literacy (–0.0917) and is followed by the tehsils of Taoru (–0.0601), Punahana (–0.0516), Hathin (–0.0447), and Nuh (–0.0424). Here, the scheduled castes literacy rate among males is higher than that of non-scheduled castes male literacy rate because of the dominance of Muslim population among non-scheduled castes.

6.5 Scheduled Castes-Non-Scheduled Castes Literacy Disparity among Females

In 2001, the index of female literacy disparity between non-scheduled castes and scheduled castes population is 0.1923. It is highest in Ratia tehsil (0.4236) and the lowest in Chhachhrauli tehsil (0.0316). Wide regional variations have been noticed in the index of female literacy disparity between non-scheduled castes and scheduled castes population. On the basis of female literacy disparity among scheduled castes and non-scheduled castes population, the tehsils of Haryana can be categorized into five parts (Table 6.6 and Map 6.5). These are:

1. Areas of Very High Disparity in Female Literacy, where the index value is more than 0.3201;
2. Areas of High Disparity in Female Literacy, where the index value is between 0.2201-0.3200;
3. Areas of Moderate Disparity in Female Literacy, where the index value is between 0.1201-0.2200;
4. Areas of Low Disparity in Female Literacy, where the index value is between 0.0200-0.1200; and
5. Areas of Negative Disparity in Female Literacy, where literacy among non-Scheduled Castes is relatively lower than that among Scheduled Castes.

1. Areas of Very High Disparity in Female Literacy (Above 0.3201)

Only four tehsils have very high literacy disparity index. Ratia tehsil has the highest female literacy disparity (0.4236) and is followed by Rania (0.3628), Sirsa (0.3337), and Guhla (0.3244) tehsils. These tehsils have very high literacy disparity index because of the high concentration of scheduled castes (above 25 per cent) in these tehsils, low status granted to women in general and of deprived sections like scheduled castes in particular, the prevalence of early marriage, prejudices against females' mobility, education and employment, and low degree of occupational participation among females. The tehsils also have the farm-based economy warranting little technical skill and are lacking in employment opportunities.

2. *Areas of High Disparity in Female Literacy (0.2201-0.3200)*

Fourteen tehsils of the State come under this category. These are Tohana (0.3111), Fatehabad (0.2805), Hisar (0.2621), Ellenabad (0.3044), and Dabwali (0.3010) tehsils in western region; Panipat (0.2567), and Karnal (0.2454) tehsils in eastern region; Ambala (0.2245), Shahbad (0.2407), and Pehowa (0.2214) tehsils in northern region; Faridabad (0.2958) tehsil in southern region; Kaithal (0.2249), Assandh (0.2680), and Rohtak (0.2251) tehsils in central region of the State.

Most of these tehsils have proportion of scheduled castes more than the State average (19.35 per cent) and are characterised with farm-based economy warranting little technical skill. In addition, low status granted to women of deprived sections like scheduled castes in comparison to men, the prevalence of early marriage especially among girls, prejudices against females' mobility, education and employment, appalling poverty of scheduled castes especially in rural areas, high cost of education, limited availability of schooling facilities, and less opportunities to participate in the family's economic struggle are the factors responsible for high disparity in female literacy (Sangwan, *et al.*, 2011).

3. *Areas of Moderate Disparity in Female Literacy (0.1201-0.2200)*

Thirty-three tehsils of the State fall under this category. These are Narwana (0.2169), Jind (0.2059), Julana (0.1417), Safidon (0.2010), Israna (0.1624), Gohana (0.1772), Maham (0.1727), Beri (0.1559), Jhajjar (0.1239), Dadri (0.1340), Bhiwani (0.1954), Bawani Khera (0.1904), Hansi (0.2189), and Narnaund (0.1820) tehsils of central

Table 6.6: Literacy Disparity among Female Non-Scheduled Castes and Female Scheduled Castes Population by Tehsils, 2001

Sr. No.	*State/Tehsil*	*Disparity Index*	*Sr. No.*	*Tehsil*	*Disparity Index*
	Haryana	**0.1923**	34.	Bahadurgarh	0.1749
1.	Ratia	0.4236	35.	Jagadhri	0.1738
2.	Rania	0.3628	36.	Maham	0.1727
3.	Sirsa	0.3337	37.	Palwal	0.1714
4.	Guhla	0.3244	38.	Sonipat	0.1699
5.	Tohana	0.3111	39.	Barara	0.1688
6.	Ellenabad	0.3044	40.	Israna	0.1624
7.	Dabwali	0.3010	41.	Gharaunda	0.1612
8.	Faridabad	0.2958	42.	Beri	0.1559
9.	Fatehabad	0.2805	43.	Julana	0.1417
10.	Assandh	0.2680	44.	Dadri	0.1340
11.	Hisar	0.2621	45.	Ganaur	0.1333
12.	Panipat	0.2567	46.	Loharu	0.1304
13.	Karnal	0.2454	47.	Kharkhoda	0.1298
14.	Shahbad	0.2407	48.	Tosham	0.1298
15.	Rohtak	0.2251	49.	Rewari	0.1287
16.	Kaithal	0.2249	50.	Siwani	0.1283
17.	Ambala	0.2245	51.	Jhajjar	0.1239
18.	Pehowa	0.2214	52.	Pataudi	0.1196
19.	Hansi	0.2189	53.	Naraingarh	0.1186
20.	Narwana	0.2169	54.	Kosli	0.1085
21.	Jind	0.2059	55.	Ballabgarh	0.1042
22.	Adampur	0.2018	56.	Mahendragarh	0.1025
23.	Safidon	0.2010	57.	Sohna	0.1006
24.	Panchkula	0.2002	58.	Samalkha	0.0991
25.	Nilokheri	0.1992	59.	Narnaul	0.0951
26.	Bhiwani	0.1954	60.	Kalka	0.0874
27.	Indri	0.1921	61.	Bawal	0.0647
28.	Hodal	0.1915	62.	Chhachhrauli	0.0316
29.	Bawani Khera	0.1904	63.	Taoru	–0.1303
30.	Thanesar	0.1869	64.	Hathin	–0.1421
31.	Narnaund	0.1820	65.	Nuh	–0.2009
32.	Gurgaon	0.1807	66.	Punahana	–0.2064
33.	Gohana	0.1772	67.	Ferozepur Jhirka	–0.2909

Source: Computed from, Census of India (2001), *Primary Census Abstract*, Haryana, Series 7, Tables A5-A8, Directorate of Census Operations, Haryana.

Note: Tehsils are arranged in descending order of disparity index, 2001.

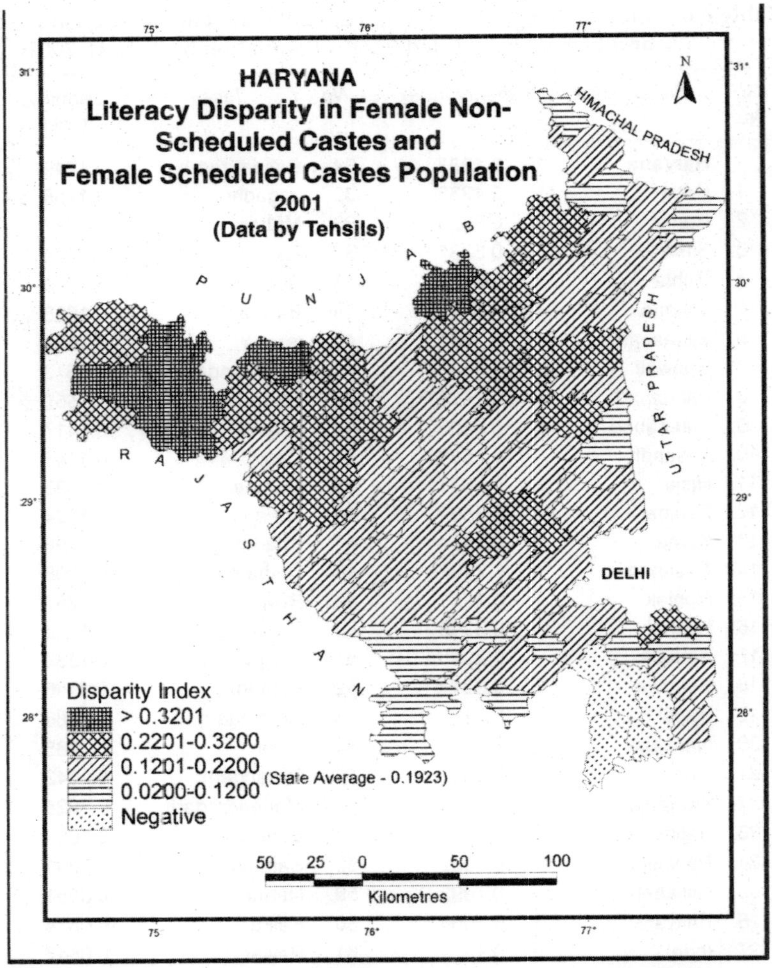

Map 6.5: Haryana: Literacy Disparity in Female Non-Scheduled Castes and Female Scheduled Castes Population, 2001

Haryana; Panchkula (0.2002), Barara (0.1688), Jagadhri (0.1738), and Thanesar (0.1869) tehsils in northern Haryana; Indri (0.1921), Nilokheri (0.1992), Gharaunda (0.1612), Ganaur (0.1333), Sonipat (0.1699), Bahadurgarh (0.1749), and Kharkhoda (0.1298) tehsils in eastern Haryana; Adampur (0.2018), Siwani (0.1283), Tosham (0.1298), and Loharu (0.1304) tehsils in western Haryana; Rewari (0.1287), Gurgaon (0.1807), Palwal (0.1714), and Hodal (0.1915) tehsils in southern Haryana.

In these tehsils, literacy disparity index among female scheduled castes and female non-scheduled castes is moderate due to the rapidly growing urbanization, rapidly increasing proportion of non-agricultural workers, improving means of transportation and communication, increasing participation of women in jobs, decision making, etc.

4. *Areas of Low Disparity in Female Literacy (0.0200-0.1200)*

Eleven tehsils of the State fall under this category. These are Ballabgarh (0.1042), Sohna (0.1006), Pataudi (0.1196), Bawal (0.0647), Kosli (0.1085), Narnaul (0.0951), and Mahendragarh (0.1025) tehsils in southern part; Samalkha (0.0991) tehsil in eastern part; Kalka (0.0874), Naraingarh (0.1186), and Chhachhrauli (0.0316) tehsils in northern part.

Low female literacy disparity index is due to Government policies for the upliftment of females among scheduled castes in particular and non-scheduled castes in general, increasing educational facilities especially for girls, increasing accessibility to schools, increasing socio-economic awareness, and engagement in economically gainful activities (Sangwan, *et al.*, 2011). In addition, sizeable proportion of female Muslim population among females of non-scheduled castes in some tehsils like Chhachhrauli (26.62 per cent), Samalkha (9.88 per cent), Sohna (8.61 per cent), and Ballabgarh (7.22 per cent) is also responsible for low female literacy disparity.

5. *Areas of Negative Disparity in Female Literacy*

Only five tehsils of Taoru (–0.1303), Hathin (–0.1421), Nuh (–0.2009), Punahana (–0.2064), and Ferozepur Jhirka (–0.2909) have experienced negative female literacy disparity index among scheduled castes and non-scheduled castes population. This could be possible because these tehsils have higher female literacy rate among scheduled castes than that of non scheduled castes because of the dominance of Muslims in non-scheduled castes population. Muslim women, generally, are not allowed much mobility and they remain confined to four walls of the house only. Also, it is very rare that a girl is sent to a school in the nearby village, if there was no school in the home village. Moreover, there is lack of educational institutions for the females along with the lack of female teachers.

6.6 Literacy Disparity among Urban Scheduled Castes and Urban Non-Scheduled Castes Population

There are noticed wide regional variations in the disparity index of urban literacy between scheduled castes and non-scheduled castes population. On the basis of disparity index value of urban literacy for the State, i.e., 0.2099, the tehsils of Haryana can be classified into six categories (Table 6.7 and Map 6.6):

1. Areas of Very High Disparity in Urban Literacy, where the index value is more than 0.3201;
2. Areas of High Disparity in Urban Literacy, where the index value is 0.2401-0.3200;
3. Areas of Moderate Disparity in Urban Literacy, where the index value is 0.1601-0.2400;
4. Areas of Low Disparity in Urban Literacy, where the index value is 0.0801-0.1600;
5. Areas of Very Low Disparity in Urban Literacy, where the index value is less than 0.0800; and
6. Totally Rural Areas.

1. Areas of Very High Disparity in Urban Literacy (Above 0.3201)

Only five tehsils of the State come under this category. Rania tehsil of Sirsa district has the highest urban literacy disparity (0.4169) and is followed by Ratia (0.3836), and Sirsa (0.3261) tehsils in western region; Assandh (0.3209) tehsil in central region; and Shahbad (0.3204) tehsil in northern region of the State. These tehsils have very high disparity in urban literacy because these are less urbanized, less industrially developed and having less educational facilities and socio-economic backwardness of the people.

2. Areas of High Disparity in Urban Literacy (0.2401-0.3200)

Only ten tehsils of the State fall under this category. This category includes Tohana (0.3181), Fatehabad (0.2884), Ellenabad (0.2795), Hisar (0.2454), and Tosham (0.2625) tehsils in western part; Guhla

Table 6.7: Literacy Disparity among Urban Non-Scheduled Castes and Urban Scheduled Castes Population by Tehsils, 2001

Sr. No.	*State/Tehsil*	*Disparity Index*	*Sr. No.*	*Tehsil*	*Disparity Index*
	Haryana	**0.2099**	34.	Thanesar	0.1883
1.	Rania	0.4169	35.	Jind	0.1826
2.	Ratia	0.3836	36.	Maham	0.1780
3.	Sirsa	0.3261	37.	Ambala	0.1771
4.	Assandh	0.3209	38.	Beri	0.1713
5.	Shahbad	0.3204	39.	Gurgaon	0.1706
6.	Tohana	0.3181	40.	Samalkha	0.1703
7.	Guhla	0.2916	41.	Jagadhri	0.1697
8.	Fatehabad	0.2884	42.	Sohna	0.1667
9.	Indri	0.281	43.	Sonipat	0.1618
10.	Ellenabad	0.2795	44.	Kharkhoda	0.1618
11.	Narwana	0.2724	45.	Bawani Khera	0.1546
12.	Tosham	0.2625	46.	Gharaunda	0.1524
13.	Kaithal	0.2547	47.	Naraingarh	0.1455
14.	Palwal	0.2537	48.	Ganaur	0.1448
15.	Hisar	0.2454	49.	Narnaund	0.1434
16.	Dadri	0.2371	50.	Taoru	0.1388
17.	Hodal	0.2352	51.	Narnaul	0.1342
18.	Safidon	0.2319	52.	Bahadurgarh	0.1211
19.	Dabwali	0.2301	53.	Ferozepur Jhirka	0.1201
20.	Rohtak	0.2265	54.	Rewari	0.1183
21.	Panchkula	0.2242	55.	Mahendragarh	0.1155
22.	Hansi	0.2198	56.	Loharu	0.1097
23.	Faridabad	0.2183	57.	Kalka	0.0948
24.	Nilokheri	0.2169	58.	Pataudi	0.0843
25.	Pehowa	0.2163	59.	Jhajjar	0.0790
26.	Julana	0.2159	60.	Bawal	0.0685
27.	Chhachhrauli	0.2097	61.	Hathin	0.0541
28.	Karnal	0.2091	62.	Nuh	0.0248
29.	Siwani	0.2022	63.	Barara	Totally Rural
30.	Bhiwani	0.199	64.	Israna	Totally Rural
31.	Gohana	0.1945	65.	Adampur	Totally Rural
32.	Punahana	0.1897	66.	Kosli	Totally Rural
33.	Panipat	0.1886	67.	Ballabgarh	Totally Rural

Source: Computed from, Census of India (2001), *Primary Census Abstract*, Haryana, Series 7, Tables A5-A8, Directorate of Census Operations, Haryana.

Note: Tehsils are arranged in descending order of disparity index, 2001.

(0.2916) tehsil in northern part; Kaithal (0.2547), and Narwana (0.2724) tehsils in north central part; Indri (0.2810) tehsil in eastern part; Palwal (0.2537) tehsil in southern part of the State.

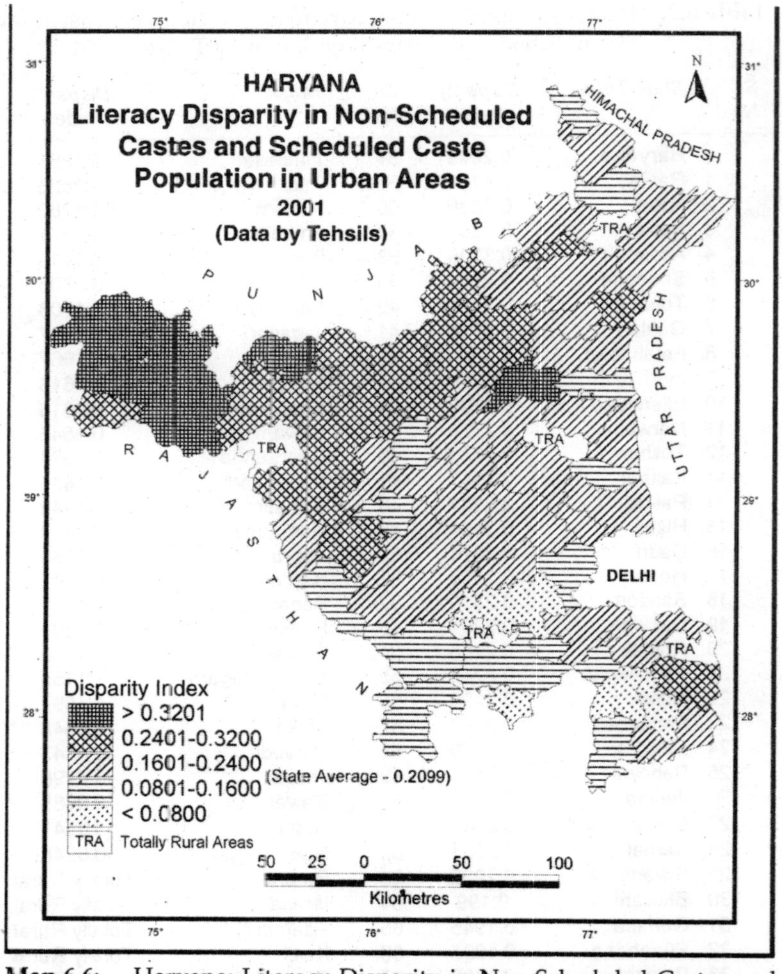

Map 6.6: Haryana: Literacy Disparity in Non-Scheduled Castes and Scheduled Castes Population in Urban Areas, 2001

In these tehsils, scheduled castes population has low level of standard of living and is mainly engaged in agricultural activities. These thesils are also backward in agriculture and industry and are less urbanized, so high disparity in urban literacy is found here.

3. *Areas of Moderate Disparity in Urban Literacy (0.1601-0.2400)*

Twenty-nine tehsils of the State fall under this category. These are

Dadri (0.2371), Bhiwani (0.1990), Beri (0.1713), Rohtak (0.2265), Maham (0.1780), Hansi (0.2198), Julana (0.2159), Jind (0.1826), Safidon (0.2319) and Gohana (0.1945) tehsils in central Haryana; Siwani (0.2022), Dabwali (0.2301) tehsils in western Haryana. Hodal (0.2352), Faridabad (0.2183), Punahana (0.1897), Sohna (0.1667), and Gurgaon (0.1706) tehsils in southern Haryana; Kharkhoda (0.1618), Sonipat (0.1618), Samalkha (0.1703), Panipat (0.1886), Karnal (0.2091), and Nilokheri (0.2169) tehsils in eastern Haryana; Pehowa (0.2163), Thanesar (0.1883), Jagadhri (0.1697), Chhachhrauli (0.2097), Ambala (0.1771), and Panchuka (0.2242) tehsil in northern Haryana.

These tehsils have moderate disparity in urban literacy due to increasing technology in agricultural economy, social awakening among people and improving transport network, and the easy accessibility of educational institutions.

4. *Areas of Low Disparity in Urban Literacy (0.0801-0.1600)*

Fourteen tehsils of the State come under this category. This category includes Bawani Khera (0.1546), and Narnaund (0.1434) tehsils in central part; Gharaunda (0.1524), Ganaur (0.1448), and Bahadurgarh (0.1211) tehsils in eastern part; Naraingarh (0.1455), and Kalka (0.0948) tehsils in northern part; Ferozepur Jhirka (0.1201), Taoru (0.1388), Pataudi (0.0843), Rewari (0.1183), Narnaul (0.1342), and Mahendragarh (0.1155) tehsils in southern part; Loharu (0.1097) tehsil in western part of the State. Here, low disparity in urban literacy is on account of increasing degree of industrialization, developing transportation facilities, increasing accessibility to schools, and increasing educational facilities.

5. *Areas of Very Low Disparity in Urban Literacy, (Below 0.0800)*

Only four tehsils fall under this category. Nuh tehsil has the lowest urban disparity in literacy (0.0248) and is followed by Jhajjar (0.0790), Bawal (0.0685), and Hathin (0.0541) tehsils. Here, very low disparity in urban literacy is because total literacy rate of scheduled castes and non-scheduled castes population is high. Many large and medium scale industries are also located in urban areas.

6. Totally Rural Areas

There are five tehsils, namely Barara of Ambala district, Israna of Panipat district, Adampur of Hisar district, Kosli of Rewari district and Ballabgarh of Faridabad district which are totally rural in character. Hence, no urban-rural disparity exists in literacy.

6.7 Literacy Disparity among Rural Scheduled Castes and Rural Non-Scheduled Castes Population

On the basis of disparity index value of rural literacy for the State i.e., 0.1190, tehsils of the Haryana can be categorized into five (Table 6.8 and Map 6.7):

1. Areas of Very High Disparity in Rural Literacy, where the index value is more than 0.2201;
2. Areas of High Disparity in Rural Literacy, where the index value is 0.1501-0.2200;
3. Areas of Moderate Disparity in Rural Literacy, where the index value is 0.0801-0.1500;
4. Areas of Low Disparity in Rural Literacy, where the index value is 0.0100-0.0800; and
5. Areas of Negative Disparity in Rural Literacy, where the literacy among rural Non-Scheduled Castes is relatively lower than that among rural Scheduled Castes.

1. Areas of Very High Disparity in Rural Literacy (Above 0.2201)

Out of sixty-seven tehsils, six tehsils of the State have very high disparity in rural literacy. Ratia tehsil of Fatehabad district has the highest disparity in rural literacy (0.3153) and is followed by Rania (0.2809), Dabwali (0.2604), Sirsa (0.2599), Ellenabad (0.2357), and Guhla (0.2306) tehsils of the State.

Very high disparity in rural literacy in these tehsils is related to poverty, less developed agriculture, low standard of living, low per capita income, high population growth rate, less educational facilities, less developed transportation and industrialization, and rigid caste system. In addition, amongst all tehsils of Haryana, Ratia tehsil has the highest proportion of scheduled castes (36.69 per cent). The other tehsils also have above average proportion of scheduled castes (19.35 per cent). Hence, very high disparity in rural literacy.

Table 6.8: Literacy Disparity among Rural Non-Scheduled Castes and Rural Scheduled Castes Population by Tehsils, 2001

Sr. No.	*State/Tahsil*	*Disparity Index*	*Sr. No.*	*Tahsil*	*Disparity Index*
	Haryana	**0.1190**	34.	Julana	0.1224
1.	Ratia	0.3153	35.	Hodal	0.1199
2.	Rania	0.2809	36.	Tosham	0.1144
3.	Dabwali	0.2604	37.	Siwani	0.1123
4.	Sirsa	0.2599	38.	Thanesar	0.1105
5.	Ellenabad	0.2357	39.	Beri	0.1070
6.	Guhla	0.2306	40.	Gharaunda	0.1043
7.	Fatehabad	0.2131	41.	Jhajjar	0.1005
8.	Tohana	0.2050	42.	Dadri	0.0988
9.	Assandh	0.2026	43.	Sonipat	0.0977
10.	Adampur	0.1916	44.	Ganaur	0.0927
11.	Hisar	0.1813	45.	Ballabgarh	0.0881
12.	Narwana	0.1751	46.	Kharkhoda	0.0874
13.	Kaithal	0.1631	47.	Gurgaon	0.0863
14.	Narnaund	0.1625	48.	Palwal	0.0812
15.	Bawani Khera	0.1600	49.	Panchkula	0.0810
16.	Shahbad	0.1551	50.	Naraingarh	0.0791
17.	Hansi	0.1530	51.	Kosli	0.0757
18.	Pehowa	0.1488	52.	Pataudi	0.0747
19.	Karnal	0.1449	53.	Mahendragarh	0.0731
20.	Panipat	0.1439	54.	Rewari	0.0704
21.	Nilokheri	0.1428	55.	Jagadhri	0.0619
22.	Jind	0.1424	56.	Faridabad	0.0541
23.	Safidon	0.1408	57.	Narnaul	0.0529
24.	Indri	0.1383	58.	Sohna	0.0493
25.	Maham	0.1368	59.	Samalkha	0.0483
26.	Bahadurgarh	0.1355	60.	Bawal	0.0318
27.	Rohtak	0.1337	61.	Chhachhrauli	0.0161
28.	Bhiwani	0.1302	62.	Kalka	0.0115
29.	Ambala	0.1267	63.	Hathin	–0.0795
30.	Loharu	0.1261	64.	Nuh	–0.0924
31.	Israna	0.1241	65.	Punahana	–0.1118
32.	Barara	0.1230	66.	Taoru	–0.1227
33.	Gohana	0.1227	67.	Ferozepur Jhirka	–0.1728

Source: Computed from, Census of India (2001), *Primary Census Abstract,* Haryana, Series 7, Tables A5-A8, Directorate of Census Operations, Haryana.

Note: Tehsils are arranged in descending order of disparity index, 2001.

2. Areas of High Disparity in Rural Literacy (0.1501-2200)

Eleven tehsils of the State have high disparity in rural literacy. It

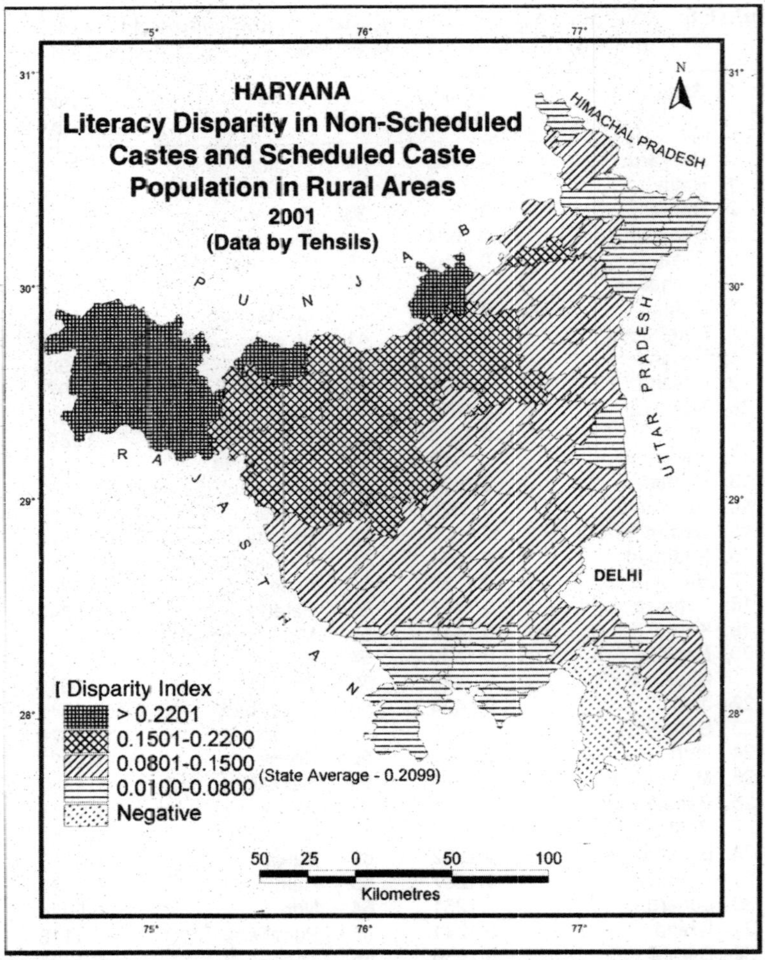

Map 6.7: Haryana: Literacy Disparity in Non-Scheduled Castes and Scheduled Castes Population in Rural Areas, 2001

has been noticed in Fatehabad (0.2131), Tohana (0.2050), Adampur (0.1916), and Hisar (0.1813) tehsils of western region; Narnaund (0.1625), Hansi (0.1530), Bawani Khera (0.1600), Assandh (0.2026), Kaithal (0.1631), and Narwana (0.1751) tehsils in central region; Shahbad (0.1551) tehsil in northern region of the State.

In these tehsils also, the proportion of scheduled castes population is high. This social group lags much behind in the race of socio-economic development. The agricultural development of the region attracted large number of relatively poor, semi-literate and illiterate scheduled castes people.

3. Areas of Moderate Disparity in Rural Literacy (0.0801-0.1500)

There are thirty-two tehsils, where disparity in rural literacy is moderate. It has been noticed in Pehowa (0.1488), Thanesar (0.1105), Barara (0.1230), Ambala (0.1267), and Panchkula (0.0810) tehsils in northern Haryana; Indri (0.1383), Nilokheri (0.1428), Karnal (0.1449), Gharaunda (0.1043), Panipat (0.1439), Ganaur (0.0927), Sonipat (0.0977), Kharkhoda (0.0874), and Bahadurgarh (0.1355) tehsils in eastern Haryana; Jhajjar (0.1005), Beri (0.1070), Dadri (0.0988), Bhiwani (0.1302), Maham (0.1368), Rohtak (0.1337), Gohana (0.1227), Israna (0.1241), Safidon (0.1408), Jind (0.1424), and Julana (0.1224) tehsils in central Haryana; Loharu (0.1261), Tosham (0.1144), and Siwani (0.1123) tehsils in western Haryana; Hodal (0.1199), Palwal (0.0812), Ballabgarh (0.0881), and Gurgaon (0.0863) tehsils in southern Haryana.

In these tehsils, the increasing awareness among all the sections of society, improving transportation network, and the increasing degree of urban-rural interaction have caused moderate disparity in rural literacy.

4. Areas of Low Disparity in Rural Literacy (0.0100-0.0800)

There are thirteen tehsils where the disparity in rural literacy is low. These are Narnaul (0.0529), Mahendragarh (0.0731), Kosli (0.0757), Rewari (0.0704), Bawal (0.0318), Pataudi (0.0747), Sohna (0.0493) and Faridabad (0.0541) tehsils in southern part; Samalkha (0.0483) tehsil in eastern part; Naraingarh (0.0791), Kalka (0.0115), Jagadhri (0.0619), and Chhachhrauli (0.0161) tehsils in northern part of the State.

Low disparity in rural literacy is associated with less concentration of scheduled castes population, commercialization of agriculture and horticulture, high per capita income, expansion of educational facilities. The increasing degree of urban-rural interaction has also caused low disparity in rural literacy.

5. Areas of Negative Disparity in Rural Literacy

In all, there are five tehsils which fall in the category of negative disparity in rural literacy. In these areas, the rural scheduled castes literacy is high than rural non–scheduled castes literacy. The negative disparity index value is found in Hathin (–0.0795), Nuh (–0.0924), Punhana (–0.1198), Taoru (–0.1227) and Ferozepur Jhirka (–0.1728) tehsils. The negative disparity in rural literacy occur here due to high concentration of Muslim population and more socio-economic awakening among rural scheduled castes.

Conclusions

The Census of India 2001 reflected that Haryana has only 55.43 per cent of the scheduled castes population as literate. The literacy rate among scheduled castes population was very low in comparison to general population. There are many reasons such as social injustice, lack of awareness, association with menial jobs and restriction to participate in economically gainful activities.

Six tehsils are characterized with very high scheduled castes literacy rate (66 per cent and above). Amongst these, Gurgaon tehsil has the highest scheduled castes literacy rate (69.35 per cent) and is followed by the tehsils of Rewari (69.32 per cent), Pataudi (68.03 per cent), Kosli (67.69 per cent), Kalka (67.30 per cent) and Bawal (66.51 per cent). High scheduled castes literacy rate in these tehsils is because these are industrially developed, economically sound and also have the favourable impact of the peripheral location of the National and State capitals of New Delhi and Chandigarh respectively. In addition to, early start of education, high job opportunities and well developed transportation network have also helped in the growth of literacy rate.

On the other hand, only five tehsils experienced very low scheduled castes literacy rates (42 per cent and below). Amongst these, Ratia tehsil of Fatehabad district has the lowest scheduled castes literacy rate (34.74 per cent) and is followed by Rania (39.57 per cent), Ellenabad (40.30 per cent), and Dabwali (41.01 per cent) tehsils of Sirsa district in western part; and Guhla (41.02 per cent) tehsil of Kaithal district in northern part of the State. These tehsils are backward in agriculture as well as in industry. Due to lack of industrialization in these tehsils, most of the people are engaged in agriculture. But agricultural operations are such that these do not have any demand of education resulting into the low level of literacy.

By comparison, in 2001 Census, 70.81 per cent of the non-scheduled castes population was able to read and write. Only two tehsils are characterized with very high non-schedules castes literacy rate (82 per cent and above). Amongst these, Gurgaon tehsil has the highest scheduled castes literacy rate (82.50 per cent) and is followed by the tehsil of Ambala (82.22 per cent), Both the tehsils are highly urbanized, industrialized and educationally developed.

On the other hand, only four tehsils of Hathin (45.01 per cent), Nuh (44.33 per cent), Ferozepur Jhirkha (39.20 per cent) and Punahana (37.00 per cent) are characterized with very low literacy rate among the non-scheduled castes population. All these tehsils are located in the southern part of the State. Very low literacy rates in these tehsils are mainly because of the dominance of Meo-Muslim population among non-scheduled castes and are also characterized with low levels of urbanization and industrialization alongwith poor development of educational institutions.

In 2001, 55.43 per cent of scheduled castes population was able to read and write as against 70.81 per cent of non-scheduled castes population giving a disparity value of 0.1550. The disparity was wider in case of females (0.1923). These disparities, although wide, have narrowed down substantially over the years. A change is in the offing and is discernible. No longer are they a subject of administrative neglect and rigidity of the caste system.

The post-Independence period has seen concession, financial assistance, reservations and other constitutional provisions being given to them. Earlier, education had never been an occupational prerequisite for the scheduled castes as its relevance was almost negligible for the menial occupation, which they were pursuing traditionally and as well as for agricultural labour, which of recent has become their major occupation. Although, a substantial proportion of scheduled castes population is still engaged in their traditional occupation, they have also witnessed occupational mobility over a period of time.

Spatially, there are wide regional variations in the disparity index of literacy between non-scheduled castes and scheduled castes population. Five tehsils of State have very high disparity in literacy (0.2501 and above). Amongst these, Ratia tehsil of Fatehabad district has the highest literacy differential index value (0.3419), and is followed by Rania (0.2985), Sirsa (0.2919), Dabwali (0.2811), and Ellenabad (0.2552) tehsils, all are situated in the western part of the State. Very high literacy disparity is mainly because of the high proportion of scheduled castes population in these tehsils. This social group lags much behind in the race of socio-economic development. Very high disparity in literacy is also related to poverty, less developed agriculture, low standard of living, low per capita income, less educational facilities, less developed transportation and industrialization, rigid caste system, subsistence farm economy, low degree of urbanization, involvement of large proportion of scheduled castes population as agricultural labour in construction activity and informal service sector.

On the other hand, five tehsils of Hathin (–0.0736), Taoru (–0.0835), Nuh (–0.0978), Punahana (–0.0994), and Ferozepur Jhirka (–0.1488) have experienced negative disparity in literacy ranging from highest (–0.0736) in Hathin tehsil to lowest (–0.1488) in Ferozepur Jhirka tehsil. In all these tehsils, the scheduled castes literacy was higher than non-scheduled castes literacy because of the dominance of Muslims in non-scheduled castes population.

In nutshell, the literacy differentials between non-scheduled castes and scheduled castes are higher in western Haryana and lower in southern Haryana, except Muslim dominated tehsils which have experienced negative disparity in literacy.

7 Summary and Conclusions

In this concluding chapter a summary of the problem under study and the conclusions derived have been presented.

During the period of united Punjab (before 1966), the part forming Haryana of today was comparatively an underdeveloped one. In 1971, though the literacy rate of Punjab was nearly 34 per cent, Haryana was nearer to 27 per cent. But after the formation of Haryana in 1966, the State government started taking care of the literacy aspect by opening up new schools in villages and towns but the impact of this growth was noticed only in 1981 when the literacy rate was 36.14 per cent as compared to 26.9 per cent in 1971. It means the literacy rate in 1981 was almost one and half times more of what it was in 1971. Not only this, but even while comparing Haryana with neighbouring States, the growth rate of literacy is very high, i.e., 35.41 per cent. This growth rate is more than the growth rate of all the adjoining States except Himachal Pradesh.

There are striking spatial variations in literacy rates within Haryana ranging from only 37.41 per cent in Punahana tehsil of Gurgaon district to 80.81 per cent in Gurgaon tehsil. It means both the highest and lowest literacy rates are found in the district of Gurgaon.

Regions having very high level of literacy are those which are industrially developed, economically sound and also have the favourable impact of big cities like Chandigarh, Delhi, Faridabad, etc. Due to these reasons, Gurgaon (80.81 per cent), Ambala (78.33 per cent) and Faridabad (77.98 per cent) tehsils have very high level of literacy in Haryana.

On the other hand, very low level of literacy is the characteristic of those regions which are industrially undeveloped and economically backward. Apart from this, the least literacy is also the outcome of the social conservatism of the people as in Meo-Muslim society who dominate in Punahana (85.23 per cent), Ferozepur Jhirka (82.54 per cent), Nuh (71.14 per cent), and Taoru (49.11 per cent), tehsils of Gurgaon district and Hathin (54.34 per cent), tehsil of Faridabad district. It means literacy rates differ strongly between various parts of the State.

The spatial pattern of literacy in Haryana is bi-modal, with literacy peaks characteristic of the zone peripheral to the union territory of Delhi and of Chandigarh. Literacy rates go on declining as one moves away from these two areas. The north-western quadrant of Haryana is the most extensive tract with low literacy, though the lowest literacy rates are characteristic of the Meo-Muslim inhabited tract in southern Haryana.

The scheduled castes, by virtue of their socially and economically deprived status, are consistently found to have association with lower levels of literacy than the rest of the population. However, there are several other communities such as Muslims and Christians whose presence in the population affects literacy levels. Thus, the percentage of Muslims has a negative association with literacy rates. Conversely, literacy tends to rise with the share of Christians in the population. Female literacy increases as the Christian proportion of the population rises. On the other hand, the presence of Muslims and scheduled castes tends to depress the level of female literacy.

There is a wide disparity between the literacy rates of rural (63.19 per cent) and urban (79.16 per cent) areas. This disparity in literacy by residence is the product of five basic factors: (i) need to get educated is more in urban areas than in agricultural countryside, (ii) educational facilities are concentrated more in urban areas while these may be completely absent in certain rural areas, (iii) urban population is socially more awakened and economically more capable of imparting education to their children in comparison to the rural counterpart, (iv) urban females enjoy relatively high status in comparison to their rural compatriots and are not denied the opportunities of educations as is the case in many rural areas, (v) many educated ruralites migrate to urban places in search of jobs outside the agricultural sector particularly when there are no avenues in the countryside as a result of which the number of literates in urban areas increase at the cost of rural areas.

The spatial patterns of both urban as well as rural literacy show marked variation. Highest urban literacy is found in Thanesar tehsil (89.11 per cent) and is followed by the tehsils of Gurgaon (86.09 per cent), Ambala (85.68 per cent), Kalka (84.32 per cent), and Rewari (82.78 per cent). Reasons for high level of literacy are the availability of more educational facilities, high degree of urbanization and good economic condition.

At the other end of the scale, the very low level of urban literacy is found in Ferozepur Jhirka tehsil (62.98 per cent) followed by Rania (63.68 per cent), Narnaund (66.06 per cent), Punahana (66.16 per cent), and Loharu (66.56 per cent) tehsils. The reasons may be lack of educational facilities and low level of urbanization alongwith the dominance of Muslim population.

By comparison, highest rates of rural literacy are found in Gurgaon tehsil (77.28 per cent) and is followed by Hodal (75.34 per cent), Rewari (74.68 per cent), Pataudi (74.45 per cent), and Kosli (74.26 per cent) tehsils. Very high rural literacy in Gurgaon may be due to its peripheral location to union territory of Delhi and tradition in army service is strong in Rewari and Kosli tehsils alongwith the availability of sufficient educational facilities.

At the other end of the scale, the tehsil of Punahana (35.33 per cent) is characterized by lowest level of rural literacy, followed by Ferozepur Jhirka (38.05 per cent), Nuh (43.62 per cent), Hathin (44.05 per cent), Ratia (49.77 per cent), and Narwana (52.86 per cent) tehsils. One of the most important causes of low rural literacy rate is the dominance of Meo-Muslim population in the tehsils of Punahana, Ferozepur Jhirka, Nuh, and Hathin.

Thus, urban literacy rates are high in big administrative, commercial and industrial towns with more educational institutions and good economic condition. By comparison, rural literacy rates are high where (i) degree of urban influence is great, (ii) proportion of non-agricultural workers is comparatively large, and (iii) tradition in army service is strong such as in Rewari and Kosli tehsils.

The analysis about literacy rates of Haryana in terms of males and females reveals the picture which is generally true for the whole India, i.e., the male literacy is higher than female literacy and the difference between two is 22.76 per cent (male 78.49 per cent and female 55.73 per cent in 1981). Appalling poverty among people and social structure of society are being considered very important among various causes responsible for the low levels of literacy in females. Poor people instead of educating their daughters prefer to educate their sons, because earning by sons will become helpful for parents adding to their income. Whereas about daughters, a feeling is there that they will have to go to others' houses ultimately. It means daughters are always considered as *Praya Dhan*.

Not only this, but the levels of literacy for both males and females vary widely within Haryana. Highest male literacy has been recorded in Rewari tehsil (89.13 per cent) followed by Gurgaon (89.12 per cent) and Kosli (88.60 per cent) tehsils, whereas the lowest literacy rate for males is found in the tehsils of Punahana (55.43 per cent) followed by Ferozepur Jhirka (58.20 per cent) in the southern part and Ratia (61.31 per cent) in the western part.

On the other hand, highest female literacy rates are found in the tehsil of Ambala (71.30 per cent) and is followed by Gurgaon (70.97 per cent), Faridabad (68.26 per cent), Panchkula (66.29 per cent) and Jagadhari (65.65 per cent) tehsils; whereas the lowest female literacy is the characteristic of Punahana (17.67 per cent) tehsil followed by Ferozepur Jhirka (19.95 per cent), Nuh (24.98 per cent), Hathin (25.64 per cent), and Taoru (39.56 per cent) tehsils.

In every tehsil, male literacy is higher than female literacy in both rural and urban populations and urban male and female populations always have a higher level of literacy than their respective rural counterpart in the same tehsil. It means the disparity in literacy by sex is larger in rural areas than in urban areas.

The sex disparity in Indian education was not of recent origin but was more marked in the medieval period. Till Independence, the country had to pass through different phases of colonial rule in which little attention was paid to the propagation of females' education and the literacy was mainly male literacy. Female literacy was practically non-existent during this period. The male-female disparity in literacy was very high in the beginning of present century due to very low female literacy. Before Independence, the educational institutions were few and far between and the socio-economic conditions were not too conducive to the growth of education, particularly for females. Undoubtedly, after

Independence, the female literacy improved a lot, yet it was far behind the male literacy.

The low level of female literacy in the country was the product of prevalence of prejudices against the females' education, mobility and employment, Inadequate schools for females, dearth of female teachers particularly in rural areas; early engagement/marriage of the females and household responsibilities of the females. Besides, the appalling general poverty and the low degree of participation of females in work were the other factors responsible for wide male-female disparity in literacy.

Like India, Haryana also has high sex disparity in literacy rate. This wide disparity between the male and female literacy was the product of heavy backlog of illiterate females population; slow and haphazard growth of educational institutions especially for females, non-availability of female teachers particularly in the countryside, prevalence of traditional prejudices against females education and their mobility; strong adherence to the tradition of early marriage; low level of urbanization and general poverty.

The male-female disparity index has been declining gradually due to the increase in female literacy in the State The disparities which have been narrowing down since independence, reflect the necessity, propensity and opportunity of various degrees for getting literate among different population groups.

The male-female disparity in literacy was inversely associated with per capita income, male literacy, general literacy, female literacy, percentage of non-agricultural workers or urban population, and it was positively correlated with the percentage of scheduled caste population.

These apart, a strong negative association between the disparity index and the level of socio-economic development could also be observed. In other words, as the general literacy decreases, the disparity index increases. But since the general literacy usually gets depressed in areas of low female literacy, the disparity index in such areas becomes high. Both the general literacy and female literacy are normally low in less developed areas where the disparity index becomes high. Thus, the male-female disparity in literacy is low in relatively prosperous areas and high in socially and economically backward areas.

Spatially, Haryana experiences a great disparity between male and female literacy rates which was 0.2233 as per 2001 Census

This wide disparity in the male-female literacy rates is the product of a variety of social and economic factors, such as prejudices against the females' mobility and education, low status granted to the females, prevalence of early marriage, appalling poverty and low degree of occupational participation among females.

In all, there are six tehsils where the male-female disparity in literacy is very high and the disparity index value was more than 0.3401. Very high disparity index is the rule of those tehsils which are either least urbanized or dominated by Muslim population. The tehsil of Punahana has the highest disparity (0.5972) between male-female literacy which is followed by the tehsils of Ferozepur Jhirka (0.5687), Nuh (0.5052), Hathin (0.4945), Hodal (0.3831), and Taoru (0.3681). These tehsils are least urbanized, whereas Meo-Muslim population dominates in Ferozepur Jhirka and Nuh tehsils. Highest sex disparity in Meo-Muslims society is mainly due to lowest female literacy which is the outcome of social conservation of these people, unequal status given to males and females and even the restriction imposed on females' mobility and education.

The disparity in male and female literacy occurs both in rural and urban areas. However, such disparities are sharper in rural areas in comparison to urban areas. In urban areas, the female literacy does not lag far behind male literacy. The relatively low disparity in urban male-female literacy may be attributed to the relatively better status of the women; availability of educational institutions equally for males and females, relatively better standard of living; increasing value of females' education for matrimonial and employment purposes and increasing degree of socio-economic awakening among urbanites.

Male-female disparity in rural literacy is also highest in the tehsils of Punhana (0.6473), Ferozepur Jhirka (0.6174), Nuh (0.5318), Hathin (0.5199), Hodal (0.4279), Taoru (0.4172) and Palwal (0.3938). This is mainly because of the reasons mentioned above in case of total male-female disparity in literacy.

Whereas in urban areas, sex disparity in literacy is very high in Punahana (0.2909), Loharu (0.2710), Ferozepur Jhirka (0.2667) and is followed by Narnaund (0.2639), Bawani Khera (0.2550), Hodal (0.2498), Hathin (0.2461), Siwani (0.2348), Bawal (0.2319), Nuh (0.2294), Beri (0.2189), Narnaul (0.2073), Mahendragarh (0.2049), Julana (0.1998) and Narwana (0.1952) tehsils (Table 4.3).

All these tehsils are least urbanised and the people are very prejudiced against the females' education.

On the other hand, very low male-female disparity in literacy is also experienced in six tehsils of the State. Ambala has the lowest sex disparity (0.1203) followed by Panchkula (0.1379), Jagadhri (0.1391), Kalka (0.1542), Karnal (0.1547) and Shahbad (0.1561). These are the areas which are industrially developed and have proximity to the union territories of Chandigarh and Delhi. Its proximity has added a new dimension to the process of propagation of literacy and education in these areas, hence characterized by very low disparity among males and females.

There are nine tehsils which have very low sex disparity in rural literacy. Ambala has the lowest sex disparity in literacy (0.1663) and is followed by Barara (0.1672), Shahbad (0.1788), Jagadhri (0.1823), Naraingarh (0.1857), Thanesar (0.1945), Panchkula (0.1982), Pehwoa (0.1987) and Kalka (0.1999) tehsils.

But as far as urban male-female disparity is concerned, it is the lowest in Ambala (0.0799) tehsil which is followed by Panchkula (0.0825), Jagadhri (0.0885), Karnal (0.0919) and Shahbad (0.0958).

It shows that the lowest male-female disparity in literacy rates for both rural and urban areas is the characteristic of those regions surrounding the industrial centres of Ambala and Jagadhri and also have proximity to Chandigarh. So, the least disparity in literacy rates is due to high degree of industrialization and urbanization of this part of the State and also due to the influence of big city of Chandigarh. Apart from this, the existing disparity between male and female literacy rates in urban areas is because of better educational facilities and general awareness towards the education among both the sexes.

Thus, the male-female disparity in literacy was low in the tehsils with high general and female literacy, good infrastructure of educational facilities, high proportion of urban population and of non-agricultural workers.

Male-female disparities in the literacy rates among the rural and urban population have gone down with the increase in general literacy rate all over the State.

Like the urban-rural disparity, the male-female disparity also varies regionally ranging from only 0.1203 (disparity index value) in Ambala tehsil to 0.5972 in Punahana tehsil of Gurgaon district.

The disparity in literacy between the two sexes across the tehsils correlates negatively with the level of literacy and that of urbanization. This relationship is observed not only in case of the total population but for the scheduled castes as well.

The urban literacy rate which was 44.7 per cent in 1961 increased to 79.16 per cent in 2001. Similarly, the rural literacy rate which was only 14.8 per cent in 1961 improved to 63.19 per cent in 2001. In other words, in 2001, while 79.16 per cent of urban population in Haryana was literate, the corresponding figure for rural population was only 63.19 per cent, implying the narrowing down of wide disparity in rural and urban literacy rates

The narrowing down of the urban-rural disparity in literacy was associated with increasing degree of rural-urban interaction, increasing socio-economic functional value of education in the countryside, improving standards of living, increasing facilities for schooling in the countryside and the waning social taboos and prejudices against females' education particularly in rural areas.

In regional perspective, the maximum urban-rural disparity in literacy rates is the rule of those areas which are either highly urbanized but dominated by Muslim population or least urbanized with high concentration of scheduled castes population in rural areas. There are five tahsils which are characterized by the highest urban-rural disparity index values (0.2401 and above). Out of these five tahsils, four tahsils namely Punhana (0.3626) Ferozepur Jhirka (0.2915), Nuh (0.2581) and Taoru (0.2521) belong to Gurgaon district and the tehsil of Hathin (0.2945) to Faridabad district in the extreme south-east of Haryana.

By comparison, the low urban-rural disparity in literacy is found in both the less developed areas and rapidly developing areas. In the former case, both urban and rural literacy rates are low and resultant differential is low. In the latter case, both the urban and rural literacy rates are high and the resultant disparity is also low. There are only seven tehsils, which are characterized by lowest urban-rural disparity in literacy. The tehsils of Pataudi (74.45 per cent), Beri (71.56 per cent), Sohna (69.61 per cent) and Kharkhoda (68.67 per cent) are characterized with rural literacy rates above the State average (63.19 per cent) and the urban literacy rates below the State average (79.16 per cent) resulting into very low urban-rural disparity in literacy. In case of remaining tehsils of Loharu, Bawani Khera and Rania, both the rural and urban literacy rates are below the State's averages (63.19 per cent and 79.16 per cent respectively). Hence, very low urban-rural disparity in literacy.

In the areas of high literacy (both urban and rural), early start of education, diversification of rural economy and relatively high degree of urbanization have their strong impact. In rural areas, commercialization of agriculture, opening of more schools, the long tradition of military service, and the waning social taboos and prejudices against females' education particularly in rural areas have played a vital role in the increase of literacy rates, thereby decreasing urban-rural gap.

The Census of India 2001 reflected that Haryana has only 55.43 per cent of the scheduled castes population as literate. The literacy rate among scheduled castes population was very low in comparison to general population. There are many reasons such as social injustice, lack of awareness, association with menial jobs and economic restriction to participate in economically gainful activities.

Six tehsils are characterized with very high scheduled castes literacy rate (66 per cent and above). Amongst these, Gurgaon tehsil has the highest scheduled castes literacy rate (69.35 per cent) and is followed by the tehsils of Rewari (69.32 per cent), Pataudi (68.03 per cent), Kosli (67.69 per cent), Kalka (67.30 per cent) and Bawal (66.51 per cent). High scheduled castes literacy rate in these tehsils is because these are industrially developed, economically sound and also have the favourable impact of the peripheral location of the National and State capitals of New Delhi and Chandigarh respectively. In addition to, early start of education, high job opportunities and well developed transportation network have also helped in the growth of literacy rate.

On the other hand, only five tehsils experienced very low scheduled castes literacy rates (42 per cent and below). Amongst these, Ratia tehsil of Fatehabad district has the lowest scheduled castes literacy rate (34.74 per cent) and is followed by Rania (39.57 per cent), Ellenabad (40.30 per cent), and Dabwali (41.01 per cent) tehsils of Sirsa district in western part; and Guhla (41.02 per cent) tehsil of Kaithal district in northern part of the State. These tehsils are backward in agriculture as well as in industry. Due to lack of industrialization in these tehsils, most of the people are engaged in agriculture. But agricultural operations are such that these do not have any demand of education resulting into the low level of literacy.

By comparison, in 2001 Census, 70.81 per cent of the non-scheduled castes population was able to read and write. Only two tehsils are characterized by very high non-scheduled castes literacy rate (82 per cent and above). Amongst these, Gurgaon tehsil has the highest non-scheduled castes literacy rate (82.50 per cent) and is followed by the tehsil of Ambala (82.22 per cent), Both the tehsils are highly urbanized, industrialized and educationally developed.

On the other hand, only four tehsils of Hathin (45.01 per cent), Nuh (44.33 per cent), Ferozepur Jhirka (39.20 per cent) and Punahana (37.00 per cent) are characterized with very low literacy rate among the non-scheduled castes population. All these tehsils are located in the southern part of the State. Very low literacy rates in these tehsils are mainly because of the dominance of Meo-Muslim population among non-scheduled castes and are also characterized with low levels of urbanization and industrialization alongwith poor development of educational institutions.

In 2001, 55.43 per cent of scheduled castes population was able to read and write as against 70.81 per cent of non-scheduled castes population giving a disparity value of 0.1550. The disparity was wider in case of females (0.1923). These disparities, although wide, have narrowed down substantially over the years. A change is in the offing and is discernible. No longer are they a subject of administrative neglect and rigidity of the caste system.

The post-Independence period has seen concession, financial assistance, reservations and other constitutional provisions being given to them. Earlier, education had never been an occupational prerequisite for the scheduled castes as its relevance was almost negligible for the menial occupation, which they were pursuing traditionally as well as for agricultural labour, which of recent had became their major occupation. Although, a substantial proportion of scheduled castes population is still engaged in their traditional occupation, they have also witnessed occupational mobility over a period of time.

Spatially, there are wide regional variations in the disparity index of literacy between non-scheduled castes and scheduled castes population. Five tehsils of State have very high disparity in literacy (0.2501 and above). Amongst these, Ratia tehsil of

Fatehabad district has the highest disparity in literacy (0.3419 per cent), and is followed by Rania (0.2985 per cent), Sirsa (0.2919 per cent), Dabwali (0.2811 per cent), and Ellenabad (0.2552 per cent) tehsils, all are situated in the western part of the State. Very high disparity in literacy is mainly because of the high proportion of scheduled castes population in these tehsils. This social group lags much behind in the race of socio-economic development. Very high disparity in literacy is also related to poverty, less developed agriculture, low standard of living, low per capita income, less educational facilities, less developed transportation and industrialization, rigid caste system, subsistence farm economy, low degree of urbanization, involvement of large proportion of scheduled castes population as agricultural labour in construction activity and informal service sector.

On the other hand, five tehsils of Hathin (–0.0736 per cent), Taoru (–0.0835 per cent), Nuh (–0.0978 per cent), Punahana (–0.0994 per cent), and Ferozepur Jhirka (–0.1488 per cent) have experienced negative disparity in literacy ranging from highest (–0.0736 per cent) in Hathin tehsil to lowest (–0.1488 per cent) in Ferozepur Jhirka tehsil. In all these tehsils, the scheduled castes literacy was higher than non-scheduled castes literacy because of the dominance of Muslims in non-scheduled castes population.

The recent trends have been such that the disparities in the literacy rates of various parts of the State are narrowing down. Areal disparities in both male and female literacy rates are also squeezing, but this process is faster in case of the latter.

It has been discussed earlier that in India, the status of women has never been at par with that of in the developed countries. Low standard of living, illiteracy, inter-spouse communication combined with economic dependence, ignorance and tradition stand in the way of improving it. Of these factors, literacy and education play a predominant role. To improve female literacy rates and scheduled castes literacy rates, following methods should be adopted:

(i) With a view to increase female literacy, government should set up separate girls high schools in rural areas and grants should be provided for the construction of these girls' educational institutions;

(ii) In girls' schools, only female teachers should be appointed;

(iii) People in villages should be enlightened about favourable aspects of female literacy. Some seats should be reserved for females in services such as teaching, medicine, etc.,

(iv) Adult education programme should be introduced in the villages and village level activists should be involved for its successful implementation; and

(v) There should be proper implementation of various scholarship schemes introduced by government for scheduled castes students and for girls.

Development of a region cannot take place till all the segments of population get equal importance. So, emphasis should be laid to improve the lot of females and of scheduled castes population. We can achieve comprehensive development only when we follow this approach.

Bibliography

Adiseshiah, M.S. (1994), "Education as a Tool for Economic Change", *Yojana*, Vol. 38, Nos. 1 and 2, pp. 18-20.

Aggarwal, J.C. (1966), *Progress of Education in India*, Arya Book Depot, Delhi.

Aggarwal, S.N. and Sinha, U.P. (1985), *India's Population Problems*, Tata McGraw Hill Publishing Company Ltd., New Delhi, pp. 160-171.

Aggarwal, Y.P. and Murlidhar, V. (1986), "A Temporal Analysis of Literacy between Scheduled Castes and Non-Scheduled Castes Population in Maharashtra", in Tilak, J.B.G. (ed.), *Education and Regional Development*, Yatan Publication, New Delhi, pp. 271-295.

Agnihotri, S.B. (2002), "High Female Literacy, Low Child Population, Does there a Threshold Effect"?, *Economic and Political Weekly*, Vol. XXXVII, No. 39, pp. 4054-59.

Ahmad, A. (1982), "Inter-Regional Inequity in Literacy Levels of Tribals and Caste Segments of Population in India, 1971", Paper Presented at Regional Workshop on *Long-Term Educational Planning*, NIEPA, New Delhi.

Ahmad, A. (1986), "Socio-Cultural Change in a Developing Society: The Case of India", in Shafi, M. and Raza, Mehdi (eds.), *Spectrum of Modern Geography*, Concept Publishing Company, New Delhi, pp. 243-268.

Ahmad, A. and Nuna, S.C. (1986), "Inequity in the Literacy Levels of Population in Maharashtra", in Raza, M. (ed.), *Educational Planning: A Long Term Perspective*, NIEPA (National Institute of Educational Planning and Administration), Concept Publishing Co., New Delhi, pp. 129-161.

Alterkar, A.S. (1957), *Education in Ancient India*, Nand Kishore Publication, Varanasi.

Arora, G.L. (1993), "Teacher Education: Search for Alternatives", *Yojana*, Vol. 37, No. 13, pp. 11-13.

Awasthi, D.N. (2002), "Indian Education System in the Global Context", *Journal of India Education*, Vol. XXVIII, No. 1, pp. 85-100.

Ayyappan, A. (1965), *Social Revolution in Kerala Village*, Asia Publishing House, Bombay.

Bahadur, K.P. (1960), *Caste, Tribe and Culture of India*, Vol. I-V, Ess Ess Publications, New Delhi.

Bailey, F.G. (1960), *Tribe, Caste and Nation*, Manchester University Press, Manchester.

Bandhopadhyay, D. (2002), "Madarsa Education and Conditions of Indian Muslims", *Economic and Political Weekly*, Vol. XXXVII, No. 16, pp. 1481-1484.

Banerjee, M. (1975), "Literacy in Singhbum, Bihar", *Geographical Review of India*, Vol. 37, No. 2, pp. 151-157.

Banerjee, R. (1997), "Why do not Children Complete Primary School? A Case Study of Low Income Neighbourhood in Delhi"?, *Economic and Political Weekly*, Vol. XXXIV, No. 32, pp. 2053-2063.

Bhandari, R.K. (1985), "Better Education, Better Nation", *Yojana*, Vol. 29, No. 7, pp. 4-8.

Bhardwaj, P.D. (1999), "Literacy in Himachal Pradesh", *Population Geography*, Vol. 21, Nos. 1 and 2, pp. 31-42.

Bhatnagar, Suresh (1983), *Indian Education: Today and Tomorrow*, Loyal Book Depot, Meerut, pp. 80-89.

Bhattacharya, A. (1978), *Population Geography of India*, Shree Publishing House, New Delhi.

Bhattacharya, R.N. (2001), "Tribal Literacy in West Bengal", *Man in India*, Vol. 81, Nos. 1 and 2, pp. 244-247.

Bishwas, A.; Dutta, S.; and Singh, R.R. (1976), *The New Education Pattern in India*, Vikas Publishing House Pvt. Ltd., New Delhi.

Blang, M. (1967), "Approaches to Educational Planning", *Economic Journal*, Vol. 77, No. 30, pp. 262-281.

Bose, A.B. (1970), "Educational Development among Scheduled Castes", *Man in India*, Vol. 50, No. 3, pp. 17-22.

Byun, H.Y. and Kim, Y.S. (1995), "Education and Worker Productivity: Socio-Economic Factors of Japan", *Asian Profile*, Vol. 23, No. 2, pp. 105-112.

Cameron, L.A. and Dowling, J.M. (2001), "Education and Labour Market Participation of Women in Asia: Evidence from Five Countries", *Economic Development and Cultural Change*, Vol. 49, No. 3, pp. 459-477.

Cameron, L.A. and Worswick, C. (2001), "Education Expenditure Responses to Crop Loss in Indonesia: A Gender Bias", *Economic Development and Cultural Change*, Vol. 49, No. 3, pp. 351-363.

Carron, G. and Ngoc, C.T. (eds.) (1980a), *Regional Disparities in Educational Development: A Comparative Issue*, International Institute for Educational Planning, UNESCO Press, Paris.

Carron, G. and Ngoc, C.T. (eds.) (1980b), *Regional Disparities in Educational Development: Diagnosis and Policies for Reduction*, UNESCO Press, Paris.

Census of India (1981), *Final Population Totals*: Paper 1 of 1982, Series-1, India, Office of the Registrar General and Census Commissioner, New Delhi.

Census of India (1991), *Final Population Totals*, Paper 1 of 1992, Vols. 1 and 2, Series 1, India, Office of the Registrar General and Census Commissioner, New Delhi.

Census of India (1991), *Final Population Totals: Brief Analysis of Primary Census Abstract*, Paper 2 of 1992, Series-1, India, Registrar General and Census Commissioner, New Delhi.

Census of India (1991), *Census Atlas*, Part XI, Series 8, Haryana, Directorate of Census Operations, Haryana, p. 18.

Census of India (2001), *Primary Census Abstract*, CDs 1-12, Office of the Registrar General and Census Commissioner, India, New Delhi.

Census of India (2001), *Provisional Population Totals*, Paper 1 of 2001, Series 7, Haryana, Directorate of Census Operations, Haryana.

Census of India (2001), *Provisional Population Totals*, Paper 2 of 2001, Series 7, Haryana, Directorate of Census Operations, Haryana.

Census of India (2001), *Primary Census Abstract*, Tables A5-A8, Series 7, Haryana, Directorate of Census Operations, Haryana.

Census of India (2001), *Final Population Totals*, Series 7, Haryana, Directorate of Census Operations, Haryana.

Census of India (2001), *Final Population Totals*, Series 1, India, Registrar General and Census Commissioner, New Delhi.

Census of India (2001), *Workers and Non-Workers: An Analysis Based on 2001 Census*, Registrar General and Census Commissioner, India, New Delhi.

Chalam, K.S. (1987), *Education and Weaker Section*, Inter-India Publications, New Delhi.

Chandna, R.C. (1980), "Distributional Pattern of Scheduled Caste Population in India", *Population Geography*, Vol. 2, No. 1, pp. 78-79.

Chandna, R.C. (1986), *A Geography of Population: Concepts, Determinants and Patterns*, Kalyani Publishers, New Delhi.

Chandna, R.C. (2000), *A Geography of Population: Concepts, Determinants and Patterns*, Fourth Edition, Kalyani Publishers, New Delhi, pp. 171-183.

Chandna, R.C. (2008), *A Geography of Population: Concepts, Determinants and Patterns*, Seventh Edition, Kalyani Publishers, New Delhi, pp. 344-377.

Chandna, R.C. and Sidhu, M.S. (1980), *Introduction to Population Geography*, Kalyani Publishers, Ludhiana, p. 96.

Chaubey, P.K. and Chaubey, G. (1998), "Rural-Urban Disparity in Literacy: Inter-State Variation in India", *Indian Journal of Regional Science*, Vol. 30, No. 1, pp. 22-39.

Chauhan, B.R. (1975), *Scheduled Caste and Education*, Anu Publication, Meerut.

Chib, S.S. (1977), *This Beautiful India: Haryana*, Light and Life Publishers, New Delhi, p. 43.

Chib, S.S. (1994), "Changing Literacy Pattern in the Trans-Himalayan Tribal Tract of Kinnaur (H.P.), A Geographical Focus," *The University Review*, (Jammu), pp. 49-62.

Chitnis, S. (1972), "Education for Equality: Case of Scheduled Castes", *Economic and Political Weekly*, Vol. 7, Nos. 31-33, pp. 1675-1681.

Chitnis, S. (1974), *Literacy and Educational Enrolment among Scheduled Castes of Maharashtra*, Tata Institute of Social Sciences, Bombay.

D'Souza, V.S. (1980a), "Rural-Urban Disparity: Education", *Demography India*, Vol. 11, No. 2, pp. 202-205.

D'Souza, V.S. (1980b), *Educational Inequalities among Scheduled Castes: A Case Study in Punjab*, Occasional Monograph, Department of Sociology, Punjab University, Chandigarh.

D'Souza, V.S. (1982), "Urbanisation and the Rural-Urban Differences in Literacy", Paper Presented at the Conference of the Indian Association for Population.

Das, M. and Nayak, D.K. (2001), "Tribal Economy and Spatial

Pattern of Literacy in Meghalaya: A Block Level Analysis", *Man in India,* Vol. 81, Nos. 1 and 2, pp. 209-218.

Datt, R. (1996), "Inequalities in Educational Development with Special Reference to Literacy Status and School Education", *Journal of Educational Planning and Administration,* Vol. 9, No. 3, pp. 225-269.

Davis, Kingsley (1951), *Population of India and Pakistan,* Princeton University Press, Princeton, pp. 150-161.

Deshpande, C.D. (1971), *Geography of Maharashtra,* National Book Trust, New Delhi.

Devi, D.R. (1991), "Literacy: A Study of South Indian Districts", *Demography India,* Vol. 20, No. 1, pp. 103-112.

Dixit, K.N. (1970), *Geography of Gujarat,* National Book Trust, New Delhi.

Dube, R.S. and Mishra, R.P. (1981), "Level of Education: A Versatile Indicator of Regional Development", *Geographical Review of India,* Vol. 43, No. 3, pp. 278-281.

Dutta, G. (1982), "Analysis of Literacy Rates in Southern Districts of West Bengal", *Geographical Review of India,* Vol. 44, No. 2, pp. 19-26.

Dutta, R.C. (1977), "Income Distribution and Economic Development in India since 1950-51", *Indian Economic Journal,* Vol. XXV, No. 2, pp. 140-164.

Evevett, J.M. (1978), *Women and Social Change in India,* Heritage Publishers, New Delhi.

Forest Survey of India (2009), *India State of Forest Report 2009,* Haryana, Chapter 7.9, Table 7.9.3, p. 88

Fraja, G.D. (2001), "Education Policies: Equity, Efficiency and Voting Equilibrium", *The Economic Journal,* Vol. III, No. 477, pp. 104-119.

Fuchs, S. (1960), *The Gond and the Bhumia of Eastern Mandla,* Asia Publishing House, Bombay.

Gandhi, M.K. (1939), *What is Women's Role,* Harijan Navjiwan Press, Ahmedabad, pp. 12-14.

Geological Survey of India (1989), *Geology and Mineral Resources of the States of India, Part-XVIII, Haryana,* Miscellaneous Publication No. 30, Director General, Geological Survey of India, pp. 2-3.

George, A. (1978), "Literacy: Doorway to Liberation", *Geographical Review of India,* Vol. 4, pp. 134-143.

Ghosh, P.K. (1997), "Problems of Primary Education in West Bengal", *Yojana,* Vol. 41, No. 9, pp. 25-27.

Gill, M.S. (1992), "Literacy in Punjab", *The Geographer*, Vol. 39, No. 1, pp. 41-53.

Goel, N.P. (1994), *Readings in Population Geography*, Mohit Publications, New Delhi.

Golden, H.H. (1955), "Literacy and Social Change in Underdeveloped Countries", *Rural Sociology*, Vol. 20, pp. 1-7.

Golden, H.H. (1968), "Literacy", *International Encyclopaedia of Social Sciences*, Vol. 9, Macmillan Company and Free Press.

Gosal, G.S. (1964), "Literacy in India: An Interpretative Study", *Geographical Review of India*, Vol. 29, pp. 276-285.

Gosal, G.S. (1964), "Literacy in India: An Interpretative Study", *Rural Sociology*, Vol. 29, No. 3, pp. 261-277.

Gosal, G.S. (1967), "Regional Aspects of Rural Literacy in India", *Transactions of the Indian Council of Geographers*, Vol. 4, pp. 1-15.

Gosal, G.S. (1979), "Spatial Perspective on Literacy in India," in Mukerji, A.B. and Ahmad, A. (eds.), *India-Culture, Society and Economy and Geographical Essays*, Inter-India Publications, New Delhi, 362-379.

Gosal, R.P.S. (1980), "Literacy in India's Scheduled Caste Population: A Spatial Analysis", *Population Geography*, Vol. 10, Nos. 1 and 2, pp. 42-60.

Gosal, R.P.S. (2002), "Sex Composition of India's Population, 2001: A Geographical Analysis", *Population Geography*, Vol. 23, No. 1 and 2, pp. 29-40.

Government of Haryana (2002), *Directory of Large and Medium Units*, Directorate of Industries, Haryana, Chandigarh.

Government of Haryana (2007), *Statistical Abstract: Haryana*, 2005-2006, Economic and Statistical Adviser, Planning Department.

Government of Haryana (2010), *Economic Survey of Haryana, 2009-2010*, Department of Economic and Statistical Analysis, Haryana, pp. 23-83.

Government of India (1999), *Ninth Five-Year Plan (1997-2002), Vol. 11, Thematic Issues and Sectoral Programmes*, Planning Commission, New Delhi.

Government of India (1999-2000), *Selected Education Statistics*, Ministry of Human Resource Development, New Delhi.

Government of India (2000-01), *Selected Education Statistics*, Planning, Monitoring and Statistical Division, Ministry of Human Resource Development, New Delhi.

Government of India (2000-01), *Statistical Abstract: India*, Central

Statistical Organization, Department of Statistics, Ministry of Planning and Programme Implementation, New Delhi.

Government of India (2001-02), *Economic Survey*, Ministry of Finance, Economic Division, New Delhi.

Government of India (2002), *National Human Development Report, 2001*, Planning Commission, Oxford University Press, New Delhi.

Hajela, P.D. (1966), "Significance of Education in Social Development," *Yojana*, Vol. 40, No. 1, pp. 26-27.

Haq, M. and Haq, Q. (1998), *Human Development in South Asia*, The Human Development Centre, Oxford University Press, Karachi.

Haryana State Gazetteers (2004), *Haryana State Gazetteer*, Vol. 1, Gazetteers Organisation, Revenue Department, Haryana, Chandigarh, pp. 119-141.

Hazra, J. (1997), "Women and Literacy," *Geographical Review of India*, Vol. 59, No. 1, pp. 62-74.

Hoselitz, B.F. (1960), "The Urban-Rural Contrast as a Factor in Social Change", *Economic Weekly*, Annual, pp. 145-152.

Hutton, J.H. (1946), *Caste in India*, Cambridge University Press, Cambridge.

Imam Ali, A.F. (1990), "Changing Social Stratification and Educational Inequality in Rural Bangladesh: A Case Study of Two Selected Villages," *Asian Profile*, Vol. 18, No. 2, pp. 163-72.

Iqbal, N. (1995), "Stir Masses against Illiteracy", *Yojana*, Vol. 30, No. 122, pp. 61-65.

Jolly, K.G. (1991), "Strategies to Attain Universal Literacy in India by 2001", *Demography India*, Vol. 20, No. 1, pp. 141-154.

Joshi, H. (2002), "Gender Related Education Development Index in Rajasthan 2000: A Geographical Analysis at Panchayat Samiti Level", *Transactions, Institute of Indian Geographers*, Vol. 24, No. 1-2, pp. 11-12.

Joshi, P.K. (2001), "Education, Technology Adoption and Agricultural Productivity", *Indian Journal of Agricultural Economics*, Vol. 56, No. 1, pp. 33-34.

Kalam, A.P.J. Abdul (1999), "Second Vision for the Nation: Developed India", *Yojana*, Vol. 43, No. 1, pp. 25-26.

Kashinath, H.M. (1997), "National Open School and Universalization of Education", *Yojana*, Vol. 41, No. 5, pp. 25-53.

Kaur, B. (2003a), "Gender Disparity in Literacy in the Indian Punjab: 2001", *The Education Review*, pp. 6-9.

Kaur, B. (2003b), *Progress of Literacy in Punjab*, Madaan Publications, Patiala.

Kaur, I. (1983), *Trends in Literacy Differentials in Patiala District: 1951-1971*, An Unpublished M. Phil, Dissertation, Department of Geography, Panjab University, Chandigarh.

Khan, A.Q. (2004), "Regional Imbalances and Changing Pattern of Literacy in Jammu and Kashmir State (1961-2001)", *Population Geography*, Vol. 26, Nos. 1 and 2, pp. 49-60.

Kingdon, G.G. (2002), "The Gender Gap in Educational Attainment in India: How Much can be Explained"? *The Journal of Development Studies*, Vol. 39, No. 2, pp. 25-53.

Kirpal, P. (1987), "The Progress of Education", *Yojana*, Vol. 31, No. 14-15, pp. 56-71.

Knight, J. and Weir, S. (2003), "The Role of Education in Facilitating Risk-Taking and Innovations in Agriculture", *The Journal of Development Studies*, Vol. 39, No. 6, pp. 1-22.

Krishan, G. (1989), "Trends in Regional Disparities in India", *Asian Profile*, Vol. 17, No. 3, pp. 243-61.

Krishan, G. (2002), "Women in Higher Education in India", *Population Geography*, Vol. 24, No. 1 and 2, pp. 99-104.

Krishan, G. and Chandna, R.C. (1974a), "Haryana: Working Force and its Occupational Structure", *Manpower Journal*, Vol. 10, pp. 50-72.

Krishan, G. and Chandna, R.C. (1974b), "Patterns of Literacy in Haryana," *Panjab University Research Bulletin (Arts)*, Vol. 5, No. 2, pp. 95-104.

Krishan, G. and Shyam, M. (1973), "Spatial Perspective on Progress of Female Literacy in India: 1901-71", *Pacific Viewpoint*, Vol. 14, pp. 203-206.

Krishan, G. and Shyam, M. (1973), "Spatial Perspective on Progress of Female Literacy in India", *Geographical Review of India*, Vol. 2, No. 1, pp. 52-57.

Krishan, G. and Shyam, M. (1974a), "Regional Aspects of Urban-Rural Differentials in Literacy", *The Journal of Development Areas*, Vol. 13, No. 1, pp. 52-57.

Krishan, G. and Shyam, M. (1974b), "Literacy Patterns of Indian Cities", *Geoforum*, Vol. 19, pp. 77-80.

Krishan, G. and Shyam, M. (1977), "Literacy in India", *Geographical Review of India*, Vol. 39, pp. 117-25.

Krishan, G. and Shyam, M. (1978), "Regional Aspects of Urban-

Rural Differentials in Literacy in India: 1971", *The Journal of Developing Areas*, Vol. 13, No. 1, pp. 11-21.

Krishan, G. and Shyam, M. (1985), "Regional Aspects of Urban-Rural Differentials in Literacy in India", in Misra, R.P., *et al.* (eds.), *Contributions to Indian Geography*, Heritage Publishers, New Delhi, pp. 317-328.

Kulkarni, M.R. and Kulkarni, S. (1986), "Are Inter-State Disparities Growing", *Yojana*, Vol. 30, No. 4, pp. 4-8.

Kumar, A.S. (1997), "Education Guarantee Scheme of Madhya Pradesh, *Yojana*, Vol. 41, No. 9, pp. 28.

Kumar, P. and Singh, J. (2004), "Educated Unemployment in Haryana", *Man and Development*, Vol. XXXVI, No. 1, pp. 21-36.

Kumar, Rana (2004), "Primary Education in Jharkhand", *Economic and Political Weekly*, Vol. XXXIX, No. 11, pp. 1171-78.

Kundu, A. and Rao, J.M. (1982), "Inequality in Educational Development: Issues in Measurement Changing Structure and Its Socio-Economic Correlates with Special Reference to India", Paper Presented at Regional Workshop on *Long-Term Educational Planning*, NIEPA, New Delhi.

Kundu, A. and Rao, J.M. (1986), "Inequality in Educational Development: Issues in Measurement Changing Structure and Its Socio-Economic Correlates with Special Reference to India" in Raza, M. (ed.), *Educational Planning: A Long Term Perspective*, NIEPA and Concept Publishing Co., New Delhi, pp. 435-466.

Kundu, A. and Raza, M. (1982), "Indian Economy: The Regional Dimension", *Spectrum*, New Delhi.

Kurrien, G. (1981), "Towards Universal Elementary Education," *Economic and Political Weekly*, pp. 1608-18.

Lal, S. (1987), *Education among Tribals*, Printwell Publisher, Jaipur.

Majumdar, D.N. (1961), *Races and Culture of India*, Asia Publishing House, Bombay.

Malhotra, O.P. (1986), *Tribal Education in Andaman and Nicobar Islands*, S. Chand & Company Limited, New Delhi.

Mathur, B.B. (1982), *Literacy Differentials in Uttar Pradesh: 1991*, An Unpublished M. Phil. Dissertation, Department of Geography, Panjab University, Chandigarh.

Mathur, B.B. (1985), "Geography of Literacy in India, A Bibliographical Note", *The Avadh Journal of Social Sciences*, Vol. 2, pp. 148-151.

McDougall, (2000), "Gender Gap in Literacy in Uttar Pradesh:

Questions for Decentralized Educational Planning", *Economic and Political Weekly*, Vol. XXV, No. 19, pp. 1649-58.

Mehta, B.C. (1996), "Free Primary Education", *Economic and Political Weekly*, Vol. XXXI, No. 16 and 17, p. 1035.

Mishra, S.K. and Chopra, A. (1978), "Dimension of Inter-District Disparities in Level of Development in Madhya Pradesh—1971", *The Indian Geographical Journal*, Vol. 53, No. 1, pp. 21-29.

Misra, (1998), "National Literacy Mission: Retrospect and Prospect", *Economic and Political Weekly*, Vol. XXXIII, No. 44, pp. 2807-15.

Misra, B. (1996), "Gandhiji's Vision of Cultural Contents in Education", *Yojana*, Vol. 40, No. 5, pp. 17-20.

Misra, S.K.; Rao, M.S.; and Dubey, V.K. (1997), "Promoting Environmental Literacy", *Yojana*, Vol. 41, No. 10, pp. 28-29.

Mohanty, B.B. (2003), "Educational Progress of Scheduled Tribes: A Discursive Review", *Man and Development*, Vol. XXV, No. 2, pp. 91-106.

Motamedi, V. and Dukshkin, L. (1996), "Dependency Theory and Education in India", *Asian Profile*, Vol. 24, No. 5, pp. 425-32.

Mukerji, A.B. (1968), "Spatial Patterns of Literacy in Andhra Pradesh, India", *Selected Papers*, 21st International Geographical Congress, pp. 181-186.

Mukherjee, A. and Vasanta, D. (2002), *Practice and Research in Literacy*, Sage Publications, New Delhi.

Naik, J.P. (1966), "Enrolment Policies in Indian Education", *Manpower Journal*, Vol. 1, pp. 88-118.

Naik, J.P. (1971), *Education of the Scheduled Castes (1965-66)*, Occasional Monograph 6, ICSSR, New Delhi.

Naik, J.P. (1978), *Education for Our People: A Policy Frame for the Development of Education (1978-87)*, ICSSR, Allied Publishers, New Delhi, pp. 1-7.

Nain, N.A. (1988), *Trends in Urban-Rural Differentials in Select Aspects of Indian Demography, 1951-81: A Spatial View.* An Unpublished M. Phil. Dissertation, Department of Geography, Panjab University, Chandigarh.

Nair, K.R. (1981), *Regional Disparities in India*, Agricole Publishing Academy, New Delhi.

Nambissan, G.B. (1966), "Equality in Education: Schooling of Dalit Children in India", *Economic and Political Weekly*, Vol. XXXI, No. 16 and 17, pp. 1011-24.

Nanjundappa, D.M. (1992), "Education Planning and the Eighth Plan", *Yojana,* Vol. 36, No. 14 and 15, pp. 64-69.

Nath, V. (2001), "First Results of the Decennial Census of Population: 2001", *Population Geography,* Vol. 23, No. 1 and 2, pp. 41-48.

Nayantara, S. (1993), "Education for the Girl Child", *Yojana,* Vol. 37, No. 10, pp. 9-13.

Neyaji, T.A. (2002), "Madarsa Education", *Economic and Political Weekly,* Vol. XXXVII, No. 38, pp. 3967-68.

Obulesn, K. (1992), "Educational Expenditure and Beneficiaries: A Case Study", *Yojana,* Vol. 36, No. 7, pp. 27-28.

Ojha, G.K. (1966), *Progress of Compulsory Education in India (1951-1966),* Universal Publication, Delhi, pp. 1-25.

Pal, M.N. (1975), "Regional Disparities in the Level of Education", *Indian Journal of Regional Science,* Vol. 11, No. 1, pp. 12-38.

Pandey, S.N. and Jain, S.K. (1998), "Common School System Needs Streaming", *Yojana,* Vol. 42, No. 5, pp. 23-26.

Parikh, K.S. (2000), *India Development Report (1999-2000),* Indira Gandhi Institute of Development Research, Oxford University Press, New Delhi.

Parlulekar, R.V. (1939), *"Literacy in India",* McMillan & Co., London, Chapters 3-5.

Petrov, V. (1985), *Literacy and Education in India: Spotlight on Population,* Progress Publishers, Moscow.

Prasad, M. (1978), "Spatial Patterns of Tribes in Chota Nagpur: A Case Study of Jharia Town", *Journal of Social Research,* Vol. XXI, No. 2, pp. 35-43.

Prema, V. (2000), "Education for Children with Special Needs", *Religion and Society,* Vol. 47, No. 1, pp. 139-50.

Premi, M.K. (1974), "Educational Opportunities for Scheduled Castes", *Economic and Political Weekly,* Vol. 45 and 46, pp. 1902-10.

Premi, M.K. (1984), "Education for the Weak", *Yojana,* Vol. 28, No. 17, pp. 13-15.

Premi, M.K. (1991), "Education for All: The Concern Areas", *Demography India,* Vol. 20, No. 1, pp. 91-102.

Premi, M.K. (2003), *Social Demography: A Systematic Exposition,* Jawahar Publishers and Distributors, New Delhi.

Pundir, J.K. (1997), *Changing Patterns of Scheduled Castes,* Rawat Publication, Jaipur.

Rajoo Krishan, S. (2002), "Literacy in India: Current Scenario and

Changes during the Last Decade", *Demography India,* Vol. 31, No. 1, pp. 51-64.

Ram, S. (1981), *Literacy Differential in Punjab: 1971,* An Unpublished M. Phil. Dissertation, Department of Geography, Panjab University, Chandigarh.

Raju, S. (1988), "Female Literacy in India: The Urban Dimension", *Economic and Political Weekly,* Vol. XXIII, No. 44, pp. 57-64.

Ram, S. and Dabral, B.M. (1995), "Progress and Pattern of Literacy in Lahaul and Spiti, (H.P.)", *Geographical Review of India,* Vol. 247, No. 2, pp. 22-27.

Ramachandran, R. and Raghu, G.V. (1987), "Regional Disparities in Chittoor District, Andhra Pradesh", *Indian Geographical Journal,* Vol. 62, No. 2, pp. 79-90.

Ramchandran, V. and Saihjee, A. (2002), "The New Segregation Reflections on Gender and Equity in Primary Education", *Economic and Political Weekly,* Vol. XXXVII, No. 17, pp. 1600-14.

Rangachar, B. (2000), "Challenges for Education in the New Millennium," *Religion and Society,* Vol. 47, No. 1, pp. 128-38.

Rao, M.S. and Misra, S.K. (1997), "Promoting Environmental Literacy," *Yojana,* Vol. 41, No. 10, pp. 28-29.

Rao, Nitya, (1993), "Total Literacy Campaign: A Field Report", *Economic and Political Weekly,* Vol. XXVIII, No. 19, pp. 914-15.

Rao, S.S. (2002), "Dalits in Education and Workforce", *Economic and Political Weekly,* Vol. XXXVII, No. 29, pp. 2998-3000.

Rao, V.K.R.V. (1966), *Education and Human Resource Development,* Allied Publishers, Bombay.

Raza, M. and Aggarwal, Y.P. (1986), "Inequalities in the Levels of Literacy in India: The Regional Dimensions", in Shafi, M. and Raza, Mehdi (eds.), *Spectrum of Modern Geography,* Concept Publishing Company, New Delhi, pp. 193-226.

Raza, M. and Aggarwal, Y.P. (1988), "An Analysis of Inequalities in the Levels of Literacy in India", in Raza, M. (ed.), *Regional Development* (Contributions to Indian Geography), Heritage Publishers, New Delhi, pp. 385-403.

Raza, M., *et al.* (1985), "Spatial Patterns of Tribal Literacy in India", *The India Geographical Journal,* Vol. 60, No. 2, pp. 103-116.

Reddy, M.M.K. (1996), *An Introduction to Demographic Behaviour in India,* Kanishka Publishers, New Delhi, pp. 53-70.

Reddy, U.B. (1985), "Regional Disparities in Educational Development in India: An Inter-State Analysis," *Geographical Review of India,* Vol. 47, No. 2, pp. 22-27.

Ryba, R. (1979), "Territorial Patterns of Diversity in Education", *Comparative Education*, Vol. 15.

Sachhidananda (1968), "Education and Changes in Social Values", *Man in India*, Vol. 48, pp. 68-71.

Sagar, P. (1984), *Changes in Female Literacy in India, 1951-81*, An Unpublished M. Phil. Dissertation, Department of Geography, Panjab University, Chandigarh, pp. 3-75.

Sagar, P. (1990), *Spatial Patterns of Literacy in India: 1981*, An Unpublished Ph.D. Thesis, Department of Geography, Panjab University, Chandigarh.

Sagar, P. (1991), "Regional Disparities in Literacy of India 1981", *Asian Profile*, Vol. 19, No. 3, pp. 253-66.

Samanta, G. (2003), "Gender Disparity in Literacy in West Bengal", *The Deccan Geographer*, Vol. 41, No. 1, pp. 31-42.

Sangwan, Sneh (1990), *Sex Disparity in the Levels of Literacy in Haryana: A Spatial Analysis*, An Unpublished M. Phil. Dissertation, Department of Geography, M.D. University, Rohtak.

Sangwan, R.S. and Sangwan, Sneh (1995), "Sex Disparity and the Levels of Literacy in Haryana: A Spatial Analysis", *East West Geographer*, Vol. 6, No. 1, pp. 31-66.

Sangwan, Sneh and Sangwan, R.S. (2003), *Rural-Urban Divide: Changing Spatial Pattern of Social Variables*, Concept Publishing Company, New Delhi, pp. 126-154.

Sangwan, Sneh and Sangwan, R.S. (2010), "Urban-Rural Differentials in Literacy", in Dubey, R.N. (ed.), *Urbanisation and Urban Planning in India: Vision and Reality*, Shree Nataraj Prakashan, New Delhi, pp. 320-333.

Sangwan, Sneh; Dabas, Anju; and Sangwan, R.S. (2011), "Literacy Differentials between Scheduled Castes and Non-Scheduled Castes in Haryana", in Anand, S. (ed.), *Ecodevelopment: Global Perspectives (Essays in Honour of R.B. Singh)*, Research India Press, New Delhi, pp. 408-427.

Sangwan, Sneh; Dabas, Anju; and Sangwan, R.S. (2011), "*Female Literacy Differentials among Non-Scheduled Castes and Scheduled Castes in Haryana: A Spatial Analysis*", A Paper Presented in 3rd International Geography Congress (under the aegis of National Association of Geographers, India (NAGI), held at Kozhikode on May 6-08, 2011 and organized by Centre for Water Resources Development and Management (CWRDM), Kozhikode (Kerala).

Sariff, A. (2000), "Indian Education Scene and Public Gap", *Economic and Political Weekly*, Vol. XXXV, No. 16, pp. 1396-1406.

Schuth, S. Katarina (1980), "Village Literacy and its Correlates: A Mysore Case Study," in David E. Sopher (ed.), *An Exploration of India: Geographical Perspective on Society and Culture*, Cornell University Press, Ithaca, New York, pp. 191-212.

Schwartzberg, J.E. (1961), "Observations on the Progress of Literacy in India: 1951-61", *Indian Population Bulletin*, No. 2, Office of the Registrar General, India, New Delhi, pp. 295-300.

Sen Gupta, P. (2002), "Enrolment, Dropout and Grade Completion of Girl Children in West Bengal," *Economic and Political Weekly*, Vol. XXXVII, No. 17, pp. 1621-37.

Shah, Maya (1981), *Economic Factors Explaining Variations in Literacy Rates in Rural Areas: A Case Study of Gujarat*, University of Baroda, Baroda.

Shah, S.Y. (1991), "Mass Literacy Campaign: Lesson of Ernakulam Model", *Yojana*, Vol. 35, No. 11, pp. 8-13.

Sharma, H.N. (1985). "Sex Disparity in Literacy and Social Topography of Assam", in Mukerji, A.B. and Ahmad, A. (eds.), India, Inter-India Publication, New Delhi, pp. 379-401.

Sharma, H.N. (2004), "Geographic Perspective on Literacy and Educational Levels in North-East India", in Neelam Grover and K.N. Singh (ed.) *Cultural Geography: Form and Process*, Concept Publishing Company, New Delhi.

Sharma, J.C. (1968), *"Literacy in Western Rajasthan", Selected Papers*, 21st International Geographical Congress, pp. 230-50.

Sharma, K.L. (1974), "Educational Inequalities among Rajasthan Scheduled Castes", *Economic and Political Weekly*, Vol. IX, No. 37, pp. 1589-92.

Sharma, K.L. (1975), "Spatial Disparities in Rajasthan", *Indian Journal of Regional Science*, Vol. VII, No. 1, pp. 70-88.

Shastri, P.S. (1985), "Patterns of Tribal Literacy in Vidarbha", *Population Geography*, Vol. 7, Nos. 1 and 2, pp. 40-59.

Shukla, S. (1995), "From Pre-Colonial to Post-Colonial: Educational Transition in Southern Asia", *IASSI Quarterly*, Indian Association of Social Science Institute, Vol. 13, No. 4, pp. 28-42.

Siddiqui, F.A. (1977), "The Geography of Literacy in U.P.", *Geographical Review of India*, Vol. 39, No. 4, pp. 374-388.

Singh, C.P. (1979), "Literacy in Rural Population in Meerut District", *Geographical Observer*, Vol. 15, pp. 32-36.

Singh, D. (1977), "Literacy in Indian Cities", *Indian Geographical Review*, Vol. 42, pp. 1-8.

Singh, Jasbir (1976), *An Agricultural Geography of Haryana*, Vishal Publications, *Kurukshetra*, pp. 32-129.

Singh, K.P. (1988), "Religion and Fertility: A Study in Differentials-Education", *Population Geography*, Vol. 10, Nos. 1 and 2, pp. 18-27.

Singh, N.K. (1979), *Education and Social Change*, Rawat Publication, Jaipur.

Singh, Nina (1998), "Female Literacy in India: The Emerging Trends", *Population Geography*, Col. 20, No. 1 and 2, pp. 23-36.

Singh, S.N. (1991), *Tribal Education in India*, Uppal Publishing House, New Delhi.

Singha, B.N. and Mishra, B.K. (1976), "Tribes of Orissa: A Geographical Analysis", *Geographical Review of India*, vol. XXXVIII, No. 2, pp. 167-87.

Sobti, Renu (1998), "Education and Nutrition", *Yojana*, Vol. 42, No. 10, pp. 37-41.

Sopher, D.E. (1974), "A Measure of Disparity", *The Professional Geographer*, Vol. 26, No. 4, pp. 389-392.

Sopher, D.E. (1980), "Sex Disparity in Indian Literacy", in Sopher D.E. (ed.), *An Exploration of India Geographical Perspectives on Society and Culture*, Cornell University Press, Ithaca, New York, pp. 130-188.

Spate, O.H.K. and Learmonth, A.T.A. (1967), *India and Pakistan*, Methuen, London, p. 535.

Sundararaman, S. (1996), "Literacy Campaigns: Lessons for Women's Movement", *Economic and Political Weekly*, Vol. XXXI, No. 2, pp. 1193-97.

Thakral, R.C. (1986), "Education: Who is at Fault", *Yojana*, Vol. 6, pp. 3-19.

Tilak, J.B.G., (1978), "Regional Inequality in Literacy in India," *Indian Journal of Adult Education*, Vol. 39, No. 1, pp. 14-22.

Tilak, J.B.G., (1981), "Inter-State Disparities in Educational Development" in Nair, K.R.G. (ed.), *Regional Disparities in India*, Agricole Publishing Academy, New Delhi, pp. 33-48.

Tilak, J.B.G. (2004), "Free and Compulsory Education: Legislative Intervention", *Economic and Political Weekly*, Vol. XXXIV, No. 7, pp. 618-20.

Tirtha, R. (1966), "Areal Patterns of Literacy in India", *Manpower Journal*, Vol. 3, pp. 88-118.

Tiwari, A.N. (1976), *Geography of Uttar Pradesh,* National Book Trust, New Delhi.

Trewartha, G.T. (1969), *A Geography of Population: World Patterns,* John Wiley & Sons, New York.

Trewartha, G.T. (1977), "Tribals: Role of Women," *Link,* Vol. 19, No. 33, pp. 23-24.

UNESCO (1957), *World Illiteracy at Mid Century—A Statistical Study,* Paris.

Usha Rao, N.J. (1982), "Inter-State Disparities in Literacy Rates in Karnataka with Special Reference to Scheduled Castes", in Bhat, L.S. (ed.), *Regional Disparities in India,* Society for the Study of Regional Disparities, New Delhi.

Vatsa, R.S. (1977), *The Depressed Classes of India,* Gitanjali Prakashan, New Delhi.

Vavrus, F. and Larsen, Ulla (2003), "Girls Education and Fertility Transitions: An Analysis of Recent Trends in Tanzania and Uganda", *Economic Development and Cultural Change,* Vol. 51, No. 4, pp. 945-76.

Venkateswarlu, N. (1992), "Financing Education: Emerging Trends", *Yojana,* Vol. 36, No. 22, pp. 7-8.

Verma, D.C. and Singh, Sukhbir (2001), *Haryana* (India—The Land and the People), 4th Edition, National Book Trust, India, New Delhi, p. 2.

Verma, H.R. and Verma, A. (1976), *Indian Women Through the Ages,* Great India Publishers, New Delhi.

Vyas, N.N. (1980), *Bondage and Exploitation in Tribal India,* Rawat Publisher, Jaipur.

Vyas, V.S. (1967), Factors Influencing the Levels of Literacy", *Arthvikas,* Vol. 3, No. 1, pp. 15-18.

Williamson, W. (1977), "Patterns of Educational Inequality in West Germany", *Comparative Education,* Vol. 13, pp. 29-44.

Youseff, N. (1971), "Social Structure and Female Labour Force: The Case of Women Workers in Muslim Middle East Countries", *Demography,* Vol. 8, No. 4, pp. 427-39.

Index